Canada: The State of the Federation 1995

D0145375

Edited by
Douglas M. Brown
and Jonathan W. Rose

Institute of
Intergovernmental
Relations

Institut des
relations
intergouvernementales

Canadian Cataloguing in Publication Data

The National Library of Canada has catalogued this publication as follows:

Main entry under title:

Canada, the state of the federation

1985-
Annual.

ISSN 0827-0708
ISBN 0-88911-579-6 (1995)

1. Federal-provincial relations – Canada – Periodicals.* 2. Federal government – Canada – Periodicals. I. Queen's University (Kingston, Ont.). Institute of Intergovernmental Relations.

JL27.F42   321.02'3'0971   C86-030713-1

The Institute of Intergovernmental Relations

The Institute is the only organization in Canada whose mandate is solely to promote research and communication on the challenges facing the federal system.

Current research interests include fiscal federalism, constitutional reform, the reform of federal political institutions and the machinery of federal-provincial relations, Canadian federalism and the global economy, and comparative federalism.

The Institute pursues these objectives through research conducted by its own staff and other scholars through its publication program, seminars and conferences.

The Institute links academics and practitioners of federalism in federal and provincial governments and the private sector.

L'Institut des relations intergouvernementales

L'Institut est le seul organisme canadien à se consacrer exclusivement à la recherche et aux échanges sur les questions du fédéralisme.

Les priorités de recherche de l'Institut portent présentement sur le fédéralisme fiscal, la réforme constitutionnelle, la modification éventuelle des institutions politiques fédérales, les nouveaux mécanismes de relations fédérales-provinciales, le fédéralisme canadien au regard de l'économie mondiale et le fédéralisme comparatif.

L'Institut réalise ses objectifs par le biais de recherches effectuées par son personnel et par des universitaires de l'Université Queen's et d'ailleurs, de même que par des conférences et des colloques.

L'Institut sert de lien entre les universitaires, les fonctionnaires fédéraux et provinciaux et le secteur privé.

CONTENTS

PREFACE

This is the tenth in the annual series of the Institute of Intergovernmental Relations entitled *Canada: The State of the Federation* appearing each fall. As with previous volumes, this year's review presents the work of a set of independent analyses commissioned especially for the series. The volume is organized into five parts. Part I comprises the overview chapter on the state of the federation, and introduces the rest of the chapters in this book. Part II presents two chapters on the Quebec referendum debate, Part III includes three chapters on the evolution of fiscal federalism, and Part IV includes chapters that address other developments in the federation. As is the tradition in this series, in Part V we continue with the chronology of events of significance for the state of the federation from July 1994 to June 1995.

The editors wish to express their thanks to the authors for their cooperation and forbearance with the editorial process. Each chapter has been read by two independent readers, and we would like to thank these readers for their important role. The preparation of this volume results from a team effort at the Institute and our colleagues at the Publishing Unit of the School of Policy Studies. Thanks to Patti Candido, Mary Kennedy, and Katherine Sharf at the Institute, and Valerie Jarus, Mark Howes, and Marilyn Banting at the School, as well as Scott Nelson for cover design and Mireille Duguay for translation.

Douglas M. Brown
Jonathan W. Rose
October 1995

CONTRIBUTORS

Gerard Boychuk is a lecturer in the Department of Political Studies, Queen's University, Kingston, Ontario.

Kathy Brock is Associate Professor of Political Science at Wilfrid Laurier University, Kitchener, Ontario.

Douglas M. Brown is the Executive Director of the Institute of Intergovernmental Relations, Queen's University, Kingston, Ontario.

David M. Cameron is Professor and Chair of the Department of Political Science at Dalhousie University, Halifax, Nova Scotia.

Susan D. Phillips is Associate Professor at the School of Public Administration, Carleton University, Ottawa, Ontario.

François Rocher is Associate Professor of Political Science at Carleton University, Ottawa, Ontario.

Jonathan W. Rose is Assistant Professor of Political Studies at Queen's University, Kingston, Ontario.

Bryan Schwartz is Professor, Faculty of Law, University of Manitoba.

Andrew C. Tzembelicos is a graduate of Political Studies at Queen's University, Kingston, Ontario.

Robert A. Young is co-director of the Political Economy Research Group and Professor of Political Science at the University of Western Ontario, London, Ontario.

I

Introduction

1

Overview of the State of the Federation, 1995

·Douglas M. Brown

Ce chapitre présente la structure et un sommaire commenté des autres chapitres de ce volume, de même qu'un survol de l'état de la fédération canadienne en 1995. Deux événements en 1995 ont alimenté un sentiment de changement déstabilisant : le budget fédéral de février 1995 et le référendum québécois d'octobre 1995. Pourtant, d'autres événements suggèrent une habileté ininterrompue du système fédéral de s'en sortir tant bien que mal.

Le débat référendaire québécois a pesé sur plusieurs autres relations intergouvernementales, retardant des décisions et augmentant l'incertitude. L'interprétation de la signification éventuelle du vote était marquée par la prévision d'un vote négatif, ce qui a soulevé des inquiétudes quant à un éventuel retour à des politiques centralisatrices par Ottawa. Cependant, le budget fédéral confirme une tendance nationale à la réduction de la taille des gouvernements et accélère la décentralisation vers les provinces des décisions et du financement des programmes sociaux. L'année à venir signifiera des négociations intergouvernementales intenses quant au partage des transferts fiscaux et quant au sort des standards nationaux qui existent encore. D'autres événements valent la peine d'être soulignés dont, notamment, trois modes importants de gestion plus progressive du changement : les négociations au Manitoba pour le démantèlement des Affaires indiennes, le renouvellement des économies provinciales par l'entremise de l'autoroute de l'information, ainsi que la mise en oeuvre de l'Entente sur le commerce intérieur. Une analyse de l'effet qu'auront sur la fédération les récentes élections provinciales, en particulier la victoire conservatrice en Ontario, conclut le survol.

INTRODUCTION

1995 was supposed to be the year of decision for Canada. At least we predicted as much in these pages in last year's review. The anticipation and uncertainty were particularly intense with respect to two key events: the federal budget of February 1995, and the referendum on sovereignty in Quebec, at point of writing still awaited on 30 October 1995. Both events have contributed to a continuing climate of change: of a sense that, however the final result works out, the universe is unfolding.... The virtue of casting back over an entire year's events is that one perceives that the life of a political system unfolds only slowly. And the message from the past year is that, as much as instability and discontinuity have been characteristic of Canadian federalism, adaptive muddling continues to have its place.

The chapters in this volume cover both the elements of instability and muddling from a variety of perspectives. This overview chapter seeks to place these perspectives within a broader framework of developments and events in the evolution of the Canadian federal system as a whole. The "Chronology of Events, July 1994 to June 1995," prepared by Andrew Tzembelicos reminds us of the many trends that bear examination in a full appreciation of the state of the federation, although only some are examined in this book. We have placed special emphasis on the two biggest issues, the debate over sovereignty in Quebec, and the fiscal policy of governments and their intergovernmental fiscal relations.

Despite the regime-threatening nature of the Quebec sovereignty debate, the past year has witnessed signs of an adapting and reacting federal system. The federal government's budget of February 1995 confirms and accelerates a clearly visible trend of the 1990s: to reduce the role of the federal government in the economy; to balance provincial budgets (and to move towards balance in Ottawa); and to significantly reduce the room for redistribution in the federal system as a whole. Fiscally driven decentralization, as many see it, is easily as important in terms of policy outcomes as any of the constitutional reforms proposed in the past decade. Intergovernmental relations, too, have had to respond to the new politics of restraint. To a degree, the reaction has been one of recrimination, but there are also signs of a determination, born of singularly strong messages from taxpayers, to get on with the task of rationalizing and harmonizing government programs.

As well as the federal government, the provincial governments are also involved, to varying degrees, in intensive change with aboriginal governments and their allied political organizations, and with local and regional governments. The fiscal agenda is as important in these relations as in the federal-provincial arena: indeed the real face of our evolving federation may be seen in the adaptations to change at this level of government and politics. But before examining these and other trends, we return to the high profile of the Quebec sovereignty debate.

THE QUEBEC REFERENDUM DEBATE

The chapter by François Rocher, "Les aléas de la strategie pré-réferendaire: chronique d'une mort annoncée," lays out in detail the pre-referendum strategy of the Parti Québécois government in office since September 1994. The sovereigntists have frequently pointed out the momentum of successive votes since 1992 which have supposedly indicated inevitable progress towards their goals. Using the hockey analogy, the first period ended in the "victory" by sovereigntists over the Charlottetown Accord in the referendum of October 1992; the second period ended with the winning by the Bloc Québécois of 54 of 75 of the Quebec seats in the federal Parliament in the election of October 1993; the third period ended in the PQ election in September 1994. In this analogy, the score at the end of the third period would have been enough to win the game. After all, the PQ under the leadership of Jacques Parizeau since 1988, had taken the position that the election of a PQ government would be sufficient to "trigger" the sovereignty process. The Rocher chapter demonstrates the difficulties of proceeding on that basis when public opinion appeared to be at best lukewarm to the sovereigntist objective. Thus, it would appear — to carry the hockey game analogy to its logical conclusion — that we are now engaged in a very long continuation of "sudden death" overtime to determine the final winner, at least in this match.

The standard interpretation of the media (particularly outside Quebec) was that the PQ electoral victory last year did not give them a mandate to pursue sovereignty — in part because the party received only 44.7 percent of the popular vote (enough to form a government but not enough to proceed to sovereignty), and in part because polling during the election campaign indicated that Quebecers thought the most important issue was to provide "good government." Rocher presents a contrary view, pointing out that the nearly 45 percent of support for the PQ is a higher threshold than the support enjoyed by the first PQ government led by René Lévesque. Rocher also notes that the election followed a campaign which, thanks to the Liberal incumbents, focused heavily on the sovereignty issue. The election produced, at 44.3 percent, an historically low level of support for the Liberal Party. This fact, when combined with the support given to the PQ (44.7 percent) and the Action Démocratique du Québec (6.5 percent) — both parties in favour of major constitutional change — would seem to indicate a rejection of "status quo" federalism. In any case, Rocher argues, the election could hardly be interpreted as illustrating the stagnation of sovereigntist support.

The year since last September has nonetheless witnessed a series of unsuccessful efforts by the PQ government (and the BQ opposition in Ottawa) to increase support for sovereignty sufficiently to call an early referendum (many expected a vote in May or June 1995). As Rocher outlines, the sovereigntist strategy has been to drive home the reality that no more offers for reform would be forthcoming from the federalists. They would thus create a coalition of hard-core separatists and softer nationalists, based on a still-potent desire for constitutional change in Quebec, and play upon the inevitable ramifications of fiscal retrenchment in Ottawa and the consequent damaging impact upon Quebec voters. Yet the new government did not move immediately to trigger the referendum process. The debate over the initial bill on sovereignty tabled in December 1994, based on a straightforward question and without formal linkage to a continuing association with Canada, failed to increase sovereigntist support. The regional commissions held in mid-winter served mainly to raise unanswered questions about the *raison d'être* of sovereignty. Even the June 1994 three-party agreement among the PQ, BQ, and ADQ to present an offer to Canada for "an economic and political partnership" did not produce the hoped-for turnaround in support, at least by the beginning of the official referendum campaign.

As for the federalists in Quebec, they have more or less stuck to the initial positions established by Daniel Johnson in the provincial election campaign of the summer of 1994. This position can be summarized as follows: the onus is on the sovereigntists to explain how their option would make life better for Quebecers; the experience of Quebecers in the federal system in Canada has not been all bad; and, while not ruling out the possibility of the ultimate recognition of Quebec's distinctiveness, the present constitution provides sufficient flexibility for change — indeed the current economic and fiscal climate demands it. The strategy has, of course, large elements of making a virtue of necessity. The prospects of any kind of constitutional reform initiative post-Charlottetown remain bleak. But as support for the sovereigntists has not been in the majority, the Liberal position has been to stay the course. The most notable source for dissent — the youth wing of the party — did succeed in getting Johnson's commitment to developing a new constitutional position,[1] but the leader has been able to put off the details until after the referendum.

For their strategy to work, the Quebec federalists had to have the support of the federal government in Ottawa and at least the tacit support of the governments of the other provinces. Such support has been relatively easy for the government of Prime Minister Jean Chrétien to provide, given the leader's promise to eschew constitutional reform in favour of policy reform. Chrétien's basic strategy has been to avoid engaging the sovereigntists over the merit of their proposals, and to avoid being drawn into debate about scenarios following a hypothetical "yes" vote. This strategy has not been followed in its entirety, and as the referendum date approaches, federalist leaders in Quebec and Ottawa have been more specific in denouncing the 12 June 1995 proposal in particular as unworkable and undesirable.[2] Nonetheless, as Robert Young outlines in his chapter, "Maybe Yes, Maybe No: The Rest of Canada and a Quebec 'Oui,'" the basic premise behind the strategy of disengagement has been to heighten the uncertainty around voting "yes."

There have been other cracks in the federalist front. In particular Preston Manning, leader of the Reform Party, has attempted to force the Chrétien government to be much more forthcoming in its reaction to a "yes" vote. The provinces have not taken Manning's lead. The premiers have largely succeeded in avoiding the issue, of keeping to the disengagement strategy, and of respectfully dismissing the "partnership" proposals of 12 June. However, as Young details, the void of official federalist comment on the consequences of a "yes" has been filled by numerous academic and other analysts. Their scenarios make different assumptions about the legitimacy of the vote, the economic damage, the acceptance or not of a "yes" vote, and so on. In particular, Young points to the importance of one group of scenarios of Quebec's secession after a "yes," but on terms that do not conform to the rosier predictions of the sovereigntists. These scenarios have been useful to the federalists, particularly in helping to sway the views of the undecided "soft nationalist" voter in Quebec.

In the meantime, however, with the referendum debate reaching its peak, it is hard to pretend that it is business as usual in the Canadian federation. Just as the five unsettling years of constitutional discussions in the period from 1987 to 1992 dominated public debate and pushed aside other public policy issues, the past year (and more if one includes the six months leading up to the September 1994 election) has placed continuing pressure on Canada. The federal system continues to muddle through, as noted above, but at a cost. The economic and fiscal costs have been obviously borne in the higher interest rates and lower Canadian dollar — although it may be impossible to separate where uncertainty over Quebec ends and unhappiness of financial markets over debts and deficits begins. But at the more mundane level of the operating system of government in Canada, once again the Quebec question looms over many decisions large and small. Policy decisions are delayed or derailed, Quebec's absence from many intergovernmental meetings distorts and also delays decision making, and courtesy of the Bloc Québécois, the daily work of Parliament is contorted to fit the mould of the federalist-sovereigntist debate.

FISCAL FEDERALISM IN EVOLUTION

While the waiting game for the referendum continues, the federal government in Ottawa has moved with more certain results on the fiscal front. The timing and nature of Ottawa's fiscal policy as announced in the February 1995 budget were shaped by the Quebec referendum politics, but have been indicative of other important influences as well.

As with many such long-anticipated events, the range of options going into the budget seemed much wider than appears in retrospect. There have been many potential reform solutions to the untenable set of fiscal arrangements between the federal and provincial governments, and to the issues surrounding the design of key social programs.[3] One only has to recall the menu of reform proposals offered by federal minister for human resource development, Lloyd Axworthy in October 1994, to find evidence of an ambitiously broad agenda.[4] According to the green paper, the following programs were up for fundamental renegotiation and reform: unemployment insurance, child tax benefits, job creation and training programs, social assistance and social service program funding, and post secondary education funding including student loans — accounting for 26 percent of total federal program spending. On top of this agenda lie federal Finance Minister Paul Martin's more discreet but no less weighty priorities for reducing the burden of the three big intergovernmental transfers: Established Programs Financing (EPF), the Canada Assistance Program (CAP) and Equalization.

The story of how much of the Axworthy agenda has been discarded and how the Finance agenda assumed its place is told by Susan Phillips in her chapter "The Canada Health and Social Transfer: Fiscal Federalism in Search of a Vision." The deficit-cutting objectives of the Chrétien government were made more urgent and more expensive in terms of program expenditure reductions by the run-up in interest rates in the spring of 1994. The collapse of the Mexican peso in December 1994 also had a sobering effect on financial markets and on the federal Cabinet, when the Cabinet was faced with key decisions about the February budget. At the same time, the pre-referendum climate in Quebec forced the Cabinet to follow advice from its Quebec members that the federal budget initiatives should not give further ammunition to the sovereigntist case of a centralist federal system, and should not impose the brunt of the cuts before the actual referendum is held.

The centrepiece of the budget, as noted, is the Canada Health and Social Transfer (CHST). The new intergovernmental transfer program combines the EPF and CAP and makes the entire amount subject to a single block transfer to the provinces. The cash amount of the transfer will be cut by six billion dollars or 37 percent over a two-year period. As such, the cost-sharing formula of the CAP will end, and with it the conditions attached. In this respect the CHST is unequivocally decentralist, finishing the job of the original EPF in 1977 to convert major cost-shared programs into block grants. The CHST also obviated many of the Axworthy reform proposals, in particular any major reform of social assistance or postsecondary education. It has also been argued that the budget as a whole leaves little room for new programs to preserve a federal role in income security beyond a further tightening of unemployment insurance provisions.[5]

Even as they instituted the CHST reductions, the federal Cabinet has been quick to claim that "national standards" for social programs must be retained. The issue of national standards as they apply to the Canada Assistance Plan is the topic of the chapter by Gerard Boychuk. In his view, critics of social programs overemphasize the existence and effectiveness of the so-called standards, when there are many other factors apart from the fiscal transfer to be considered. The provinces have widely varying programs which are not necessarily reflective of provincial wealth or ideology, but more rooted in unique provincial social and economic conditions. Reforms of social assistance now underway in all provinces will also reflect this diverse reality. Boychuk's chapter thus reminds us of the limitations of pursuing national standards in social programs.

Whether such analysis has an impact on the national political stage remains to be seen. The federal minister of health, Diane Marleau obtained the insertion of the word "health" in the CHST title, and continues to maintain that the terms of the *Canada Health Act* will apply to the reduced transfers. The federal legislation enacting the budget also provides for the negotiation of "national principles" for social assistance. As Boychuk argues, the results of such negotiation on social assistance are very unlikely to be more restrictive than the current conditions. But as Phillips argues, the federal Liberals and the provinces are very well aware of the continuing strong political support of Canadians for a universal health-care plan. The federal government, therefore, can be expected to keep to the high road of claiming to maintain national standards for health care, with the knowledge that the provinces will nonetheless cut more deeply into education and social assistance/services funding.

The rigorous review of all federal programs, with first phase results released with the budget, also indicates a root and branch reform of the role of the federal government in the economic and social life of Canadians. As the capstone of these reforms, the federal budget reverses some 50 years of federal fiscal policy, signalling an end to an era of federal spending in areas of provincial jurisdiction and of social policy expansionism.[6] Indeed the budget was probably the first in a generation not to make a single new policy promise or pronouncement. According to Phillips, the message was direct: aimed as much at citizens as at financial markets: Ottawa is rapidly getting out of the redistribution business and Canada is becoming an even more decentralized federation.

The reaction of the provinces to the budget has been muted. All of the provinces except Ontario and Quebec have balanced their budgets in the past fiscal year, in response to the combined pressure of taxpayers and bondholders. With the election of the Conservative government in Ontario (see below) that province is likely not far behind and it could be argued that only the referendum is delaying a more determined deficit reduction effort in Quebec. Thus the provinces could hardly attack the federal government for getting its fiscal house in order, and they seem to have realized that they cannot also argue that intergovernmental transfers remain untouched. Besides, the budget remains quite popular both with the Canadian public and the financial markets.

Still, the budget will force painful changes at the provincial level. The extent of such change is well documented in David M. Cameron's chapter on "Nova Scotia and the Fiscal Challenge." In that province, perhaps more severely than others, the recent and impending federal transfer reductions have led to a major restructuring of the delivery system for health care, municipal services, and education, to take three prominent examples. Such rationalization of public services is completely changing the political and administrative landscape in the province. It remains to be seen if the structural adjustments will be sufficient to handle the conflict between reduced resources and increased need.

For all of the provinces, the consequences of the budget are sinking in as the day of reckoning approaches. Each province is staking out its position for the difficult negotiations to come. The annual Premiers' Conference, held in St. John's, Newfoundland, foreshadows the debate. The provinces will accept the cuts but not being told how the remaining funds are to be spent.[7] The issue of how the CHST is allocated among the provinces may also be hotly contested, although it did not get any public airing at the Premiers' Conference. Because of the "cap" on the CAP (in place since 1989) and the cost-matching features of the transfer, the provincial shares vary widely on a per capita basis. Ontario in particular, but also the other richer provinces, will argue that the CHST must provide equal per capita shares to the provinces — leaving interregional distribution to the equalization program. Quebec and, to a lesser extent, some other provinces benefit more significantly from the CAP, and will likely resist such an approach.

Nor is it likely that the equalization program, ostensibly untouched by the 1995 budget, will remain unscathed by these negotiations. As the second largest intergovernmental transfer, it remains a target not only for further federal cost-cutting to come, but also as a source of funds to help achieve an equality of per capita shares among the provinces in the CHST. It may be argued that equalization, by providing for at least a minimum of program expenditures across the provinces, is the most important assurance of national standards of all of the federal programs; and that an erosion of funding in this area would have a much more serious impact upon the delivery of harmonized social programs. But it seems unrealistic to think that the current terms of the program will remain unchanged beyond 1996-97.

Thus, the 1995 federal budget illustrates a number of current developments in the federal system. First, the continuing sensitivity to politics in Quebec played an important role in federal decision making, and perhaps even a decisive role in the design of the CHST. Second, the outcome of the budget in terms of the redistributive role of the state is to leave more or less intact the regional underpinning of redistribution (notably through equalization) while steadily reducing the basis for interpersonal redistribution.[8] Third, and related to the last point, the budget opens the potential for a damaging interregional conflict over "fair shares" of intergovernmental transfers. Look for Ontario and the other richer provinces to be tougher than in the past. And fourth, room continues to exist, if somewhat reduced, for creative solutions to social policy problems to complete the social security review agenda and to make realistic adjustments to such national citizen entitlements as universal health care. This can only occur, however, if the parties to the negotiations neither deify nor demonize "national standards" and remain open to the inevitable need for differentiated solutions in Quebec.

In any case, the stage is set for a difficult set of negotiations about refinancing the federation. In the period leading up to the next two rounds of federal and provincial budgets, governments face an intensive agenda of discussions affecting not only the fiscal transfers but also the related and unfinished business of the social security review, as well as potential tax reform to replace the GST, opening other negotiating possibilities for different sorts of tax-based solutions to the fiscal transfer agenda. There are also many continuing issues rippling from the federal review of its other expenditure and regulatory programs.

OTHER DEVELOPMENTS

As noted in the introduction, apart from the two big issues of the referendum and the budget, there have been other significant developments which illustrate the continuing process of coping with change and muddling through. Three chapters in this volume — by Kathy Brock, Jonathan Rose, and Bryan Schwartz — illustrate these trends with respect to aboriginal government, provincial economic renewal, and internal trade.

The chapter by Kathy Brock, "Taking Control: Dismantling Indian Affairs and Recognizing First Nations Government in Manitoba," covers one of the most important current initiatives affecting Aboriginal Peoples. The Manitoba exercise seeks to dismantle the Department of Indian Affairs with respect to the Manitoba First Nations, and is being scrutinized carefully by First Nations across Canada. In Brock's view, the initiative is important both in its own right and for setting a potential pattern for the evolution of self-government by "status Indians" elsewhere. The negotiations are nowhere near to completion, but if successful, the Manitoba initiative will be an important step in applying the inherent right of self-government. Other important developments affecting Aboriginal Peoples during the past year have been the ongoing treaty negotiations in British Columbia involving the province, the federal government and the First Nations, and land settlement negotiations in Saskatchewan.

Indeed, in almost every province (and in the north with respect to the implementation of the Nunavut government) there are ongoing important negotiations on comprehensive claims, the scope of self-government and specific grievances related to land and other rights. However, in many aboriginal communities alternative groups in opposition to the Band Councils established under the *Indian Act* are taking more direct action. These groups feel that progress on recognizing their rights, including self-government, is far too slow. But without a firmly established basis for a new relationship, it is difficult to move quickly on implementing self-government or on expanding the exercise of treaty rights. The final reports of the Royal Commission on Aboriginal Peoples, expected in late 1995 or early 1996, may provide acceptable recommendations for such a foundation.

Over the years, the *State of the Federation* series has included chapters dealing with individual provinces or regions, in an attempt to discern provincial trends and developments in a federal context. The chapters by Cameron, noted above, and to an extent the chapter by Brock, provide such a perspective in this volume. Jonathan Rose's chapter, "Selling New Brunswick: Fibre Optics or Optical Illusion" also presents a similar focus, in this case examining a province that is attempting to reinvent itself in an age of information technology. New Brunswick's efforts towards economic renewal are born of a determination to break the cycle of dependence, both of individuals and of the provincial government. The government of Premier Frank McKenna can be credited for being out in front of economic and fiscal trends; it was one of the first provinces in the 1990s to balance its budget, and to adapt government operations, the education system, and large parts of its industrial infrastructure to the "information highway." As Rose makes clear, it is still too early to judge whether the McKenna approach will permanently and fundamentally transform the provincial economy. But in the meantime the government has changed the image of the Maritime province and, increasingly, the way in which New Brunswickers think of themselves.

The final substantive chapter in this volume deals with an important development in 1994: the signing of the Agreement on Internal Trade by the federal, provincial, and territorial governments. Bryan Schwartz' chapter "The Agreement on Internal Trade: The Case for a More Perfect Union" provides an analysis and summary of the agreement, in the context of the constitutional framework for free trade within Canada. Schwartz finds the agreement falls short in many respects in providing the "more perfect" economic union he thinks Canadians need. In his view, there is room for a more aggressive jurisprudence on interprovincial trade, in order to breathe life into the federal trade and commerce power. The new agreement, which only took effect on 1 July 1995, while complex and comprehensive, is replete with exceptions and exemptions and much unfinished business (for example, the agriculture and energy sectors). Schwartz finds the provisions overly weak and complicated, but recognizes that the agreement stands as a positive demonstration of cooperative federalism. However, he argues that the agreement will become an effective tool for preserving and extending the economic union only if the governments take seriously both the task of implementation and the current negotiations to expand its scope and enforceability.

While not the subject of chapters in this year's review, another important set of developments within the federation have been recent provincial elections. The past year has seen incumbent provincial governments returned to power in Manitoba, Saskatchewan, and New Brunswick, and two new governments elected in Quebec and Ontario. The elections in New Brunswick and Manitoba indicate the staying power of fiscal conservatism among these two relatively "have-not" provinces; in both cases the governments were returned for a third term, an unusual event in Canadian politics. When coupled with the re-election of the New Democratic Party government of Premier Roy Romanow in Saskatchewan on a platform of continued fiscal probity, these three provincial contests are evidence of the importance to voters of the less-is-more mode of governance.

The election of the Parti Québécois in Quebec was expected after the two-term Liberal rule. This government's sovereigntist agenda, discussed above, has tended to eclipse the extensive governmental restructuring underway (including health care and municipal financing among other sectors). One can expect an even sharper focus on such efforts after the referendum.

The Ontario election results, however, were the biggest political surprise of the year. The surprise was not that the NDP was defeated after only one term in office but that the centrist Liberals who had led the polls for two years prior to the election call were bypassed in favour of a majority Conservative government. The new government under Premier Michael Harris has pledged to dramatically reduce taxes and cut public spending, to bring in a balanced budget within its mandate, and to pare back what is perceived to be the intrusive role of the state in the lives of Ontario citizens. Observers predict a rough ride for the government and the people of Ontario akin to the experiences of the past two years of deficit cutting in Alberta.

The consequences of the Ontario election for intergovernmental relations and the federal system are less obvious. On the one hand, the return of the Conservatives to power in Ontario, with the Liberals again in power in Ottawa, harkens back to the long postwar electoral balancing of Ontarian voters. And now with three Conservative provincial governments, there is the glimmer of hope for a provincially-led recovery for the federal Conservative Party. Some observers also see in the Harris victory the chance to turn the clock back to the Davis years (1971-85). But on the other hand, the Harris government, with its neoconservative determination to dramatically reduce the size and role of the public sector, may reflect a similar trend across the country rather than represent a return to the past. The effects on intergovernmental relations will likely be to reinforce provincial opposition to new or retreaded national standards, a clear departure from the NDP government of Premier Bob Rae. The Harris government will also likely reinforce the fiscal conservatives among the Chrétien government, and be a more willing ally in tax reform.

With respect to the other provinces, one can expect a tough stance on "fair shares" from intergovernmental transfers, although probably not much different than their predecessors' position — except, as one columnist has noted, that had the Liberals won in Ontario, the Chrétien government might have found it more difficult to criticize Ontario.[9] As for Quebec and the referendum debate, the Harris government has been rather quiet, and in the first few months in office has not met some fears that it would be less sympathetic to Ontario's francophone minority or to Quebec itself.[10] Perhaps the most significant impact of the Ontario election for the federal system would be after a "no" vote in the referendum. Ontario could be an important ally for Quebec, if it wants one, for resisting centralizing schemes out of Ottawa. But if the Conservative promises of a rebound in private sector investor confidence are realized, the example will force the government of Quebec to follow suit in terms of competitive fiscal, economic and, social policies.

CONCLUSION: YES, NO, MAYBE...

This volume is being completed at the beginning of the Quebec referendum campaign and without knowledge of its outcome. By way of conclusion, therefore, it is appropriate to pause briefly at this moment in time, when different outcomes are still possible and before the backward glance interprets all events as leading in the same path.

As the polls have for some months indicated that a "yes" vote is unlikely, the full ramifications of a "yes" have not been absorbed, either in Quebec or in the rest of Canada. Thus even a close "yes" vote would come as a shock to Canadians and the international community. The emotional fallout in "English Canada" would be substantial and conflicted: there would be disbelief and denial, along with resentment and recrimination in many quarters. Such reactions would argue for a difficult separation with minimal ties. In other quarters there would be a desire for reconciliation with Quebec, to make fresh offers — to deliver a new partnership, even possibly within the federal framework, i.e., what the moderate sovereigntists and soft nationalists have been wanting all along. But beyond recognizing that there would be these two camps outside Quebec, the outcome of the conflict between the camps is impossible to predict and, from Quebec's perspective, impossible to control. A "yes" vote, even a very close one, opens Pandora's box. It may seem to empower Quebec, but key decisions about the future would be made elsewhere.

The "no" vote is also fraught with some uncertainty, if less so than the "yes." A strong "no" vote, particularly one that is close to the 1980 vote (say anything greater than 55 percent) brings with it the dangers of federal triumphalism about the death of separatism and an endorsement of the unreformed federal system. Unlike the 1980s, the federal government does not have the money to launch a renewed use of the federal spending power, but might be tempted to pursue regulatory centralism. Such a trend would be resisted, perhaps as much by Ontario and other provinces as by the government of Quebec. And in any case such centralism could be strongly counterproductive in quelling nationalism in Quebec. Because the "no" result had in fact been expected for many months, and such outcomes as those just described have been part of the public debate, it seems likely that the reaction to a "no" would be more measured, and more of a continuation of current trends towards fiscal decentralization. A close "no" vote would place the lid more securely on federal centralist tendencies, while keeping the door open to a modest effort at reconciliation of Quebec's traditional demands. In the short term, either a big or a little "no" would force major political realignments in Quebec as the sovereigntist referendum coalition self-destructs.

Finally, a possibility for a "maybe" occurs, but this seems the slimmest chance of all. A very close vote might produce the climate for a compromise solution. Elements in the sovereigntist camp will attempt to put a favourable spin on the meaning of a yes vote during the campaign, just as moderate nationalists can take comfort from a very close no. But there is no real way of knowing what the electorate has in mind apart from disposing of the question at hand, and as noted already, even a close yes could unleash a furious reaction outside Quebec.

To conclude, the current Quebec verdict on its nationalist aspirations comes at the end of the postwar era of state expansion, and amidst an emerging era of intense global competition that challenges the welfare state. This is where the two biggest issues of this year in the state of the federation intersect. During the current referendum campaign the sovereigntists have played upon class conflict and drawn the worst-case scenarios of federal spending cuts, and have promised a more supportive and coherent state role in an independent Quebec. Whatever the outcome, Quebecers will soon have to focus more squarely on the difficult choices which other Canadians are facing about the role of the state in their lives and the economic and social costs of alternative policy directions. The participation of Quebec in the Canadian solutions to these choices may not change the basic policy directions, but will make an enormous difference in the specific nature of our adaptation to global trends. The decision in Quebec will determine whether Canadians are to layer onto this existing governmental challenge the diverting task of another round of intense constitutional politics which could result in two or more new states. Most likely Canadians and their governments will return to the more normal Canadian activity of muddling through.

NOTES

1. *La Presse*, 14 August 1995.

2. See, for example, reports in *The Globe and Mail*, 14 June 1995 covering Prime Minister Chrétien and QLP Leader Daniel Johnson; 15 June 1995 covering premier-elect of Ontario, Michael Harris; 25 August 1995 covering the Premiers' Conference; and 27 September 1995 covering federal minister of finance, Paul Martin.

3. For one comprehensive set of analyses on the options see Keith Banting, Douglas Brown and Thomas Courchene (eds.) *The Future of Fiscal Federalism* (Kingston: School of Policy Studies, Queen's University, 1994).

4. Government of Canada, *Improving Social Security in Canada: A Discussion Paper* (Ottawa: Minister of Supply and Services, 1994).

5. See Kenneth Battle and Sherri Torjman, *How Finance Re-Formed Social Policy* (Ottawa: Caledon Institute of Social Policy, 1995).

6. For a commentary on this point see Arthur Kroeger, "The 1995 Federal Budget — Recognition of Reality, or Threat to the Federation?" *Opinion Canada/ Canada Opinion* 3, 2 (April, 1995).

7. See the 36th annual Premiers' Conference, *Final Communiqué*, St. John's Newfoundland, 23-25 August 1995, pp. 1-3.

8. Keith Banting, "Who 'R Us ?" paper prepared for a Forum on the Federal Budget, John Deutsch Institute for the Study of Economic Policy, Queen's University, 31 March 1995.

9. For comments, see column by Chantal Hébert in *La Presse,* 9 June 1995, p. A1.

10. Ibid.

II

The Pre-Referendum Debate

2

Les aléas de la stratégie pré-référendaire : Chronique d'une mort annoncée

François Rocher

This article traces developments in the pre-referendum debate, from the election of the Parti Québécois in September 1994 to the end of summer 1995. While the PQ has always signified its intention to hold a popular vote on Quebec's political status, it has followed a path marked by numerous delays on the referendum date and the substance of the question, among other things. The first part of this chapter discusses how the brief victory of September 1995 led the sovereignty camp to abandon their initial strategy, then looks at the bill on sovereignty and at the attempt to align moderate nationalists with the péquiste process. It also reviews the context in which the regional commissions had to work and the little impact they had on public opinion, and examines both the stategic "turning" of Lucien Bouchard and the report of the National Commission on the Future of Québec. Finally, it provides an analysis of the tripartite agreement PQ-BQ-ADQ and demonstrates the necessity of avoiding a split between Mr. Parizeau and Mr. Bouchard.

The chapter concludes that the agreement is not sufficient to convince a majority of Quebecers to support the sovereignty option. The weak progress of the sovereignty option followed by a plateau explains the strategic reversals and uncertainties that marked the pre-referendum stage. Thus, the PQ slowly transformed the approach it favoured during the election campaign to expand the sovereignty coalition, and even more importantly, to take into account the attachment that many Quebecers felt towards Canada. The federalist forces have concentrated on contesting the idea that the federal experience has been a failure for Quebec, opting instead to defend its flexibility. An anticipated failure of the sovereignty option could not be interpreted as support for the constitutional status quo by Quebecers, as they will always prefer a renewed Canada to constitutional impasse.

L'élection du Parti Québécois (PQ) le 12 septembre 1994 a marqué le coup d'envoi de la campagne pré-référendaire au Québec. La victoire péquiste représente le troisième épisode d'une saga marquée par l'échec de l'entente de Charlottetown et l'élection d'un fort contingent de députés du Bloc québécois

(BQ) lors des élections fédérales d'octobre 1993. Ces événements démontrent qu'une large proportion de la population québécoise est insatisfaite de l'immobilisme constitutionnel et n'adhère pas à la vision qui s'est imposée dans le reste du Canada quant à la nature des rapports qui doivent lier les différentes communautés politiques [1]. L'élection de septembre 1994 a porté au pouvoir un parti politique dont la raison d'être est l'accession du Québec à la souveraineté. Ce succès électoral n'est pas sans rappeler celui remporté par René Lévesque 18 ans plus tôt. Tout comme en 1976, le PQ a promis de tenir un référendum pour trancher la «question nationale». De la même manière, toute l'activité gouvernementale est jugée à l'aune des gains pouvant être obtenus au moment du référendum. Avant même que la campagne référendaire ne soit officiellement lancée, les tenants de la souveraineté ou du maintien du Québec dans l'espace politique canadien fourbissent leurs armes et cherchent à développer des stratégies gagnantes.

Toutefois, le contexte social, économique et politique de la fin des années 1970 ne peut se comparer à celui du milieu des années 1990. L'insécurité linguistique qui a marqué les années 1960 et 1970 s'est atténuée suite aux différentes législations qui ont renforcé le statut du français au Québec, dont la pierre angulaire fut la *Charte de la langue française*. Les thèses néolibérales dominent largement le discours sur le rôle de l'État. Le Canada a approfondi son intégration économique continentale en adhérant à l'Accord de libre-échange Canada-États-Unis puis à l'Accord de libre-échange nord-américain. Les crises économiques ont lourdement hypothéqué les finances publiques, réduisant d'autant la marge de manoeuvre dont disposait antérieurement les gouvernements pour élaborer leurs stratégies de développement économique. Par ailleurs, les lendemains du référendum québécois de 1980 ont grandement affaibli le rapport de force du Québec dans la fédération canadienne. Le rapatriement de la Constitution en 1982 et les modifications constitutionnelles ont profondément transformé le paysage politique canadien. L'État du Québec a vu ses pouvoirs en matière de législation linguistique érodés et la nouvelle *Charte canadienne des droits et libertés* a accru l'influence du gouvernement central et diminué celle des provinces. Ce processus a particulièrement affecté le Québec [2]. Le double échec des tentatives d'amender la Constitution canadienne, qui visaient entre autres à accorder au Québec le statut d'une «société distincte», fait en sorte qu'au projet souverainiste s'oppose maintenant le *statu quo* constitutionnel.

Comme le soulignait notamment Peter Russell, le défi des forces souverainistes est de convertir le sentiment de mécontentement à l'endroit du régime fédéral en un appui au projet souverainiste [3]. Toutefois, le succès électoral du BQ tout comme le rejet de l'entente de Charlottetown par plus de 55 pour cent de l'électorat québécois ne signifient pas un appui proportionnel à l'idée de la souveraineté. Qui plus est, toute stratégie référendaire gagnante doit reposer sur les quatre éléments suivants : 1) convaincre une majorité de citoyens que l'expérience fédérale est un échec pour le Québec; 2) démontrer que le Québec a le droit de faire la souveraineté; 3) qu'il en a les moyens; et, 4) que cela est réalisable à court terme. C'est sur ces quatres fronts que se situent les principaux éléments qui ont marqué les débats politiques au cours de la période préréférendaire.

Par ailleurs, le projet souverainiste est associé depuis les années 1970 à la construction et à la consolidation de l'État du Québec. Reprenant un argument bien connu, Robert Boily affirmait aux lendemains du référendum de 1980 que les Québécois «savent qu'ils constitueront, à l'intérieur du Canada, une minorité de moins en moins forte. Ils croient que le seul État sur lequel ils peuvent exercer un contrôle demeure celui du Québec. Marqués profondément par les effets de l'industrialisation et du colonialisme, ils ont mis, dans l'intervention de l'État et dans le système coopératif, leur espoir de développer une influence plus grande sur leur avenir économique et leur développement» [4]. Or, avec le désengagement graduel de l'État, ou plus justement à cause de la réorientation de ses activités [5], le mouvement souverainiste ne porte plus un projet de société intimement lié à un accroissement du rôle de l'État québécois inspiré des idéaux de la social-démocratie. Cette nouvelle donne oblige le camp souverainiste à insister davantage sur les économies pouvant être réalisées en éliminant les dédoublements et les chevauchements et sur les nouvelles façons de faire que mettrait en place le nouvel État, que sur le potentiel de développement découlant d'une totale maîtrise des leviers étatiques. En d'autres mots, on insiste davantage sur le «mieux faire» que sur le «faire plus». Le discours est donc alimenté par une approche économiste et bureaucratique, centrée sur une reconfiguration particulière du rôle de l'État d'inspiration néolibérale, loin des préoccupations de la société civile. On assiste donc à une césure entre les objectifs du mouvement souverainiste issu de la Révolution tranquille selon lequel la réalisation de la nation passait obligatoirement par la constitution d'un État en possession de tous ces moyens et les objectifs mis aujourd'hui de l'avant par ses principaux porte-parole. C'est dans ce contexte que plusieurs posent la question suivante : «la souveraineté, pour quoi faire?». Cette interrogation, maintes fois entendue au cours des derniers mois, illustre le paradoxe dans lequel se trouve le camp souverainiste pour qui la construction de l'État québécois constituait l'une des raisons d'être.

La stratégie préréfendaire, d'abord définie au cours de la campagne électorale par le PQ secondé par le BQ, s'est butée à une dure réalité : l'appui à la thèse souverainiste s'est graduellement atténué depuis la mort de l'Accord du lac Meech, alors que la souveraineté-association obtenait 60 pour cent dans les sondages et la souveraineté pas moins de 57 pour cent [6]. Alors qu'initialement M. Parizeau s'était présenté comme le porte-étendard d'un projet souverainiste dénué de toute ambiguïté, la nécessité d'élargir le plus possible le bassin des adhérants à l'idée de souveraineté l'a conduit à modifier le programme constitutionnel du PQ et à l'adapter aux exigences de ses partenaires.

L'objet de ce chapitre est donc d'analyser les principaux événements survenus entre l'élection du PQ et l'élaboration de la position tripartite PQ-BQ-Action démocratique du Québec (ADQ) à la mi-juin 1995.

L'ÉLECTION DE SEPTEMBRE 1994 :
UNE VICTOIRE PÉQUISTE MOINS IMPOSANTE QUE PRÉVUE

En dépit du fait que le chef du Parti libéral du Québec (PLQ) ait insisté tout au long de la campagne électorale sur la nature référendaire de l'élection, le PQ a pour sa part soutenu que l'élection ne portait par sur la souveraineté. Son slogan «L'autre façon de gouverner», comme le soutiennent Bousquet et Monière, «permettait d'associer dans l'esprit des électeurs la critique du bilan libéral, le choix d'une nouvelle équipe gouvernementale et l'option souverainiste» [7]. Le thème de la souveraineté a continuellement été martelé par les libéraux provinciaux qui rappelaient le programme du PQ selon lequel «[l]'élection d'un gouvernement du Parti québécois signifiera notamment que la population du Québec a choisi de se doter d'un gouvernement souverainiste» qui aura non seulement le mandat de préparer la souveraineté mais aussi «d'en faire la promotion, de préparer et de tenir un référendum qui permettra de la réaliser» [8]. Même si la campagne électorale constituait une occasion pour M. Jacques Parizeau de persuader l'électorat de la pertinence de la souveraineté après le double échec constitutionnel depuis 1990, l'essentiel du message véhiculé par le PQ portait sur la nécessité de changer l'équipe gouvernementale et la critique de la gestion libérale. Mais la souveraineté était omniprésente dans le discours. Par exemple, le rétablissement de la confiance des citoyens en leurs institutions est associé à la construction d'un «pays normal»; la souveraineté passe par la lutte au cynisme des électeurs.

Sur la question constitutionnelle, la campagne portait sur deux options diamétralement opposées. La position de M. Daniel Johnson est limpide : le Québec peut très bien s'accommoder de l'actuelle Constitution dans la mesure où le fédéralisme est, par nature, en constante évolution. Il a laissé clairement savoir que, comme premier ministre, il ne brandirait jamais la menace souverainiste devant le reste du Canada pour obtenir des gains dans des discussions constitutionnelles. Pour lui, l'indépendance n'est pas un moyen d'atteindre l'égalité. De là les efforts déployés par M. Johnson pour modifier l'équation présentée par son prédécesseur lors de la campagne référendaire sur l'accord de Charlottetown en 1992, selon qui un «non» allait permettre aux souverainistes d'opposer la souveraineté au *statu quo*, au fédéralisme irréformable [9], d'où la nécessité de discréditer l'idée du *statu quo* et de lui substituer celle du «fédéralisme évolutif». Cette évolution est possible par voie d'ententes administratives sur des questions bien précises, telles la formation de la main-oeuvre, l'environnement, les communications ou l'immigration. Il propose de mettre fin aux chevauchements et aux dédoublements. C'est sur cette base que le Québec doit renouveler ses liens historiques et naturels avec ses partenaires canadiens. M. Johnson adopte le discours de l'autonomie provinciale : «À l'évidence, le Québec est une société distincte. Notre avenir est lié à la reconnaissance de cette caractéristique. Tous les gestes que nous faisons, toutes les discussions que nous avons dans quelque forum que ce soit, s'alimentent constamment de l'exercice de la plus grande autonomie, par le Québec, de ses compétences» [10]. En clair, la «reconnaissance de cette caractéristique» passe par l'exercice de l'autonomie provinciale. C'est à travers cette quête d'autonomie que doit être compris les thèmes du rejet du *statu quo* et du «fédéralisme évolutif». Il n'est pas anodin de constater que le principal problème, selon lui, relève du pouvoir fédéral de dépenser qui a permis à ce dernier d'intervenir dans des champs de compétences provinciales.

Le programme du PQ était néanmoins clair quant à la stratégie qui devait être adoptée entre son élection et la tenue du référendum. Trois étapes étaient identifiées : 1) l'adoption par l'Assemblée nationale d'une déclaration solennelle affirmant la volonté du Québec d'accéder à la pleine souveraineté; 2) l'établissement de l'échéancier et des modalités de transfert des pouvoirs et des fonctionnaires ainsi que les règles de partage de l'actif et des dettes; 3) l'adoption d'une loi instituant une commission constitutionnelle ayant le mandat de rédiger un projet de Constitution du Québec souverain. Le premier élément, aux yeux de M. Parizeau, était d'abord et avant tout de nature symbolique, ne liant en aucune manière la population qui devra se prononcer sur la question par voie de référendum. Quant à la seconde étape, elle dépendait bien entendu de la volonté du gouvernement central d'entamer de telles négociations. Bien que se montrant sceptique quant à une éventuelle participation du gouvernement fédéral à de telles discussions, l'inclusion de cet élément visait à montrer la bonne volonté du Québec à l'endroit de ses obligations. La troisième étape cherchait tout simplement à entamer le travail de précision quant à l'environnement institutionnel d'un Québec souverain.

Pour ce qui était de la date du référendum, M. Parizeau a fait savoir à maintes reprises que le plus tôt serait le mieux, évoquant la tenue de la consultation populaire dans les huit à dix mois suivant l'élection ou à tout le moins, comme il le précisait en fin de campagne, au cours de l'année 1995.

Le PLQ n'a eu de cesse de dénoncer le premier élément du programme, brandissant face à l'électorat le fait qu'en élisant l'équipe péquiste, le processus d'accession à la souveraineté serait «enclenché» sans que le gouvernement n'ait obtenu un mandat en ce sens. Cette manoeuvre fut qualifiée d'anti-démocratique puisqu'elle présumait de la volonté des Québécois d'appuyer l'option péquiste. Pour le PQ, soutenu en cela par le BQ, il s'agissait essentiellement d'une déclaration d'intention à portée symbolique.

L'approche péquiste était plus proche des attentes des Québécois. Un sondage réalisé à la mi-août indiquait que 49,4 pour cent (contre 35,3 pour cent) des électeurs étaient en désaccord avec l'idée de M. Daniel Johnson de refuser toute négociation constitutionnelle avant 1997; 64,5 pour cent se disaient plutôt d'accord pour qu'il reprenne les revendications traditionnelles du Québec (contre 21,1 pour cent) et même 48,1 pour cent étaient plutôt favorables à ce qu'il organise un référendum sur la souveraineté du Québec (contre 44 pour cent). Par ailleurs, les quatre éléments de la stratégie péquiste obtenaient un appui important : 56,3 pour cent (contre 37,7 pour cent) pour que M. Parizeau tienne un référendum sur la souveraineté; 47 pour cent (contre 43,6 pour cent) étaient plutôt d'accord avec son intention de faire adopter une résolution par l'Assemblée nationale; 49,2 pour cent (contre 41,4 pour cent) pour qu'il entame des discussions avec le gouvernement central; 46,9 pour cent (contre 44,3 pour cent) pour qu'il entreprenne la rédaction d'un projet de Constitution d'un Québec souverain [11]. Malgré la proximité de l'approche péquiste face aux attentes de l'électorat, le soutien à l'option souverainiste ne dépassait pas le seuil des 45 pour cent dans les sondages [12].

Dans un éditorial rédigé une semaine avant les élections, Lise Bissonnette rappelait le dilemme dans lequel était plongé les électeurs et les problèmes stratégiques des deux principales formations politiques. Le moratoire constitutionnel avancé par M. Johnson ne répond pas à l'insatisfaction des Québécois à l'égard de l'arrangement fédéral actuel. Mais il y a plus : «pareil temps d'arrêt n'a aucun sens au moment où la machine fédérale, elle, se prépare à bouleverser les données du jeu sur le terrain avec son train de réformes». Quant à la stratégie péquiste, elle pourrait de nouveau mener à l'impasse si le PQ, en monopolisant l'idée de souveraineté, «exclut tout rapprochement avec ses alliés d'hier, les libéraux déçus des manoeuvres» constitutionnelles ayant conduit aux accords de Charlottetown : «la "question claire" des péquistes promet de s'attirer une réponse tout aussi claire des électeurs, qui pourraient se refuser le changement de crainte d'en obtenir trop» [13]. En somme, le succès de la démarche souverainiste passe par la constitution d'une large coalition qui obligera à remettre en question non seulement l'échéance référendaire du PQ, mais aussi la formulation de la question et à préciser la raison d'être de la souveraineté. Il s'agissait là du premier écueil de la stratégie mise de l'avant par une formation politique dont l'option, telle que formulée, ne recueillait pas l'appui de la majorité de la population.

Dans l'ensemble, ce sont surtout les libéraux qui ont centré leur campagne sur la souveraineté. Ils ont insisté sur les coûts et les dommages irréversibles qu'engendrerait la séparation du Québec et dénoncé «l'enclenchisme» que représenterait l'adoption d'une déclaration solennelle de souveraineté par l'Assemblée nationale. Pour leur part, les péquistes se sont surtout efforcés de faire le bilan de l'administration libérale tout en invoquant les arguments positifs en faveur de la souveraineté, notamment au chapitre de l'élimination des dédoublements de programmes dans le domaine de la formation de la main-d'oeuvre. Tous les sondages réalisés au cours de la campagne accordaient une avance au PQ, situant l'appui de l'électorat entre 48 et 50 pour cent, à l'exception d'un sondage CROP fait au début septembre qui n'accordait qu'une avance de 3 points de pourcentage aux péquistes face aux libéraux. L'ADQ récoltait de 6 à 9 pour cent des faveurs de l'électorat [14].

Le soir du 12 septembre, les résultats de l'élection furent bien en-deçà des attentes du PQ qui ne récolta que 44,7 pour cent des voix et fit élire 77 députés. Le PLQ réussi à s'assurer le soutien de 44,4 pour cent de l'électorat pour un total de 47 sièges alors que l'ADQ ne faisait élire qu'un seul député, le chef de la formation politique, M. Mario Dumont. Ce nouveau parti réussit néanmoins à s'assurer 6,5 pour cent des voix même s'il n'a présenté des candidats que dans seulement 80 des 125 circonscriptions. Bien qu'inférieure aux espoirs du PQ, cette victoire se distingue de celle arrachée en 1976 à double titre. D'abord, alors qu'à cette époque le PQ avait fait campagne sur le thème du «bon gouvernement» et avait mis son option en veilleuse, l'élection de 1994 portait en grande partie sur la question de la souveraineté — le PLQ en ayant fait son principal cheval de bataille. En ce sens, le PQ et l'option souverainiste font meilleure figure avec près de 45 pour cent des voix en 1994 qu'avec 41 pour cent en 1976. Ensuite, la présence de l'ADQ a contribué à accroître la défaite du PLQ dans la mesure où ce parti est le fruit du schisme survenu au sein des libéraux aux lendemains de la défaite de Charlottetown. Cela peut expliquer en partie pourquoi le PLQ a obtenu l'un des pires scores de son histoire. À l'exception de deux élections générales (1952 et 1976), jamais ce parti n'avait recueilli moins de 45 pour cent de l'appui populaire [15]. L'élection de 1994 ne peut donc pas être interprétée comme illustrant la stagnation de l'option souverainiste, contrairement à ce qu'ont laissé entendre de nombreux commentateurs politiques à l'extérieur du Québec.

La courte victoire péquiste a néanmoins amené M. Jacques Parizeau à revoir les éléments de sa stratégie. Tout en réitérant son intention de tenir le référendum dans les délais annoncés, il est revenu sur son intention de faire adopter par l'Assemblée nationale une résolution solennelle affirmant la volonté de faire du Québec un pays dans le but d'éviter une inutile confrontation. Pour sa part, M. Lucien Bouchard, prenant bonne note du niveau d'appui à l'option souverainiste, interprétait le résultat électoral comme l'expression de la volonté des Québécois de donner priorité à l'économie plutôt qu'au débat référendaire. Il allait toutefois plus loin en affirmant que le référendum ne devrait être tenu que s'il pouvait être gagné, questionnait l'engagement de tenir cette consultation au cours de l'année 1995 et liait cette victoire à la performance du gouvernement péquiste [16].

Sur le front des relations fédérales-provinciales, M. Parizeau annonça qu'il ne voulait pas provoquer de confrontation et qu'il agirait dans le respect des institutions fédérales. Néanmoins, cette approche pragmatique, dictée aussi bien par le fait que le Canada d'aujourd'hui sera le principal partenaire d'un Québec souverain que par l'inefficacité de la confrontation pour convaincre les Québécois du bien fondé de la souveraineté, n'empêchera pas le Québec de vouloir défendre de manière agressive les intérêts du Québec et de participer aux seules conférences où les intérêts du Québec sont en jeu. Conscient du fait que l'idée de souveraineté ne recueillerait toujours pas 50 pour cent de l'appui de la population, le chef du PQ ouvrait ce qu'il appelera les «voies parallèles sur l'autoroute de la souveraineté». S'adressant aux fédéralistes autonomistes — que certains qualifient de «fatigués» —, il leur promit de fournir toutes les informations nécessaires pour qu'ils puissent prendre une décision éclairée et nomma Richard Le Hir ministre de la Restructuration, responsable notamment de préparer des études sur les enjeux de la souveraineté. Cette tentative d'ouverture à l'endroit des Québécois fut mal accueillie aussi bien par le chef de l'ADQ qui affirma que les 250 000 votes obtenus par son parti «ne sont pas à vendre» alors que les libéraux autonomistes préféraient chercher à amener le PLQ à revoir sa plate-forme constitutionnelle [17]. Des quatre éléments portant sur le thème de la souveraineté avancés lors de la campagne électorale (déclaration solennelle; échéances et modalités quant au transfert des pouvoirs, des fonctionnaires, de la dette, des actifs; commission constitutionnelle; référendum en 1995), seule la promesse de la tenue du référendum, bien que tempérée par M. Bouchard, tenait toujours.

Au lendemain de l'élection de septembre, deux défis attendaient les forces souverainistes : d'abord combattre le sentiment de morosité suite aux résultats décevants de l'élection et, ensuite, convaincre les Québécois que la souveraineté ne peut être prisonnière d'un seul parti, que les péquistes ne détiennent pas le monopole de cette option. Cette dernière nécessité pouvait potentiellement poser un problème à M. Parizeau, peu enclin à diluer son option et à envisager des scénarios différents du sien pour faire triompher l'objectif de la souveraineté. Dès novembre 1994, au Conseil national du PQ, il enjoignit ses troupes à «ouvrir les bras aux souverainistes d'autres horizons» dans le but de former une «coalition arc-en-ciel» comparable à celle qui avait permis de défaire l'entente de Charlottetown lors du référendum de 1992 [18]. Lors de la même rencontre, des militants proposèrent une motion visant la création d'une commission itinérante ayant pour objectif de recréer un *momentum* comparable à celui qui avait caractérisé les travaux de la Commission Bélanger-Campeau. Cette approche fut rejetée par les militants qui y voyaient une acceptation du programme de l'ADQ, allant à l'encontre de l'appel lancé par M. Parizeau qui les invitait à oublier l'esprit de chapelle qui caractérise le PQ.

EN QUÊTE D'UN *MOMENTUM* :
L'AVANT-PROJET DE LOI SUR LA SOUVERAINETÉ

Lors du discours inaugural, le premier ministre québécois fait connaître son intention de déposer à l'Assemblée nationale un document qui servira de base à la participation populaire au débat préréférendaire : «Nous voulons ouvrir un dialogue avec tous les Québécois sur ce contenu. Un Québec souverain, pour en faire quoi, au juste? Pour qu'il soit porteur de quelles valeurs, de quels principes, de quels objectifs?» [19]. Quelques jours plus tôt, il indiquait avoir trouvé un moyen astucieux de disposer de la fameuse déclaration solennelle affirmant la volonté du Québec d'accéder à sa pleine souveraineté prévue au programme du PQ. Le 6 décembre, il annonce son plan de match reposant sur la tenue d'un vaste processus de consultation devant être tenue entre janvier et mars 1995. Le gouvernement comptait former au moins 15 commissions consultatives régionales composées de parlementaires et de personnes issues du milieu. Il conviait tous les Québécois à débattre du contenu d'un projet de loi et à participer à la rédaction de la Déclaration de souveraineté. C'est ainsi que M. Parizeau invita la population québécoise tout comme tous les partis politiques, y compris le Parti libéral du Canada et le Parti conservateur, à faire valoir leurs vues sur l'Avant-projet de loi sur la souveraineté du Québec. Suite à la consultation, le document deviendra un projet de loi, sera adopté par l'Assemblée nationale puis soumis aux Québécois par référendum. Le premier ministre déposa la question référendaire qui devrait être la suivante : «Etes-vous en faveur de la loi adoptée par l'Assemblée nationale déclarant la souveraineté du Québec? Oui ou Non?».

L'Avant-projet de loi sur la souveraineté du Québec compte 17 articles. Il affirme en son article 1, le plus court, que «[l]e Québec est un pays souverain». Le second article porte sur l'association économique et autorise «le gouvernement à conclure un accord consacrant le maintien de l'association économique entre le Québec et le reste du Canada». Les autres articles abordent, dans l'ordre, les questions suivantes : l'élaboration d'une nouvelle constitution du Québec; le territoire; la citoyenneté; la monnaie; la participation aux traités et aux alliances internationaux; la continuité des lois; le partage des actifs et des dettes; et, enfin, les modalités d'entrée en vigueur de la loi, soit un an après la tenue du référendum à moins que l'Assemblée nationale n'en décide autrement. L'article 3, portant sur la nouvelle constitution précise qu'«elle doit garantir à la communauté anglophone la préservation de son identité et des institutions. Elle doit également reconnaître aux nations autochtones le droit de se gouverner sur des terres leur appartenant en propre. Cette garantie et cette reconnaissance s'exercent dans le respect de l'intégrité du territoire québécois» [20]. Outre les travaux des commissions régionales, la stratégie péquiste comptait sur la publication de travaux d'experts, dont plusieurs recrutés à l'étranger, pour démontrer la faisabilité de la souveraineté et les inconvénients du fédéralisme.

Les libéraux provinciaux et fédéraux ont refusé de participer à la démarche de consultation populaire, qualifiant celle-ci de frauduleuse, d'illégitime et semant la confusion. Pour M. Daniel Johnson, la démarche était trop orientée vers la souveraineté et il n'entendait pas engager ses troupes dans une vaste opération de manipulation et de propagande. C'est sur cette dernière base que les troupes fédéralistes ont boycotté la démarche proposée par le PQ. Force est d'admettre que la démarche référendaire, si «astucieuse» soit-elle, s'inscrivait dans une tradition de consultation que le gouvernement fédéral avait instaurée quelques années plus tôt suite à l'échec de l'Accord du lac Meech, d'autant plus que les Canadiens étaient appelés à se prononcer sur une question de facture semblable en 1992. La question était tout de même plus ambiguë en 1992 puisqu'elle demandait aux Canadiens de se prononcer «sur la base» d'une entente dont le texte officiel n'a été rendu public qu'en cours de référendum.

Faute de pouvoir proposer de nouveaux arrangements constitutionnels, les forces fédéralistes ont plutôt misé sur l'éloge du caractère évolutif du fédéralisme en faisant valoir les changements pouvant être obtenus dans le cadre des mécanismes politiques déjà en place [21]. Ils ont pu compter sur le soutien tacite du milieu des affaires [22] ainsi que sur les craintes exprimées à maintes reprises par les porte-parole des nations autochtones. Ceux-ci avaient déjà rappelé au cours de la campagne électorale qu'ils entendaient faire reconnaître leur droit de demeurer dans la Confédération si telle était leur intention. Cette revendication fut réitérée par les chefs de l'Assemblée des premières nations qui rédigeaient une courte déclaration commune à la mi-octobre où on pouvait lire qu'ils rejetaient le concept de l'intégrité territoriale du Québec tout en considérant toutes les options présentes : «Nous seuls, les peuples indigènes, déterminerons l'avenir de nos enfants sur des principes d'égalité et de coexistence pacifique. [...] Nous défendrons nos droits et notre droit de choisir avec qui nous désirons nous associer. [...] Toute modification du cadre constitutionnel politique exigera le consentement des peuples autochtones» [23].

Mais au plan de la stratégie sur le terrain, le camp fédéraliste a surtout insisté sur les incertitudes qui accompagneraient la constitution du nouvel État, cherchant manifestement à jouer sur les craintes exprimées par les indécis : renégociation défavorable au Québec de l'Accord de libre-échange nord-américain, perte d'emplois, illégalité de la sécession, perte du dollar canadien, difficultés du partage de la dette et des actifs et pressions fiscales que cela créerait au Québec, remise en question des programmes sociaux, diminution des investissements étrangers, menace sur les pensions de vieillesse versées par le gouvernement fédéral et finalement perte de la citoyenneté canadienne.

L'unique représentant de l'ADQ à l'Assemblée nationale et chef de ce parti a quant à lui adopté une approche plus conciliante en posant cinq conditions à sa participation aux commissions : que le mandat de la commission soit élargi et que des discussions puissent avoir lieu sur la date, le contexte le plus propice et les circonstances dans lesquelles serait tenu le référendum; qu'il soit possible de discuter du bien fondé de la souveraineté; qu'il soit possible de présenter d'autres options; que soit distribué un document présentant la position des autres partis dans tous les foyers québécois et que les présidents des

commissions ne soient pas nommés unilatéralement par le gouvernement [24].
La position de l'ADQ s'inspire de l'expérience de l'Union européenne et propose la mise sur pied d'un parlement commun où les deux entités politiques délégueraient certains pouvoirs, concernant notamment les domaines suivants : la libre circulation des personnes, des biens des services et des capitaux, le commerce international, la politique douanière et tarifaire; le remboursement de la dette conjointe; le maintien d'une monnaie commune, d'une banque centrale et la réglementation des banques à charte; la citoyenneté; l'armée; les politiques générales en matière d'immigration et l'établissement de normes environnementales. Néanmoins, la souveraineté est une condition préalable à l'offre de partenariat.

L'initiative de M. Mario Dumont de participer aux travaux des commissions régionales à condition que son option y soit débattue et la réception positive que lui a réservé M. Parizeau eurent pour effet d'isoler les libéraux mais aussi d'associer les nationalistes modérés à la marche à suivre gouvernementale. Cela a permis de lever l'hypothèque qui pesait sur la démarche péquiste en permettant de discuter des options qui ne se situaient pas expressément dans la mouvance péquiste. Le chef du PLQ revint à la mi-janvier sur sa position qui consistait en un boycott intégral des commissions en invitant les fédéralistes à y témoigner sur une base individuelle.

LES COMMISSIONS RÉGIONALES :
UN EXERCICE DE RENFORCEMENT POSITIF

La mise en branle des commissions régionales visait aussi à élargir le plus possible la coalition souverainiste. C'est ainsi que Jean-Paul L'Allier, maire de la ville de Québec et ex-ministre libéral, M. Marcel Masse et Mme Monique Vézina, ex-ministres du gouvernement conservateur de Brian Mulroney, furent choisis pour présider les commissions sur la souveraineté de Québec, de Montréal et des aînés. Dans la même veine, la présidence de la Commission de Laval fut attribuée à M. Philippe Garceau. ancien membre de l'exécutif du PLQ et Mme Diane Viau, ex-vice-présidente du PLQ, fut nommée à la vice-présidence de la Commission régionale de la Montérégie. Le tandem PQ-BQ pouvait aussi compter sur l'appui du mouvement syndical même si le soutien du milieu des affaires continuait à lui faire défaut. Le mouvement Desjardins, dont le président avait appuyé l'option souverainiste lors de la Commission Bélanger-Campeau, décidait quant à lui de rester neutre.

Cette démarche cherchait aussi à apaiser les craintes des Québécois quant à l'impact économique de la souveraineté. Un document interne du PQ recommandait de «relever le niveau de fierté des Québécois» et de gagner la bataille économique en démontrant que la souveraineté ne ferait pas baisser le niveau de vie. Finalement, il importe d'amener les indécis à «voter contre» le

fédéralisme actuel en insistant sur le *statu quo* endossé par les forces fédéralistes [25]. Le public cible était donc composé des nationalistes qualifiés de
«mous» qui ont le profil suivant : âgés de 18 à 45 ans, peu politisés et infor-
més, moins instruits, économiquement fragiles, souvent socialement démunis
qui craignent la part de dette que le Québec devrait assumer, la fermeture des
frontières et la violence que pourrait provoquer la souveraineté, que les programmes sociaux soient menacés, que les taxes augmentent, qu'ils perdent
leur identité canadienne, que le Québec soit isolé en Amérique du Nord et que
les réactions des autochtones soient négatives.

C'est pourquoi l'argumentaire souverainiste reposait sur la démonstration
que le Québec est en avance sur le reste du Canada dans bien des secteurs et
peut se passer de la tutelle du gouvernement central (notamment dans les domaines de la santé, des services sociaux, de la formation de la main-d'oeuvre).
Prenant appui sur les contraintes fiscales imposées par les politiques fédérales, il s'agissait aussi de faire savoir qu'Ottawa n'a plus les moyens de ses
ambitions bien qu'il continue à s'ingérer dans les champs de compétences
provinciales et d'imposer des normes dites «nationales». En somme, il est
plus facile de relever les défis à partir d'un seul gouvernement plutôt que
d'essayer de dégager des consensus à l'échelle canadienne. Les commissions
sur la souveraineté invitaient donc surtout le citoyen moyen, non partisan, à
faire valoir ses vues mais surtout à s'informer sur les différentes dimensions
du projet souverainiste afin de diminuer les appréhensions et de clarifier les
enjeux. Pour M. Parizeau, le discours souverainiste doit «rassurer sur l'impact économique de la souveraineté, le maintien de leur niveau de vie, de leur
emploi» et doit «relever le niveau de fierté des Québécois et répondre à leurs
préoccupations quant à l'avenir de la langue et de la culture, à l'impossibilité
d'acquérir plus de pouvoirs dans le régime fédéral actuel» [26]. Voilà posée la
raison d'être des commissions régionales sur la souveraineté.

Les stratégies souverainiste et fédéraliste n'ont que peu modifié l'état de
l'opinion publique. Les cinq sondages réalisés entre l'élection du PQ et la fin
décembre 1994 montrent une stagnation de l'option gouvernementale alors
que l'appui à la souveraineté fluctue, avant la répartition des indécis, entre 32
et 36 pour cent et que l'appui au Non varie entre 54 et 42 pour cent. Les
indécis — ou les discrets — ont plutôt tendance, dans une proportion d'environ
60 pour cent, à rejoindre le camp fédéraliste. Par ailleurs, au cours de cette
période, les Québécois appuient majoritairement la démarche péquiste, ce
soutien variant de 55 à 58 pour cent [27], même si un bon nombre juge toujours
la question confuse (44 pour cent contre 53 pour cent qui trouvent la question
claire)[28] et voudraient une question dont le libellé serait «Voulez-vous que le
Québec se sépare et devienne un pays indépendant?», soit 62 pour cent des
répondants. Un sondage réalisé à la mi-janvier révélait que seulement 46 pour
cent des Québécois, après relance et répartition des indécis, auraient répondu
positivement à la question référendaire de l'Avant-projet de loi sur la

souveraineté, bien qu'une majorité en faveur du Oui se dégageait dans toutes les régions à l'exception de l'Estrie, Montréal et l'Outaouais et que 40 pour cent auraient voté Oui à une question plus dure portant sur la séparation du Québec [29].

Ces sondages permettent de mesurer le chemin parcouru par les souverainistes depuis le référendum de 1980. À cette époque, la question portait sur un mandat de négocier la souveraineté-association et il était encore possible de rêver à une éventuelle refonte du régime fédéral. En 1995, deux Québécois sur cinq appuient l'idée de séparation pure et simple. C'est dire que le PQ peut maintenant compter sur un noyau solide d'indépendantistes nettement supérieur à celui qui existait il y a quinze ans. Néanmoins, l'espoir de voir la Constitution canadienne amendée et l'attachement au Canada demeurent vifs. Parmi les options constitutionnelles privilégiées par les Québécois, l'obtention de plus de pouvoirs pour la province devance celle de la souveraineté-association (respectivement 35 et 33 pour cent). De même, les deux tiers des Québécois souhaitaient que le gouvernement fédéral présente des offres constitutionnelles au Québec avant le référendum [30]. En cela, le camp souverainiste n'est pas parvenu à accréditer l'idée voulant que l'expérience fédérale soit un échec pour le Québec et que toutes les issues soient bouchées. Qui plus est, une majorité de Québécois (51 pour cent) croient que le *statu quo* est préférable à la souveraineté et que le Québec à plus à perdre en devenant un pays indépendant. Cet attachement au Canada s'exprime aussi lorsqu'on associe la souveraineté au maintien de l'union économique canadienne : 55 pour cent appuieraient la souveraineté s'ils étaient à peu près certains que le reste du Canada maintiendrait une association économique avec un Québec souverain. De la même manière, l'insécurité culturelle des Québécois francophones n'est pas, à elle seule, suffisante pour faire pencher la balance : seulement 55 pour cent voteraient Oui s'ils avaient la certitude que le statut du français s'améliorerait dans un Québec souverain. Comme le rappelait pertinemment la journaliste Chantal Hébert : «[l]e sondage identifie l'absence de motivation concrète comme un des talons d'Achille du projet souverainiste» [31]. C'est dire que pour obtenir un score référendaire autour des 55 pour cent, les forces souverainistes doivent jouer sur plusieurs tableaux à la fois et faire la démonstration, hors de tout doute, qu'il serait possible de maintenir l'union économique, de conserver la citoyenneté canadienne (ou à tout le moins l'usage de son passeport), d'améliorer le sort du français et de conserver le territoire actuel.

Dès la mi-février, le gouvernement envisageait la possibilité de reporter à l'automne le référendum que M. Jacques Parizeau aurait voulu tenir en juin 1995. Le plafonnement de l'option souverainiste dans les sondages n'était certes pas propice à un «référendum gagnant», selon l'expression de M. Lucien Bouchard pour qui la victoire référendaire est plus importante que les échéances. Les commissions régionales n'ont pas permis de modifier les tendances lourdes qui se manifestaient dans l'opinion publique. Le premier message du chef du BQ lors de sa rentrée sur la scène politique après une absence de deux mois et demi suite à une terrible maladie invitait à une reformulation de la stratégie souverainiste et à une reformulation de la question à poser au référendum. Au cours de l'entrevue accordée à l'émission *Le Point* de la télévision de la SRC, il déclarait sur la question qu'«il y a des critères, il faut que la réponse permette de sortir du marasme actuel, du *statu quo*, qu'elle soit positive» et invitait les Québécois à conjuguer les deux démons qui les affligent : l'indécision et la division [32].

Au sein du camp souverainiste, on pouvait voir les premiers signes de rapprochement avec l'ADQ découlant de la nécessité d'élargir le soutien populaire à l'endroit de l'option souverainiste. M. Lucien Bouchard évoquait la possibilité de lier la question référendaire à la notion d'union économique avec le reste du Canada. M. Mario Dumont suggérait de poser aux Québécois une question à trois volets comprenant la souveraineté, une union politique et économique avec le reste du Canada ou le maintien du *statu quo*. Plusieurs ministres du PQ se disaient ouverts à la possibilité de modifier la question afin de proposer un «projet rassembleur», véritable hantise devant les signes avant-coureurs d'une défaite référendaire. Mais il n'en demeure pas moins que l'option de l'ADQ ne semblait pas avoir reçu un accueil enthousiaste lors des travaux des commissions régionales. C'est ce qui faisait dire au ministre et leader parlementaire, M. Guy Chevrette, que «sa proposition n'a pas reçu l'adhésion qu'il [Mario Dumont] attendait. Je pense que les citoyens, qui se sont exprimés librement, considèrent qu'il y a un palier de gouvernement de trop. Ça ressort d'une façon très évidente» [33]. Pour M. Jacques Parizeau, il était hors de question de tenir une consultation sur une nouvelle union politique. Il rappelait que l'Avant-projet de loi prévoyait la négociation d'une union politique avec le reste du Canada advenant la souveraineté. À la fin de l'exercice de consultation, la démarche n'avait pas réussi à recréer un *momentum* favorable aux souverainistes, ces derniers affichant publiquement leurs interrogations à la fois sur la question à poser et sur les moyens à prendre pour élargir un soutien populaire qui tardait à se manifester.

Au moment de la conclusion des travaux de la commission régionale de Montréal, son président, M. Marcel Masse, soulignait le fait que les Québécois n'étaient pas encore prêts à se prononcer sur la souveraineté et que le débat devrait inclure la définition d'un projet de société : «Et ça, c'est nouveau par rapport à 1980, alors que les gens s'attardaient davantage à l'idée d'un pays. Cette fois-ci, on dit : Un pays, oui, mais pour en faire quoi» [34]. Cette intervention faisait écho aux multiples appréhensions exprimées devant les commissions et la préférence des Québécois pour une rupture tranquille et sans douleur.

Les travaux des commissions ont permis à plus de 55 000 personnes de participer aux activités publiques et plus de 5500 mémoires ont été déposés.

Ce sont surtout les questions relatives à la décentralisation, aux garanties quant aux bénéfices et aux coûts de la souveraineté et au projet de société qui ont retenu l'attention. La lecture des sondages unanimement défavorables à l'option souverainiste a amené le gouvernement à reporter à l'automne la tenue du référendum. Dans un rappel haut en couleur de la fameuse Bataille de Balaklava pendant de la Guerre de Crimée au cours de laquelle les troupes britanniques furent massacrées, le vice-premier ministre M. Bernard Landry dira : «Je ne veux pas être le commandant en second de la brigade légère qui fut exterminée en Crimée en vingt minutes à cause de l'irresponsabilité de ses commandants» [35]. À compter de cette date, le sort d'un référendum en juin était scellé, les souverainistes invoquant le besoin d'informer davantage la population pour en justifier le report. Un sondage venait confirmer cette réalité car même après deux mois de commissions régionales, seulement 48 pour cent affirmaient en savoir suffisamment sur le projet du PQ pour prendre une décision et 24 pour cent disaient pouvoir changer d'idée s'ils disposaient de plus d'information [36]. Par delà la lecture stratégique de ces données, ils soulignent le peu d'attention portée par bon nombre de citoyens à la question du statut politique du Québec, traduisant soit une fatigue à l'endroit des questions constitutionnelles ou le fait qu'ils sont peu intéressés par les détails nombreux et complexes qui l'entourent.

LE «VIRAGE» DE LUCIEN BOUCHARD :
LES ACTEURS SE REPOSITIONNENT

Le deuxième article de l'Avant-projet de loi indiquait que le gouvernement serait «autorisé à conclure avec le gouvernement du Canada un accord consacrant le maintien d'une association économique entre le Québec et le Canada» [37]. Cet article ne précisait pas la nature ou l'étendue de l'association souhaitée, bien qu'il semblait s'agir d'une association essentiellement économique, tout en conférant une marge de manoeuvre importante au gouvernement quant à la forme que pourrait prendre une telle association [38]. Comme nous l'avons souligné, la question de l'association économique a constitué l'un des aspects ayant marqué les débats devant les commissions sur l'avenir du Québec, et plus particulièrement au sein des régions qui partagent une frontière avec les autres provinces canadiennes. Par ailleurs, le thème d'un nouveau partenariat Québec-Canada constituait la pierre d'assise de la plate-forme constitutionnelle de l'ADQ, joueur minoritaire mais tout de même indispensable à l'élargissement de la clientèle souverainiste.

Lors de son allocution prononcée devant 1400 délégués au moment de l'ouverture du premier Congrès national du BQ au début avril 1995, M. Lucien Bouchard indiquait son intention de voir les forces souverainistes opérer un virage et proposer, aux lendemains de la souveraineté, une forme de

partenariat qui prendrait la forme d'une union politique inspirée du traité de
Maastricht :

> [...] l'examen des recommandations des commissions régionales ainsi que les
> discussions tenues à la Commission nationale révèlent que nos concitoyens
> veulent donner des assises plus élaborées à l'Union économique Québec-Canada.
> Compte tenu de l'ampleur de l'espace économique commun, il nous faut réflé-
> chir davantage sur les moyens concrets de le consolider. Il importe d'examiner
> sérieusement l'opportunité de l'encadrer par des institutions communes, voire
> de nature politique [39].

S'inspirant du document publié par le BQ en 1992 [40], M. Bouchard évoquait
la mise sur pied d'une Conférence parlementaire pour débattre des questions
d'intérêt commun, d'un secrétariat pour gérer un accord global entre les deux
parties et d'une cour de justice commune pour interpréter les ententes et arbi-
trer les différends. Cette approche avait jusqu'à présent soulevé peu d'intérêt
de la part de M. Parizeau, celui-ci ayant plutôt manifesté beaucoup de mé-
fiance à l'endroit de la notion d'institutions politiques communes entre un
Québec souverain et le Canada. Elle forçait ce dernier à s'aligner sur les priorités mises de l'avant par son plus sûr allié, par surcroît plus populaire dans
l'opinion publique.

La proposition du chef du BQ a fait mouche. M. Mario Dumont indiquait
Après avoir exprimé publiquement à maintes reprises des doutes sur la tenue d'un référendum en juin, M. Bouchard orientait à nouveau le débat et
obligeait le camp souverainiste à évaluer l'avenue d'une éventuelle union
politique. Certains commentateurs politiques y ont vu les signes d'une lutte
de pouvoir opposant les deux leaders souverainistes [41]. D'autres ont plutôt
souligné que le BQ ouvrait une porte que le PQ n'aurait pu franchir sans perdre
sa crédibilité [42]. Quoi qu'il en soit, cette manoeuvre, présentée par les uns
comme un «virage» et par les autres comme un «éclaircissement», avait pour
objectif d'attirer la sympathie des Québécois pour qui l'appartenance au
Canada demeure un élément important de leur identité et «d'améliorer les
chances de tenir un référendum gagnant», de l'aveu de M. Bouchard [43]. Ces
gens, peu attirés par la souveraineté, n'en manifestent pas moins un profond
mécontentement à l'endroit du régime politique actuel et cherchent à obtenir
des aménagements reflétant un rapport égalitaire entre les sociétés québécoise et canadienne. En plaçant l'accent sur une éventuelle union politique,
l'approche du BQ interpellait aussi l'ADQ qui voulait faire porter le référendum sur une nouvelle union, à la différence près que pour M. Bouchard la
souveraineté était posée comme un préalable à toute offre de partenariat.

La proposition du chef du BQ a fait mouche. M. Mario Dumont indiquait
d'abord qu'il se joindrait au camp du Oui si le virage vers une union économique et politique était inscrit dans le projet et la question référendaire [44]. Il
continua par la suite à faire valoir qu'il préférerait un référendum sur une
offre de partenariat qui, si elle était rejetée par le Canada, devrait conduire à

une déclaration de souveraineté ou à un autre référendum [45]. Il devait finalement admettre qu'il était inspiré par la question soumise par un proche conseiller de M. Parizeau lors des audiences de la Commission Bélanger-Campeau qui souhaitait un référendum portant sur l'indépendance du Québec advenant un échec des négociations portant sur une entente de souveraineté-association avec le reste du Canada [46].

Par ailleurs, un sondage publié dans le *Toronto Star* révélait qu'une question incluant la notion d'association récoltait 51 pour cent d'appuis contre 39 pour cent pour une question ne portant que sur la souveraineté [47]. Le changement de cap amorcé par Lucien Bouchard découlait d'une lecture attentive des sondages d'opinions.

LE RAPPORT DE LA COMMISSION NATIONALE SUR L'AVENIR DU QUÉBEC

À la mi-avril, la Commission nationale sur l'avenir du Québec déposait son rapport. On peut y lire, sans surprise, que «[l]'article 1 de l'avant-projet de loi édictant que "le Québec est un pays souverain" a reçu la faveur d'une nette majorité des interventions faites par les individus» [48]. S'enracinant dans le rejet du *statu quo*, la souveraineté est présentée comme indispensable à la sauvegarde de l'identité du peuple québécois et à l'épanouissement de sa culture. Les commissaires notent toutefois que «le résultat des négociations avec le reste du Canada, quant à l'association économique et au partage de la dette, suscite de nombreuses questions relatives aux coûts éventuels de la souveraineté en matière économique et sociale» [49].

Dans l'ensemble, les 40 recommandations formulées par la Commission nationale n'étaient pas discordantes avec l'Avant-projet de loi. Plusieurs d'entre elles précisaient toutefois la portée de certaines dispositions soumises à l'attention de la population et reprenaient certains thèmes qui ont dominé les débats publics au cours des derniers mois. C'est ainsi que la Commission recommandait que la Déclaration de souveraineté tienne compte des attentes exprimées lors des audiences concernant, notamment, le statut du français. Cet aspect était absent de l'Avant-projet de loi, ce qui n'a pas manqué d'être souligné par de nombreux intervenants issus du milieu des arts et de la culture, de telle sorte que la Déclaration devrait rappeler que le français est la langue commune et officielle des Québécois. Faisant écho à l'idée du projet de société, il était aussi proposé d'inclure dans la Déclaration une référence au fait que les principes de l'égalité des hommes et des femmes, de la lutte à la pauvreté et à l'exclusion sociale, le respect de l'environnement ainsi que la solidarité internationale étaient partagés par la population. De la même manière, le *Rapport* invitait, bien que dans des termes généraux, le gouvernement à esquisser un projet de société pour le Québec de demain. Sur la question de l'union économique, l'une des craintes majeures ressentie par les Québécois, la Commission recommandait au gouvernement de préciser la nature des institutions communes, dont un tribunal de résolution des conflits. La Commission se mettait au diapason du «virage» proposé par le BQ et tendait la main aux partisans de l'ADQ qui avaient participé au processus de consultation en recommandant que «la souveraineté sera, pour le Québec, le signal d'un nouveau départ dans un partenariat avec le Canada qui n'exclurait pas éventuellement une forme d'union politique» [50]. C'est ainsi qu'un Québec souverain pourrait proposer des structures politiques communes au reste du Canada. Finalement, c'est au chapitre des relations avec les nations autochtones que la Commission a formulé le plus de recommandations, soit six sur un total de 40. La pierre angulaire des recommandations est la reconnaissance des droits des autochtones et la nécessité de négocier avec eux dans le respect de la constitution, du territoire et des lois du Québec. La Commission invitait à plus de clarté et demandait à l'État du Québec d'expliciter «davantage sa vision des rapports que le Québec devrait entretenir avec la population autochtone»[51].

Du document de 102 pages, ce sont surtout la réaffirmation de la souveraineté comme «seule option apte à répondre aux aspirations des Québécois», l'allusion à une éventuelle union politique et le chapitre relatif à la décentralisation qui ont retenu l'attention. Les fédéralistes y ont vu un rapport qui ne reflétait pas les positions de 60 pour cent des Québécois et les adéquistes la prise en compte de leurs propositions. L'éditorial du quotidien *La Presse* résume bien la réaction des premiers. Pour Mme Agnès Gruda, il s'agissait d'«[u]n exercice astucieux et vicié dès le départ, qui a donné au point d'arrivée les résultats auxquels on pouvait s'attendre : une allusion au consensus autour d'une option qui, pourtant, ne réussit pas à "lever" au-delà du traditionnel 40 p. cent» de telle sorte qu'«à quelques détails près, tout cet exercice aura servi à entériner une démarche déjà engagée. [...] Même son ouverture à une éventuelle union politique [...] a été grandement surestimée, tant elle est bardée de conditions» [52].

L'ENTENTE TRIPARTITE : À LA RECHERCHE D'UNE FUYANTE MAJORITÉ

Deux semaines après le Congrès du BQ (tenu du 7 au 9 avril), M. Jacques Parizeau adhérait totalement à l'idée de présenter une offre de partenariat au Canada. Il rappelait toutefois que la souveraineté demeurait un préalable à cet exercice qui fournirait la preuve que les souverainistes sont des «gens raisonnables et que nous avons l'intention de proposer des façons dont les deux pays pourraient être associés» [53]. Un proche collaborateur du premier ministre, M. Bernard Landry, faisait savoir que cette décision avait été extrêmement difficile à prendre. Elle était pourtant dictée par une double nécessité : éviter une rupture entre MM. Parizeau et Bouchard quant à la stratégie à adopter et rassembler les conditions permettant de franchir le cap fatidique des 50 pour cent favorables à l'option souverainiste. Cette adhésion du chef du gouvernement aux *desiderata* de son principal allié illustre bien la complexité de l'équation souverainiste. Le premier ministre québécois, chef du PQ et principal porte-étendard du Oui est placé dans une position qui le force à faire des compromis. Le projet souverainiste «rassembleur» n'est possible qu'à ce prix.

Il aura fallu moins d'un mois pour que se dégage un consensus au sein du camp du Oui sur la question de l'union politique et que s'amorce un rapprochement avec l'ADQ. Au début de mois de mai, M. Bouchard affirmait que le virage était terminé et qu'il n'envisageait aucun autre ajustement significatif au projet souverainiste : «Les éléments de souplesse, ils sont contenus dans le projet dont M. Parizeau et moi avons convenu. [...] Il peut y avoir des nuances de mécanismes, mais fondamentalement, il s'agit d'un référendum qui permettra à l'Assemblée nationale de proclamer la souveraineté et de faire au Canada anglais une proposition qu'il prendra ou ne prendra pas» [54]. Le contenu de l'offre de partenariat devrait être connu avant le référendum même si elle ne sera transmise au Canada qu'après la tenue de celui-ci. De la même manière, les développements survenus au cours du dernier mois ont amené les forces souverainistes à repenser les termes de la question à poser lors du référendum. Elle devrait tenir compte aussi bien de la souveraineté que de l'offre de partenariat pour la création d'institutions conjointes de gestion de l'association. Cette démarche est différente de celle proposée par le PQ en 1980 puisque la souveraineté n'est pas conditionnelle à l'assentiment du Canada et à son acceptation de l'offre.

Le calendrier référendaire prévoit les étapes suivantes : présentation d'un projet de loi et de la question au début septembre, un débat parlementaire suivi du déclenchement du référendum entre la mi-septembre et le début octobre, pour la tenue de la consultation populaire au plus tard à la mi-novembre. D'ici là, le gouvernement a l'intention de produire un document esquissant ce que devrait être un «projet de société» d'un Québec souverain [55].

Le BQ établissait lors de son Congrès un groupe de travail sur l'union économique qui joua notamment un rôle d'entremetteur auprès des instances politiques de l'ADQ. Ces négociations conduisirent à la conclusion d'une entente de principe conclue par MM. Jacques Parizeau, Lucien Bouchard et Mario Dumont le 12 juin 1995. Reprenant le thème du changement, par opposition au *statu quo* constitutionnel qui caractérise les forces fédéralistes, les trois partis réussirent à s'entendre sur les termes du virage proposé par M. Lucien Bouchard moins de deux mois plus tôt : «Nous convenons de conjuguer nos forces et de coordonner nos efforts pour qu'au référendum de l'automne 1995, les Québécois puissent se prononcer pour un véritable changement : faire la souveraineté du Québec et proposer un nouveau partenariat économique et politique au Canada, visant notamment à consolider l'espace économique actuel» [56].

Cette entente s'inspirait largement du document de réflexion déposé par l'ADQ au début mai [57]. Les domaines relevant de cette nouvelle instance supranationale comprendraient l'union douanière, la libre circulation des biens, des personnes, des services et des capitaux ainsi que la politique monétaire, la mobilité de la main-d'oeuvre et la citoyenneté. De plus, les intérêts communs des deux États membres pourraient les conduire à s'entendre dans d'autres domaines : commerce intérieur et international, représentation internationale, transport, défense, institutions financières, politiques fiscales et budgétaires, protection de l'environnement, etc.

Cette entente prévoit la conclusion d'un traité avec le Canada qui ouvrirait la voie à la création et les règles de fonctionnement de quatre institutions communes : le Conseil du partenariat (instance décisionnelle composée de ministres délégués, chaque État membre disposant d'un veto), le secrétariat permanent (qui aurait une fonction de liaison et assurerait le suivi des décisions du Conseil), l'Assemblée parlementaire (formé de députés délégués au sein duquel le Québec détiendrait 25 pour cent des sièges) et le Tribunal de règlement des différends dont les décisions lieraient les États membres. Cette offre de partenariat serait présentée au Canada après une victoire du Oui au référendum et le Québec déclarerait sa souveraineté après entente sur les termes du traité. En cas d'échec des négociations, le Québec déclarerait tout de même sa souveraineté «dans les meilleurs délais». Par ailleurs, un comité d'orientation et de surveillance des négociations comprenant des personnalités indépendantes des trois partis sera créé pour conseiller le gouvernement et informer le public.

La conclusion de l'entente tripartite marquait la fin d'une longue période d'arrimage au sein de ce que les leaders de la mouvance souverainiste ont qualifié de «camp du changement». Les observateurs n'ont pas été longs à faire remarquer que la souveraineté constituait l'étape décisive et que le partenariat était conditionnel à la volonté du Canada de participer ou non à la construction d'une instance politique supranationale. Ils ont aussi souligné le caractère stratégique de la démarche. Dans un éditorial du quotidien *Le Devoir*, M. Gilles Lesage rappelait que «[c]e qui est important [...] c'est que l'option souverainiste est tirée de l'impasse où elle s'enlisait et que le cul-de-sac largement appréhendé s'estompe quelque peu. Bien sûr, cette entente vise à élargir la base des appuis, à rassurer les nationalistes dits "mous", inspirer confiance pour la suite des choses, advenant un vote OUI, autour de la mi-novembre, probablement. Et pourquoi pas?» [58]. Ce n'est pas sans hésitations que les instances péquistes ont approuvé l'entente qui faisait une large place à la notion d'union politique, allant ainsi beaucoup plus loin que le principe d'association économique inscrit au programme [59]. Par ailleurs, les militants de l'ADQ réunis en Congrès général ont manifesté de la suspicion à l'égard de M. Jacques Parizeau et de sa volonté de mener à bon port de telles négociations avec le Canada. La création d'un comité d'orientation et de surveillance est perçue comme une police d'assurance contre les dérapages que pourrait être tenté de provoquer M. Parizeau [60].

Il semble que ce projet constitue une condition essentielle à l'obtention d'une majorité et que les stratèges souverainistes aient visé juste. Ce réalignement stratégique répond au désir d'une écrasante majorité de Québécois (près de 80 pour cent) d'offrir au Canada une association économique advenant la souveraineté. Reste à savoir si cette condition est suffisante. Même si l'idée d'une offre d'association politique recueillait plus de 60 pour cent d'appui d'après un sondage tenu à la mi-juin[61], elle n'a guère réussi à accroître la popularité de l'option souverainiste. En dépit du fait que la souveraineté assortie d'un projet association ralliait entre 52 et 57 pour cent des Québécois au début de l'été 1995[62], le camp fédéraliste semblait avoir une légère avance à la mi-août, 50,5 pour cent des électeurs ayant mentionné leur intention de voter «non» contre 49,5 pour cent «oui»[63]. La solidité des appuis au camp du «oui» était par ailleurs moins bien assurée que celle des fédéralistes, 81,6 pour cent de ceux qui s'opposent à la souveraineté affirmant ne pas avoir l'intention de changer d'idée comparativement à 68,4 pour cent de ceux qui ont l'intention de voter «oui». Des universitaires et spécialistes en sondages proches de la famille souverainiste faisaient remarquer que les enquêtes d'opinion publique ont toujours systématiquement surévaluées le vote nationaliste en répartissant inadéquatement les indécis de telle sorte que l'écart entre les deux camps pourrait être différent le soir du référendum, à l'avantage du camp fédéraliste. Ils soulignent aussi «l'effet de tassement» qui ne peut que se produire lorsque les forces du Non clameront inlassablement leur opposition à toute forme de partenariat, insécurisant ainsi le centre de l'électorat plus fragile, conservateur et moins politisé[64].

Ces éléments démontrent qu'une victoire référendaire, dans la meilleure des hypothèses, ne pourrait dépasser la barre du 50 pour cent que par quelques points. Pour leur part, les fédéralistes tenteront sûrement de démontrer les faiblesses du projet d'association et l'improbabilité que celle-ci aille jusqu'à une union politique afin de gruger les appuis fraîchement acquis par le camp souverainiste. La bataille référendaire aura pour cible les indécis ou les convertis de la dernière heure.

CONCLUSION

À la fin juin 1995, la stratégie souverainiste est maintenant précisée : le cap sur la souveraineté est maintenu même si cette dernière est maintenant assortie d'une offre de partenariat. L'échéancier et la stratégie préréférendaire définis lors de la campagne électorale de septembre 1994 ont été substantiellement modifiés. La courte victoire électorale et les pressions exercées par les alliés fédéraux en ont décidé autrement. Les efforts conjugués du BQ et de l'ADQ ont amené le PQ a revoir l'un des aspects majeurs de son projet en le forçant à tenir compte du désir de nombreux Québécois de maintenir une forme d'association formelle avec le reste du Canada. L'adhésion de l'ADQ au camp souverainiste ne peut qu'élargir la base des appuis à cette option. Contrairement aux propos de l'éditorialiste en chef de *La Presse* qui a qualifié l'ADQ de marginal [65], il n'en demeure pas moins que ce parti recueille entre 10 et 15 pour cent de la faveur de l'électorat et qu'environ un tiers de ses sympathisants sont tentés par l'aventure souverainiste. Il s'agit sans nul doute du membre minoritaire de l'entente tripartite, mais tout de même du joueur indispensable. À cet égard, la mention du terme association dans la question référendaire fait passer, soutiennent les sondeurs, l'appui à la souveraineté au-delà de la barre fatidique des 50 pour cent [66]. Néanmoins, plusieurs écueils se profilent à l'horizon. D'abord, les Québécois ont toujours majoritairement manifesté un plus grand penchant à l'endroit d'un réaménagement du fédéralisme qui soulève, bon an mal an, plus d'intérêt que la souveraineté «pure et dure». Ensuite, l'élargissement de la coalition souverainiste est le fruit des efforts consentis par l'élite politique, quoiqu'en dise M. Parizeau qui en appelle au «consensus» dégagé lors de l'exercice de consultation tenue au cours de l'hiver. Par ailleurs, le gouvernement québécois devra tenir sa consultation hypothéqué par un bilan de réalisations qui n'ont pas toujours été accueillies favorablement dans la population, notamment aux chapitres de la gestion des services de santé, de l'éducation et de la réforme de l'aide juridique. De plus, ni les commissions régionales, ni les multiples appels à la fierté n'ont réussi à recréer un *momentum* favorable à l'option souverainiste comparable à celui qui a marqué l'échec de l'Accord du lac Meech. Finalement, le camp fédéraliste est resté plutôt effacé au cours de la campagne préréférendaire et ses interventions ont consisté à faire porter le fardeau de la preuve aux seuls souverainistes.

En somme, l'appui qui se dégage des sondages à l'égard de l'idée d'union politique risque de fondre comme neige au soleil lorsque la véritable campagne référendaire sera lancée. Le camp du Non n'est par ailleurs pas exempt de contradictions qui risquent de briser l'unanimité qui semble se dégager à l'heure actuelle. D'une part, il devra mettre tout en oeuvre pour éviter de se faire accoler l'étiquette du camp du *statu quo*. Cette option est largement rejetée par une majorité de Québécois. On comprend aisément les libéraux fédéraux d'éviter de promettre des changements qui seraient indubitablement mal reçus de la part des Canadiens qui ont reporté aux calendes grecques toute réforme constitutionnelle majeure puisqu'ils n'en voient pas la nécessité. On ne peut en dire autant des libéraux provinciaux qui ont une position menant à un cul-de-sac [67]. Ils souhaitent un régime fédéral plus décentralisé et plus flexible mais sont incapables de fournir des garanties quant aux probabilités de changement dans le temps [68]. D'autre part, la stratégie qui a consisté depuis l'élection du PQ à insister uniquement sur les coûts de la séparation «pure et dure», option qui recueille le moins d'appuis, ne tient pas compte des attentes profondes d'une majorité de Québécois [69]. En d'autres termes, pour avoir la certitude de gagner, il n'est pas suffisant de faire l'éloge du régime fédéral. Si les Québécois demeurent attachés au Canada, ils trouvent néanmoins dysfonctionnels les arrangements actuels. Dans ce contexte, les forces fédéralistes devront aussi préciser le sens à donner à une victoire du Non. Si tel n'est pas le cas, bon nombre d'indécis pourraient être tentés par le changement proposé par le camp souverainiste auquel il sera facile d'opposer l'immobilisme des fédéralistes.

Une victoire du Non au référendum ne pourrait être interprétée comme la manifestation de la volonté des Québécois d'adhérer à la Constitution de 1982. Au mieux, elle marquerait un retour à la case départ et confirmerait l'absence d'un rapport de force favorable au Québec dans le régime fédéral. Au pire, elle ouvrirait la porte à une autre offensive du gouvernement fédéral dans les champs de compétence provinciale. Il est aussi possible que le camp du Oui, appréhendant une défaite, reporte la tenue du référendum ou que celui-ci n'ait jamais lieu. M. Bouchard demeure un élément important de la coalition souverainiste et pourrait fort bien juger que les conditions ne sont pas réunies pour un «référendum gagnant». Un report *sine die* du référendum ne ferait que perpétuer la situation actuelle faite d'insatisfactions, de récriminations constantes et d'espoirs frustrés. Cela serait sûrement interprété par le camp fédéraliste comme un aveu d'impuissance. Toutefois, la charge symbolique d'un référendum perdu serait plus importante que celle associée à un événement non tenu. Un tel report ne menacerait pas à court terme la raison d'être du BQ et de l'ADQ. Il en serait autrement pour le PQ qui devrait traverser une crise existentielle profonde.

Les termes du «projet rassembleur» sont maintenant connus et ne pourront qu'être marginalement modifiés. Il reste maintenant à attendre un momentum qui tarde à venir.

NOTES

1. François Rocher et Miriam Smith, «Four Dimensions of the Canadian Constitutional Debate», dans F. Rocher et M. Smith (sous la direction de), *New Trends in Canadian Federalism* (Peterborough: Broadview Press, 1995), pp. 61-64.

2. F.L. Morton, *Federalism and the Charter of Rights: Empowering the Centre* (Montréal : Communication présentée au Congrès annuel de l'Association canadienne de science politique, Juin 1995).

3. Peter Russell, *Constitutional Odyssey. Can Canadians Become a Sovereign People?* (Toronto : University of Toronto Press, 1993), p. 230.

4.   Robert Boily, «Un fédéralisme en éclatement», *Un pays incertain. Réflexions sur le Québec post-référendaire* (Montréal : Québec/Amérique, 1980), p. 44.

5.   Il semble en effet qu'en dépit du discours dominant, le développement de l'État s'est davantage stabilisé que réduit. Les politiques de déréglementation et de privatisation ont plutôt conduit à une reformulation des objectifs et des instruments de contrôle étatique, accroissant la puissance d'intervention de l'État au lieu de la réduire. Voir à ce sujet Robert Bernier et James Ian Gow (sous la direction de), *Un État réduit? A Down-sized State?* (Sainte-Foy : Presses de l'Université du Québec, 1994).

6.   Édouard Cloutier, Jean H. Guay et Daniel Latouche, *Le virage. L'évolution de l'opinion publique au Québec depuis 1960 ou comment le Québec est devenu souverainiste* (Montréal : Québec/Amérique, 1992), pp. 45-46.

7.   André Bousquet et Denis Monière, «Les visées stratégiques des partis», dans Denis Monière et Jean H. Guay, *La bataille du Québec. Deuxième épisode : les élections québécoises de 1994* (Montréal : Fides, 1995), p. 27.

8.   Michel Venne, «Pas de souveraineté sans référendum», *Le Devoir*, 7 août 1994, p. A1 et A10.

9.   Michel Venne, «Le Canada évolutif de Johnson», *Le Devoir,* 15 juin 1994, p. A1.

10.   Paul Cauchon, «Johnson promet d'oeuvrer au respect du Québec comme société distincte», *Le Devoir*, 19 août 1994, p. A10.

11.   Pierre O'Neil, «Constitution : les Québécois rejettent le moratoire prôné par Johnson», *Le Devoir*, pp. A1-A2.

12.   Daniel Latouche, «Regardez les chiffres», *Le Devoir*, 4 septembre 1994, p. A8.

13.   Lise Bissonnette, «Le choix. 8- Le statut du Québec», *Le Devoir*, 4 septembre 1994, p. A8.

14 . Denis Monière, «Le déroulement de la campagne électorale», Monière, Guay, op. cit., pp. 39-71.

15.   Jean H. Guay, «L'analyse des résultats électoraux», Monière et Guay, op. cit., p. 210.

16.   Michel Venne, «Vers la souveraineté sans confrontation», *Le Devoir*, 15 septembre 1994, p. A1-A6.

17.   Michel Venne, «Quatre fronts, quelques écueils», *Le Devoir*, 1er octobre 1994, p. A1.

18.   Michel Venne et Pierre O'Neil, «Parizeau s'en prend à l'esprit de chapelle du PQ», *Le Devoir*, 7 novembre 1994, p. A1-A10.

19.   De large extraits du discours d'ouverture de la 35e législature de l'Assemblée nationale du Québec furent reproduit dans *Le Devoir* du 30 novembre 1994, p. A9.

20.   Québec, *Avant-projet de loi sur la souveraineté du Québec* (Québec : Éditeur officiel, 1994).

21.   Voir à cet égard la synthèse de Ronald Watts, «What is the Status of the Status quo?», *Policy Options Politiques* (vol. 16, no. 3, avril 1995), pp. 28-31.

22. Le Conseil du patronat du Québec faisait connaître son opposition à l'indépendance du Québec au début mars 1995. Pour le CPQ, la souveraineté entraînerait des coûts et une baisse du niveau de vie que la population québécoise n'est pas prête à assumer. Voir le résumé de la Déclaration de principe du CPQ dans *Le Devoir*, 7 mars 1995, p. A7.

23. Cette déclaration fut reproduite dans *Le Devoir*, 14 octobre 1994, p. A5.

24. Michel Venne, «Démarche référendaire. Mario Dumont pose ses conditions», *Le Devoir*, 8 décembre 1994, p. A6.

25. Denis Lessard, «Pour les souverainistes, la victoire du OUI passe par l'économie», *La Presse*, 21 janvier 1995, p. A21.

26. Michel Venne, «Après les purs et les durs, les "mous"», *Le Devoir*, 22 janvier 1995, pp. A1-A12.

27. Michel Venne, «Quatre fronts : 2) Le grand ralliement. Il manque des couleurs à la coalition arc-en-ciel», *Le Devoir*, 4 janvier 1995, pp. A1-A8.

28. Pierre O'Neil, «La question remise en question», *Le Devoir*, 26 janvier 1995, p. A1-A10.

29. Mario Fontaine, «54% des Québécois disent Non à Parizeau», *La Presse*, 26 janvier 1995, p. B1.

30. Au début mars 1995, ce sentiment n'avait guère changé puisque 63 pour cent des Québécois souhaitaient toujours obtenir de nouvelles offres constitutionnelles avant le référendum. Néanmoins, 49 pour cent auraient opté pour la souveraineté. Konrad Yakabuski, «Sondage CROP-*L'Actualité*. 63% des Québécois souhaitent une réforme constitutionnelle». *Le Devoir*, 4-5 mars 1995, pp. A1-A10.

31. Chantal Hébert, «Les Québécois préfèrent le statu quo», *La Presse*, 17 février 1995, p. B5. Voir aussi Michel Venne, «Sondage CROP-Environics-Radio-Canada. 51% des Québécois préfèrent le statu quo à la souveraineté», *Le Devoir*, 17 février 1995, pp. A1-A12.

32. Stéphane Baillargeon, «Il ne faut pas "exposer les Québécois à un Non". Lucien Bouchard s'interroge sur la stratégie référendaire», *Le Devoir*, 20 février 1995, pp. A1-A8.

33. Gilles Normand, «Union économique : la suggestion de Bouchard est une idée parmi d'autres», *La Presse*, 2 mars 1995, p. A2.

34. Paul Roy, «Le Québec a besoin d'un projet de société», *La Presse*, 6 mars 1995, p. A1-A2 et Pierre O'Neil, «Les Québécois ne sont pas prêts à voter», *Le Devoir*, 4-5 mars 1995, pp. A1-A10.

35. Konrad Yakabuski et Jean Dion, «Tenue du référendum. Landry penche pour l'automne», *Le Devoir*, 28 mars 1995, pp. A1-A8.

36. Mario Fontaine, «59% des Québécois s'opposent encore à la souveraineté», *La Presse*, 7 avril 1995, p. B4.

37. Québec, *Avant-projet de loi sur la souveraineté du Québec*, op. cit., p. 5.

38. Daniel Turp, *L'Avant-projet de loi sur la souveraineté. Texte annoté* (Montréal : Les Éditions Yvon Blais, 1995), pp. 17-20.

39. Dans son édition du 11 avril 1995, *La Presse* reproduisit de larges extraits du discours de M. Bouchard, p. B3.

40. Bloc québécois, *Un nouveau parti pour l'étape décisive* (Montréal : Éditions Fides, 1992).

41. Lysiane Gagnon, «Virage ou lutte de pouvoir?», *La Presse*, 11 avril 1995, p. B3.

42. Chantal Hébert, «Bouchard attend un signal», *La Presse*, 10 avril 1995, p. A1-A2; voir aussi l'éditorial de Claude Masson, «Le "virage" de l'option souverainiste», La Presse, 10 avril 1995, p. B2

43. Gilles Gauthier, «Le "virage" Bouchard adopté, on craint les chausse-trappes», *La Presse*, 10 avril 1995, p. A5.

44. Pierre Avril, «Le "virage" de Bouchard séduit Mario Dumont», *La Presse*, 11 avril 1995, p. B5.

45. Suzanne Dansereau, «Dumont propose un référendum sur une union politique avec le Canada», *La Presse*, 22 avril 1995, p. A19.

46. Philippe Cantin, «Un rapprochement se dessine entre Dumont et Parizeau», *La Presse*, 28 avril 1995, p. B1.

47. Gérald Leblanc, «L'association fait la différence», *La Presse*, 19 avril 1995, p. B1.

48. Commission nationale sur l'avenir du Québec, *Rapport* (Québec : Éditeur officiel, 1995), p. 14.

49. Ibid., p. 15.

50. Ibid., pp. 65 et 81.

51. Ibid., p. 80.

52. Agnès Gruda, «Les marchands d'illusions», *La Presse*, 21 avril 1995, p. B2.

53. Denis Lessard, «Québec fera des propositions au Canada avant le référendum», *La Presse,* 25 avril 1995, p. B1.

54. Pierre O'Neil, «Le virage est terminé», *Le Devoir*, 2 mai 1995, p. A1-A8.

55. Michel Venne, «L'association dans la question», *Le Devoir*, 19 mai 1995, pp. A1-A12; Gilles Normand, «Une question à deux volets», *La Presse*, 19 mai 1995, pp. A1-A2.

56. Le texte intégral de l'entente fut reproduit dans *La Presse*, 10 juin 1995, p. B3; voir aussi Philippe Cantin, «La triple alliance est scellée», *La Presse*, 10 juin 1995, pp. A1-A2.

57. Les principaux extraits du document intitulé *La nouvelle Union Québec-Canada. Institutions et principes de fonctionnement* ont été publié dans *Le Devoir*, 12 mai 1995, p. A9.

58. Gilles Lesage, «Du virage aux convergences», *Le Devoir*, 12 juin 1995, p. A8.

59. Michel Venne, «"L'essentiel est préservé"», *Le Devoir*, 12 juin 1995, pp. A1-A10.

60. Konrad Yakabuski, «L'entente tripartite. Hésitants, les militants de l'ADQ se rangent derrière Dumont», *Le Devoir*, 12 juin 1995, p. A3.

61. Richard Mackie, «Quebeckers want referendum to offer links to Canada», *The Globe and Mail*, 23 juin 1995, p. A1-A3.

62. Chantal Hébert, «Le OUI rebondit», *La Presse*, 30 juin 1995, p. B1.

63. Hugh Winsor, «Sovereignty drive seems to be stalled. Yes and No votes almost tied», *The Globe and Mail*, 25 août 1995, pp. A1 et A4.

64. Jean-Herman Guay, Pierre Drouilly, Pierre-Alain Cotnoir et Pierre Noreau, «Référendum 1995. Le courage de dire "une prochaine fois". Les souverainistes se dirigent vers un autre échec», *Le Devoir*, 28 août 1995, p. A7.

65. Alain Dubuc, «L'alliance PQ-ADQ-BQ : une pizza "all-dressed"», *La Presse*, 17 juin 1995, p. B3.

66. Denis Lessard, «La balle passe dans le camp fédéraliste», *La Presse*, 13 juin 1995, p. B4; «Selon un sondage mené pour le compte d'Ottawa — La souveraineté avec l'association recueille 54%», *Le Devoir*, 19 juin 1995, p. A3.

67. François Rocher, «De Daniel Johnson à Daniel Johnson : retour vers le futur», *Bulletin d'histoire politique*. (à paraître)

68. Lise Bissonnette, «Parlant de malhonnêteté», *Le Devoir*, 16 juin 1995, p. A10.

69. C'est pourtant ce que se contente de faire une campagne publicitaire lancée fin juin dans tous les quotidiens québécois par le Comité des Québécois et Québécoises pour le NON. Michel Venne, «Le camp du NON s'attaque à l'entente PQ-BQ-ADQ», *Le Devoir*, 27 juin 1995, p. A4; Philippe Cantin, «Le Non réplique au Oui par la pub», *La Presse*, 28 juin 1995, p. B1.

3

"Maybe Yes, Maybe No":
The Rest of Canada and a Quebec 'Oui'

Robert A. Young

Cet article traite des conséquences d'un vote majoritaire en faveur du Oui lors du référendum au Québec. Pendant la campagne, l'attention portera inévitablement sur ce qu'un Oui pourrait entraîner, ce qui ouvrira une porte pour des manoeuvres stratégiques des deux côtés.

La première partie de l'article analyse la position fédéraliste face à un éventuel Oui, position qui consiste pour l'essentiel à caractériser toute la question d'hypothétique et à refuser d'en discuter. L'objectif de cette stratégie est de maintenir l'incertitude qui aidera à guider les Québécois vers un vote négatif. Mais l'éventualité d'un Oui a amené plusieurs politologues et commentateurs à créer des scénarios au sujet des événements qui suivraient un tel résultat. Ces scénarios ont été analysés par Stéphane Dion. La deuxième partie de l'article décrit ses catégories de «l'impossible séparation» (le Québec ne voudrait pas ou ne pourrait pas se séparer à la suite d'un Oui) et de la «séparation inévitable» (la séparation du Québec se produirait rapidement, quoique pas sans anicroches, à la suite d'un Oui). Ces scénarios sont fondés sur des postulats différents quant à la légitimité du vote, aux problèmes économiques qu'il provoquerait et à l'effet qu'aurait sur l'opinion publique au Québec et ailleurs au Canada un refus du gouvernement fédéral d'accepter le verdict populaire.

Ce qui est au moins aussi important que ces scénarios d'universitaires est la façon dont ils s'inscrivent dans le débat référendaire. La troisième partie de l'article démontre comment le scénario de «l'inévitable séparation» est supérieur pour les fédéralistes parce qu'il séduit le plus important groupe d'électrices et électeurs, les «nationalistes mous» qui demeurent sensibles aux arguments souverainistes. L'utilité de ce scénario semble maintenant avoir été saisie par le côté du Non.

INTRODUCTION

As the Quebec referendum campaign heats to a boil,[1] attention will focus more and more closely upon a single question — what are the consequences of a Yes vote? This is the crucial issue in the debate among politicians, not because of any conscious collective choice but because of the logic of the two sides' arguments in the campaign. Adherents of both the Yes and the No options seek to influence the Quebec electorate, and predictions about the consequences of a Yes are deployed to push or entice voters in the desired direction. As discussed in the next section, each side in the political debate manoeuvres strategically around the other's rhetoric about a Yes. But this issue has also generated a secondary debate in the analytical sphere, among political scientists and other commentators. Several have laid out scenarios about what would happen after a Yes vote, and these differ sharply about whether such a result would be accepted by ROC (the Rest of Canada). These scenarios are explored in section two. Finally, the political campaign and the academic debate about the referendum's consequences have become intertwined to an unusual degree, and so the third part of this analysis assesses the practical political merits of the academic scenarios.

THE FEDERALIST STRATEGY AND THE OUI

The essential federalist position has been to remain quite mute about the consequences of a Yes majority in the referendum. Before his October 1993 election victory, Jean Chrétien dismissed as irrelevant any questions about the constitution, and since then he has consistently rejected speculation about a sovereignist victory as purely hypothetical. So have his ministers. A typical example was provided by Marcel Massé when he was pressed about the possibility that Ottawa might hold its own referendum on Quebec separation: "Si je ne nous réponds pas, c'est parce que je ne veux pas vous répondre, et si je ne veux pas vous répondre, c'est parce qu'actuellement ce n'est pas la question."[2] In Quebec, the federalists have adopted basically the same position, though they face greater direct pressure from the sovereignists to respond to predictions about the consequences of both a Yes and a No, and consequently have lapsed on a few occasions.

The logic of the federalist strategy is straightforward. It is to argue and demonstrate that the present constitutional structure is adequate and flexible. It is to place the burden of proving the benefits of sovereignty upon Mssrs. Parizeau, Bouchard, Dumont, and their allies. It is to label a Yes vote as a vote for "separation," however much the sovereignists try to muddy the waters with promises of economic and political association with ROC. And it is, above all, to reinforce the sense of uncertainty with which the undecided Quebec voters — the "soft nationalists" — regard the project of sovereignty. A Yes represents a leap into the unknown, with unforeseeable and possibly disastrous economic and political consequences.

This position concedes some strategic ground to the sovereignist forces, because there is much support in Quebec for a constitutional decentralization of powers (as there is in ROC as well). It also leaves the federalists exposed to that widespread strain of Quebec nationalism in which Canada is regarded as the creation of two founding peoples, and Quebec is definitely not a province like the others. These notes of pride and dignity are powerfully sounded by Lucien Bouchard, and they underlie the appeal to the swing voters of the triumvirate's promise that a Yes would produce negotiations with Canada on a new basis — *"égal-à-égal."*

But it seems clear that the current federalist strategy remains the best one for the No forces. Most undecided voters have proven risk-averse in the past. The sovereignists are pushed on the defensive in trying to clarify the objectives of sovereignty (through a *projet de société* that must be either hopelessly unrealistic or sure to alienate some segments of an alliance split by class and regional cleavages). And, by maintaining a wall of silence around the consequences of a Yes vote, the federalists aim to heighten the uncertainty that consistently has made a majority of the electorate opt for the constitutional status quo rather than for "separation" or for "sovereignty" *tout court*. A considerable bureaucratic apparatus and much liaison work have been devoted to maintaining consistency and solidarity on this core federalist position (even as the sovereignists have made the various strategic changes described by François Rocher in this volume). As one clever journalist has put it, separation, in the federalists' strategic discourse, "is not so much an evil as a non sequitur"[3]

An intriguing feature of the referendum debate is such strategic silences. They arise when politicians cannot make certain arguments or respond to their opponents because to do so would be to counter or dilute previous or more basic arguments and commitments. The PQ, for example, has declared federalism to be terminally unworkable, and so cannot respond to demonstrations of its flexibility and effectiveness. Similarly, their line that federalism involves *"un gouvernement de trop"* leaves them vulnerable to scorn for proposing yet another level of political structures to manage the association they now seek. For their part, the federalists in Ottawa have declared a Yes majority to be hypothetical, and so cannot respond to suggestions like those of Mario Dumont that a Yes could result in a substantial rearrangement of ROC-Quebec relations within the existing constitutional framework — that there could be, as he once put it, sovereignty but not separation.[4] The federalists cannot spell out what a Yes vote would entail, other than massive risk. They cannot say what margin of victory, if any, would suffice for sovereignty to be accepted by ROC, or who would negotiate with Quebec, or what the preferred outcomes would be on dossiers such as the national debt, the army, borders, Aboriginal Peoples, commercial relations, and so on. To speak about any of these matters would reduce Quebecers' uncertainty, and, presumably, to increase the Yes vote.

There are other reasons for this silence, of course. Discussions about what to do if the campaign were lost would absorb time and energy, and leaks could help the sovereignists by making secession seem more plausible. Such discussions also would weaken the No side's unity, which is based in the shared conviction that secession is dangerous. And, frankly, many political leaders are simply unwilling to contemplate a Yes result: better to concentrate on preventing it, by stressing the advantages of Canada and the unknowable dangers of separation.

While it appeared that the PQ was set for a June 1995 referendum, the basic strategy held rock-solid, despite the "astute" tactics of Jacques Parizeau in coupling the declaration of sovereignty in the draft bill presented to the National Assembly with a set of proposals about economic relations with ROC. As Bouchard's *virage* pulled the PQ towards offering common political structures (a position derided by Jean Paré of *l'Actualité* as a "unilateral declaration of association"), and as Dumont came to emphasize the negotiations that would follow a Yes rather than the sovereignty promised by his partners, the basic federalist strategy remained firm. There was some stumbling — Deputy Prime Minister Sheila Copps' suggestion of a federal referendum if the question were not clear, and Daniel Johnson's brief inclination towards making pre-referendum constitutional offers — but the position held. Even as Chrétien blasted the sovereignists' "contempt for democracy" in trying to trick Quebecers with offers about association, there was no clear statement from Ottawa about the effect of a Yes. No speculation, no lifting of uncertainty.

As the campaign heats up, there seems little doubt that this position will be maintained, despite the sovereignists' concerted effort to focus the debate on the implications of a Yes or a No. Parizeau will insist that secession can be accomplished with minimal disruption, because common economic rationality will dictate cooperation to maintain existing links of trade and regimes of economic regulation; Dumont will argue that a Yes will finally reinforce Quebecers' constitutional bargaining power; and Bouchard will proclaim that a No vote would cripple Quebec's leverage within the federation forever, exposing the province to the triumphalist tendencies of ROC and the reflex propensity of Chrétien to centralize power. The federalists have no 1980-style promise of constitutional reform to offer. They will stress the flexibility of federalism, the benefits of Canada, and the terrible, unknowable consequences of voting Yes to "separation."

The Quebec electorate will be confused and irritated by this debate, and by its strategic silences. (Many Quebecers no doubt are resentful that they are being forced to choose at all — and forced to have their Sunday dinners spoiled again by intra-family political disputes — and this may be the jack, if not the ace, in the federalist hand.) As the sovereignists broaden the scope of the association sought with Canada, it becomes harder for them to justify sovereignty. They may also denounce a domineering Ottawa, but the public will find it hard to discern such a stance when many central-government functions are being wound down. On the other hand, frustration will also grow as the federalists maintain their silence about the consequences of a Yes. Quebec voters will want what many English-Canadians sought desperately during the 1987-88 debates about the Canada-U.S. Free Trade Agreement — accurate, credible information about what the future will hold if the choice is Yes or No; that is, precisely the information needed to assess the consequences of their decision, and so to make up their minds. Of course this is impossible to provide. No one knows what would happen in the wake of a Yes vote or a No vote. But Quebecers will still want to know. Since they are familiar with the status quo, they can extrapolate from it with relative certainty to the consequences of a No, and so the search for information will be concentrated intensely on the implications of a Yes. Moreover, because so much rides on it after the *virage*, they will be most interested in ROC's reaction to a Yes. What would the rest of Canada do if Quebecers voted Yes? That's the question. But the federalist side has no interest in providing any answers, or at least any answers that would alleviate the uncertainty that pushes Quebecers towards the No.

TWO SCENARIOS ABOUT A YES

Into this vacuum have been drawn many actors. Several provincial premiers have replied disparagingly to the sovereignists' proposals for a post-Yes association, but they have been restrained by discussions with federal leaders as well as their own independent perceptions that interventions could backfire if they are perceived in Quebec as threats or rebuffs. The media have acted on three fronts: they have described the federalist strategy; they have predicted very little post-separation cooperation after a messy "divorce"; and they have sometimes lambasted those who deviate from the official line.[5] But, of course, there is no organized coherence to the Canadian media: even in the ROC newspaper of record, *The Globe and Mail*, the "separatists" decried in editorials are "secessionists" at the bottom of the page, while pompous analyses of Quebecers' interests are pricked in the weekly column of Daniel Latouche, noted separatist/secessionist.

The serious work on the consequences of a Yes has been done by academics and journalists. The first wave of contributions emanated from the C.D. Howe Institute and the York University Constitutional Reform Project, largely in response to the Bélanger-Campeau Commission. The second wave accompanied the revival of the sovereignists' fortunes, and it has swelled since the election of the *Parti Québécois*.

Recently, Stéphane Dion has categorized and analyzed these latter studies.[6] Dion, of course, is a respected Université de Montréal political scientist. He is also a visible and outspoken advocate of the federalist cause, and in the context of the referendum debate his long review is of more than academic interest.

Dion divides academic studies of post-Yes scenarios into two types — those depicting the "impossible secession" and those that predict the "inevitable secession." In the first, secession would not or could not take place after a Yes vote; in the second, secession would occur, and quickly if not smoothly. In the first camp are works by Marcel Côté, Jean-Pierre Derriennic, and Patrick Monahan; in the second are those by Gordon Gibson, Alan Freeman and Patrick Grady, and myself.[7] These schools of thought differ along several dimensions.

In the "impossible secession" scenario, says Dion, a Yes vote would be of questionable legitimacy. There is doubt that Quebec has the legal or moral right to self-determination and secession, the question posed by the PQ government can be attacked as ambiguous, and minorities — including Quebec's Aboriginal Peoples — can claim the right to remain in Canada. So a Yes majority result would be fiercely contested. Second, a move towards secession would have severe economic repercussions, with the dollar plummeting and interest rates rising from the moment the result was announced, and this crisis would deepen as the implications of the Yes sank in. Negotiations between ROC and Quebec would be slow to start, or they might not start at all. There would be shock and confusion in ROC, and there is no obvious interlocutor for Quebec. Ottawa has no mandate to negotiate, and neither do the provincial governments, whose interests in Quebec and reactions to the Yes would vary in any case. Inevitably ROC-Quebec negotiations would break down, because the agenda would be too crowded, the players too numerous, and the issues — especially the debt — too difficult.[8] Then Quebec could be forced into a unilateral declaration of independence (UDI), which Canada probably would not recognize. The two sides could then enter a contest for authority over the territory, one that would cause enormous economic damage and one raising the spectre of "the violence we must fear," as Dion puts it.[9] In Monahan's account, Quebecers in the end could not "endure the kinds of costs and disruptions that secession from Canada would necessarily entail," and when this is fully understood "there seems little or no likelihood that Quebec will actually secede from Canada."[10] The most probable outcome is that the Quebec government would withdraw the UDI and return to the bargaining table.[11] In part this is because "Canadian leaders would make it clear that they would be forced to take whatever steps might be necessary to induce Quebec to withdraw the UDI and come back to the negotiating table."[12] In Dion's own view, Quebec voters probably would have discovered before matters reached this point that Parizeau's promised smooth secession was not materializing. Support for sovereignty would wane, and this change would be registered either through a new referendum or through a federal election: a separatist defeat then would "nullify the referendum victory."[13] So secession would not occur after a majority Yes vote.

In the "inevitable secession" scenario, ROC would not refuse a Yes majority vote. A Yes would produce severe economic uncertainty throughout the country (and among international investors and foreign governments). This uncertainty would generate support for some positive action to resolve it very rapidly, and only ROC's acceptance in principle that separation would occur could accomplish this. In any case, the alternatives — including some of those envisaged phlegmatically by the "impossibility" theorists — are even less palatable than accepting the Yes. Once the principle was settled, events would be marked by polarization between the Canadian and Quebec communities as negotiations proceeded. There would be internal divisions within each, but these would be overcome in the short run by the solidarity produced through confronting the "Other" and by the urgent need to settle outstanding issues. After synchronized announcements that international obligations would be met and the separation would be achieved lawfully, and subsequent immediate agreements on basic issues such as Quebec's borders and the disposition of the army, the negotiations about the terms of secession would take place quickly (though they would be very difficult). In ROC, the provinces would not impede this process initially, and they could not do so as it gathered momentum.[14] After all, two separate negotiating agendas would be involved. The first would concern the terms of Quebec's separation, where most matters — provisional recognition of the new country, the debt, monetary policy, trade relations, citizenship, and the Aboriginals — fall squarely within federal jurisdiction (though some provincial governments would have firm views about them). The other negotiations would concern the reconstitution of Canada, and after the immediate emergency was past these would be Canadians' top priority, because there would be overwhelming public sentiment that Canada should carry on as a going concern. Reconstituting Canada would involve rewriting the constitution to excise Quebec (and this would achieve its constitutional secession), and the provincial governments would have to be fully involved in this because the necessary amendments would require unanimous provincial consent. In this process, some interests would be ignored and some arguable rights would be infringed, but this is inescapable: the need to resolve uncertainty would dictate the first steps of the separation, and once the process was underway it would not be reversed. As Kenneth McRoberts put it:

> In the last analysis, I would argue, Canada's interest would lie in a rapid agreement on the terms of Quebec accession to sovereignty and in the pursuit of amicable relations which would allow the free movement of goods and people across the borders. The obstacles to attaining these objectives are very substantial. But with determination on both sides, and a bit of luck, they could be reached.[15]

Of course Dion's dichotomy — let alone the abbreviated version just provided — crudely forces substantial and nuanced analyses into two camps. There are very large differences between the views of Monahan and Derriennic, for example.[16] But Dion's analysis does have the virtue of focusing attention on some critical assumptions made by each "side," and some of these ultimately are empirical issues that would become all too real were the referendum to produce a Yes majority.

One is the legitimacy of the Chrétien government after a referendum defeat. Would the prime minister be blamed for the federalists' failure, or would Canadians in ROC — perceiving separation to be irrational and the fault of Quebecers — rally around a decisive Ottawa prepared to cope with the crisis? Another concerns the legitimacy of the question: after a campaign in which the No side has insisted that a Yes represents a vote for "separation," could it then refuse to accept a Yes result on the grounds that some Quebecers did not know what they were voting for? A third issue involves the severity and distribution of the immediate economic losses of a Yes vote. Those who hold that Ottawa and/or other governments in ROC could "wait out" the sovereignists tend to assume either that the economic uncertainty which ensued would not be so massively disruptive as to make imperative an immediate acceptance (or rejection) of the result or else that the damage would be concentrated in Quebec. But is a run on the Montreal branches of the Bank of Montreal a Quebec problem or a Canadian one?

Many important assumptions have to do with public opinion. It is possible for those painting scenarios to deploy lots of polling data about attitudes towards aboriginal claims to Quebec territory, the margin necessary for secession to be legitimate, and even the length of time that people expect negotiations would take. (One noteworthy contribution to this burgeoning literature has assessed all polls on ROC attitudes towards economic association after a Quebec secession.)[17] But these are weak straws for the most part. Except on basic issues confirmed by many polls, such as Canadians' sense of identification with their country or region, public opinion data are not reliable guides to what people would do or what policies they would support during the course of a secession. The questions are hypothetical. The respondents are not in the context of a momentous event, as they would be following a Yes vote. Poll data also do not allow for the trade-offs that would have to be made in the actual context of a Yes: there might be considerable support in the abstract for northern Quebec Aboriginals to remain in Canada, but would this stand up if the value of people's houses and savings were declining sharply? And, out of context, neither do poll data allow for the changes in opinion that can be brought by persuasive leaders in uncertain times.

Undoubtedly the most important assumption about public opinion highlighted by Dion's dichotomy concerns how Quebecers would react to the non-acceptance by ROC of a Yes result. The "impossible secession" scenario generally has negotiations beginning slowly, if at all. In Côté's account, for instance, it could possibly take ROC several years to decide what and how to negotiate with Quebec. By then, the mandate of the PQ government would have expired. Dion's own scenario has the economic repercussions of the Yes vote persuading Quebecers of their mistake; then they demonstrate this shift by voting against sovereignty in a federal election or referendum. Now the "inevitable secession" scenario also envisages that Quebecers — and all Canadians — would suffer economic losses after a Yes vote. The key question is whether Quebecers would blame ROC for these. If the losses were accumulating as ROC refused to negotiate or to clearly accept or reject the Yes vote in principle, would Quebec voters blame Canada for the costs caused by its inaction? Or is Dion correct in claiming that "[m]ost Quebeckers will not hold the ROC, or Ottawa, or Jean Chrétien politically responsible for a flight of capital, or a liquidity crisis where large numbers of Quebeckers decide they want to transfer their Canadian dollars to bank accounts outside of Quebec. Those difficulties will be created by the economy itself, not by federal politics."[18]

Interestingly, this question has had a trial run in Quebec. One of the many conferences held in Canada during the pre-referendum period took place at the C.D. Howe Institute in Toronto in March 1995. Here the possible responses of Canada to a Yes vote were quite frankly analyzed. The views of Stanley Hartt and Michel Bélanger, among a few others, were that Ottawa could and would and should adopt precisely the strategy envisaged by some advocates of the "impossible secession" scenario; that is, wait out a Yes vote and allow economic damage to change Quebecers' minds. These views were reported, and a brief but intense skirmish followed.[19] Parizeau seized upon the story.[20] Both moderate and sovereignist columnists were stirred to write blistering columns against the strategy.[21] Quickly, Daniel Johnson and Michel Bélanger, who presumably are pretty well attuned to public opinion, distanced themselves from the concept: the former was even moved to say that he hoped a clear decision on a clear question would be recognized: "c'est un principe démocratique de base."[22] Though hardly conclusive, the incident was instructive.[23] Following a non-recognition of a Yes vote, there certainly would be rhetorical room for arguing to Quebecers that the economic damage was resulting not from impersonal market forces but from Canadian inaction, and these arguments could make inroads among federalists. If so, non-recognition of a Yes would rally moderate Quebec nationalists towards secession rather than discouraging them from the project. As political scientists all know, agents can be held responsible for exercising power through inaction, and resentment and resistance can ensue.

THE SCENARIOS IN THE REFERENDUM DEBATE

As a political scientist I am obviously on the side of Dion's "inevitable secession" scenario (though I hardly regard my own predictions as inevitable, and
my work makes this quite clear). But the debate about ROC's reaction to a Yes
result is much more important than a normal academic dispute. It raises the
question of which scenario is likely to be most persuasive in the referendum
campaign. This matter now deserves as much analysis as the relative academic merits of Dion's two scenarios.

Clearly, the "impossible secession" scenario appears to reinforce the federalist side. It fits well with the essential strategy of emphasizing uncertainty,
because it provides no predictable outcome whatsoever, especially if the Quebec government enters the dangerous and uncharted waters of a UDI. But it is
not a scenario that is likely to persuade the critical voters. To put it crudely, an
account like Côté's might filter down to reinforce the fears that help animate
the 40 percent of hard-core No voters, but it seems unlikely to draw into the
Yes column the "soft nationalists" who are susceptible to the arguments and
counter-arguments of the sovereignists.

One aspect of the "impossible secession" line that could alienate some voters is its central assumption that a Yes vote might not be accepted by Canada,
at least in the short run. Arguments to the effect that ROC is structurally incapable of responding to a Yes may have some validity, but they are unlikely to
persuade those voters in Quebec who see Ottawa as the natural interlocutor.
Beyond this, there is the basic democratic principle that the majority rules. In
the view of analysts like Dion and Derriennic it may be "unwise" or illegiti-
mate to proceed with secession after a close vote for the Yes, because
democratic norms require concern for minority rights and also widespread
participation in the negotiations. However, close referendum votes determined
fundamental decisions about EEC membership in several Scandinavian countries, and nearer to home Clyde Wells appears set to eliminate denominational-
school rights in Newfoundland after a narrow Yes on a low turnout in his
referendum. There is no doubt that a 48-percent Yes would lose the referendum. Is it not insulting to suggest that a 52-percent Yes would be met in the
end by inaction, economic sanctions, or force? These suggestions are very
threatening, and perceived malevolence contradicts the sense of affection for
Canada that the No campaign is meant to heighten and that is genuinely felt
by many swing voters. The "impossible secession" scenario may paint a Canada
to which many Quebecers would prefer not to remain attached.

A related problem with this scenario is its casual assumption that ROC is
stronger than Quebec, and less economically vulnerable. After a Yes vote, the
costly effects of political uncertainty would weigh more heavily upon
Quebecers, and it is the soft sovereignists who would then be driven to cede.
But while ROC may be larger and stronger (on paper), the deployment of this

argument could be counter-productive to the cause of unity. As has already been suggested, the entanglement of the two economies would lead to heavy losses in ROC in the event of a Yes vote. Would ROC, so fragile in some variants of the "impossible secession" scenario, be able to maintain its coherence in the face of losses, or would pressure to eliminate Quebec mount in the land as the value of real estate, pensions, and savings plummeted? In theory, it could be that the societal capacity to bear the losses resulting from a stand-off depends on the ratio of the losses anticipated by giving in to the actual losses being incurred. In this case, Quebecers, though losing more, could perceive themselves as having more to lose, and they could become more solidaristic than the citizens of ROC. To put it another way, consider the example of the rugby coach who heard a player boast that he'd given an opponent a tremendous punch in the face during a scrum: the coach replied that in rugby, the winner is not the side that can deliver the harder punch, but the side that can take it. Solidarity lets a society take it. ROC may be bigger, but not stronger; in fact, there is much in some variants of the "impossibility scenario" to suggest that it would buckle before Quebec. In any event, to simply assume that it would not do so because it is bigger and stronger is irritating to the swing voter, and conducive to the polarization that plays into the sovereignists' hands.

Yet another problem with the saleability of the "impossibility scenario" is the sovereignist argument that it is a bluff. This is a long-standing position, and one that has been well disseminated in Quebec. It is very hard for the federalists to counter. Its essence is that ROC would have to negotiate economic and perhaps political arrangements in the wake of a Yes vote, out of a normal preoccupation with its self-interest. The argument runs that it is perfectly rational for ROC to threaten economic losses (contrived or not) before the referendum is held. This is part of a strategy to increase fear and uncertainty, and the No vote along with them, and it makes sense because a Yes vote would impose some costs upon ROC. The sovereignist counter-argument starts with the fact that Quebecers have heard such threats before, but have defied them — notably in 1976 and 1992 — without suffering negative repercussions. More logically, sovereignists point out that the federalist threat makes sense only until the moment that the Yes vote is registered; at that time, to avoid losses, the rational ROC strategy is to negotiate cooperative arrangements about economic management and commercial links. In other words, once the bluff has been called by a Yes, ROC would enter into economic arrangements to maintain the status quo ante.

This argument is totally false.[24] It errs in equating rationality with cooperation. In reality, some forms of non-cooperation can be entirely rational. For example, an actor who will face another in repeated interactions might rationally refuse to cooperate at some time or about a particular dossier in order to gain its larger objectives later, or about another dossier. But the superficial logic of the argument has been effectively propagated throughout nationalist circles in Quebec, and in its light the threat that is more or less explicit in the "impossible secession" scenario is simply a bluff that is transparently part of a strategy to make Quebecers vote No. This is a big defect — in practical politics if not in reality — of the scenario that has ROC refusing to negotiate with Quebec in the event of a Yes.

This leads to the next problem that the "impossibility scenario" encounters in the political marketplace. It cannot predict anything with precision. It has the Yes resulting in a mess, or the status quo after a messy interlude. The most striking example, perhaps, is found in the essay of Derriennic, who argues that if the margin of the Yes is narrow, Quebecers should be afforded the opportunity to reverse themselves in a provincial or federal election, a contest in which the federalist theme would be that "tout est devenu trop compliqué, il faut en finir avec l'idée de séparation."[25] Since confusion and loss would lead to a sovereignist cave-in after a Yes, Quebecers should envisage this now and vote No. This line of argument has all the rhetorical defects described above: lack of democracy, ROC as a bully, and the strategy of bluff. Voters susceptible to these sovereignist arguments would prefer more precise predictions about what would happen were ROC to confront a Yes verdict. If ROC did not accept it, there would be a costly mess. But what if, as the sovereignists claim, it did accept the Yes? What if it did so in a civilized, egalitarian, and self-interested way — the best of all possible worlds for the sovereignists?

About this prospect, the "impossibility" theorists must remain mute. The precise outcome of Canada-Quebec negotiations simply cannot be predicted under this scenario. And so the strategic silence is filled by the sovereignists' assurances about ROC's need to negotiate, the importance of maintaining its economic and political links with Quebec, and the inevitability of cooperation. This is a void, in short, into which members of the sovereignty camp can spin their predicted webs of ROC-Quebec association. And these predictions seem to have increased the Yes support substantially.

Under the "inevitable secession" scenario, however, counter-predictions can be made about the equilibrium outcomes on a number of dossiers about which Quebecers, including the swing voters, care deeply. First, if the secession is accepted in principle by ROC, Ottawa and the provinces would pass constitutional amendments that would make Quebec an independent, sovereign state, with no constitutional relationship to Canada. Second, and more precisely, the terms of the separation are foreseeable. In my own account these include: (i) a forced choice of citizenship within two years, (ii) no economic integration beyond NAFTA and some transitional arrangements in agriculture and financial services, (iii) acceptance of a per capita share of the national debt, (iv) guaranteed access for Canadians across Quebec territory, (v) full Quebec responsibility for Aboriginal Peoples and their claims, (vi) a limited say for Quebec in Canadian monetary policy, (vii) no international (i.e., Canada-Quebec) mobility rights, and (viii) no common political institutions.[26] I believe that these predictions are credible, in that they represent the likely outcomes were ROC to accept a Yes vote in principle. If the soft nationalists really want all of this, let them vote for it.

The final weakness of the "impossibility scenario" is its vulnerability to the most dangerous argument of the triumvirate. The softest wing of the Yes camp suggests that a Oui vote would permit — indeed, force — serious nego-tiations about Quebec's status in Canada. A Yes would be followed by ROC-Quebec dealings — *égal-à-égal* — that could produce a basic change in the Canadian constitutional order, without actually fracturing it. This argu-ment, essentially, is that a Yes (Dumont) would make ROC listen. (Its counterpart is that a No (Bouchard) would vitiate forever Quebec's capacity to make credible constitutional demands.) The only possible counter-argument is that a vote for the Yes is a vote for "separation," as the federalists do say. "Vote Yes and you're out" — to put it crudely again. And yet how credible are such statements when the "impossibility scenario" predicts that the Yes would not be definitive? For example, in Monahan's flow-chart of post-Yes alterna-tives, the stage labelled "Quebec chooses date for declaration of independence" is followed by two possible alternatives: (i) "Constitutional negotiations be-gin" (and this is followed by either impasse or agreement on the terms of secession), or (ii) "Agreement reached whereby Quebec will remain within Canada: secession avoided."[27] This is not the kind of argument that would peel away the swing voters whom Dumont has been able to attract, even were it advanced by an equally telegenic political entrepreneur. On the contrary, the argument leaves the door wide open to the prediction that a Yes vote would finally produce constitutional movement on the part of ROC. In the "inevita-ble secession" scenario, there is no such opening: a 51-percent Yes vote means that separation happens, period. And this means that wanting to reform the Canadian constitution is the worst possible reason for voting Yes.

Just as this paper is being finished, some of these arguments appear to have been recognized. Television reports break the news that Mme Robillard has stated clearly that the federal government will accept (or "respect") a Yes verdict. She thereby acknowledges the right to self-determination of Quebecers, and accepts, implicitly but inescapably, that the referendum process and the question are legitimate. Chrétien, in the *arrière-plan*, maintains his basic line about the hypotheticality of a Oui, but does not repudiate her. So his own options are open — and one of them, of course, is repudiating her later. At the same time, Johnson has replied to the introduction of the question, and has affirmed both Quebecers' right to self-determination and the fact that Quebec is a distinct society. Suddenly, the No side has exploded like a Roman candle. It has become a triumvirate too, with messages distinct enough to contradict Mssrs. Parizeau, Bouchard, and Dumont (along all the lines sketched above), and still contradictory enough to maintain the essential uncertainty about the consequences of a Yes. The battle is well and truly joined. And in this campaign,

the two post-Yes scenarios may prove complementary. If they are, the enormous costs of testing which is true will be less likely to materialize.

CONCLUSION: THE USEFULNESS OF THE SCENARIOS

A third criterion for choosing between scenarios is not based on which is
more realistic or persuasive, but which is more useful. If there actually is a
Yes vote, politicians will need some guidance. How might an actual void in
planning — as opposed to a strategic silence — be filled? Here there is not
much to say in this regard, as the predictions of political scientists fade all too
easily into prescription. In Dion's view, for example, an ambiguous question
may make it *"justifiable* to take the time to clarify the entire issue" [emphasis
added], and he advocates that an election or referendum be held to do just
that.[28] Representatives of the "inevitable secession" scenario, in contrast, would
advise Ottawa to accept in principle a majority Yes. This would be a horren-
dous decision to have to make. However, precisely because of the larger mess
foreseen by the "impossibilists" if the Yes is resisted — and both resistance
and a mess are real possibilities — acceptance in principle is the superior
response. But no one knows what ROC's response would be to a Oui from
Quebec.

NOTES

1.   This article was completed 12 September 1995.

2.   Jean Dion, "Ottawa renvoie la balle à Parizeau," *Le Devoir*, 8 December 1994,
     p. A1.

3.   Paul Wells, "Be vewy, vewy quiet," *Saturday Night*, September 1995, 17-21: 17.

4.   *The Globe and Mail*, 16 September 1994. On this contention, see Robert Young,
     "Six Big Lies in the Referendum Debate," *Policy Options* 16, 3 (April 1995):
     12-16.

5.   The main example here is the *The Globe and Mail*, whose editorialist, in a
     Canada-Day rant, lumped Joe Clark together with Parizeau as enemies of Canada.

6   Stéphane Dion, "The Dynamic of Secessions: Scenarios after a Pro-Separatist
     Vote in a Quebec Referendum," *Canadian Journal of Political Science* 28,3 (Sep-
     tember 1995): 533-51.

7.   Marcel Côté and David Johnston, *If Québec Goes...The Real Cost of Separation*
     (Toronto: Stoddart, 1995); Jean-Pierre Derriennic, *Nationalisme et Démocratie*
     (Montréal: Boréal, 1995); Patrick J. Monahan, *Cooler Heads Shall Prevail: As-
     sessing the Costs and Consequences of Quebec Separation*, C.D. Howe Institute
     Commentary No. 65 (Toronto: C.D. Howe Institute, 1995); Gordon Gibson, *Plan
     B: The Future of the Rest of Canada* (Vancouver: The Fraser Institute, 1994);

Alan Freeman and Patrick Grady, *Dividing the House: Planning For a Canada Without Quebec* (Toronto: HarperCollins, 1995); Robert A. Young, *The Secession of Quebec and the Future of Canada* (Montreal-Kingston: McGill-Queen's University Press with the Institute of Intergovernmental Relations, 1995). See also Kimon Valaskakis and Angéline Fournier, *Le Piège de l'Indépendence* (Montréal-Paris: L'Étincelle, 1995); Daniel Drache and Roberto Perin (eds.), *Negotiating with a Sovereign Québec* (Toronto: James Lorimer, 1992); Kenneth McRoberts (ed.), *Beyond Quebec: Taking Stock of Canada* (Montreal-Kingston: McGill-Queen's University Press, 1995) and the various contributions made throughout 1995 in the "Referendum Papers" of the C.D. Howe Institute's *Commentary* series and the publication *Choix* (Série Québec-Canada) of the Institute for Research on Public Policy.

8. This conclusion resembles that of Michael Lusztig in "Constitutional Paralysis: Why Canadian Constitutional Initiatives Are Doomed to Fail," *Canadian Journal of Political Science* 27, 4 (December 1994): 747-71.

9. Dion, "The Dynamic of Secessions," p. 537.

10. Monahan, *Cooler Heads Shall Prevail*, p. 5.

11. Monahan, Ibid., p. 30.

12. Monahan, Ibid., p. 27.

13. Dion, "The Dynamic of Secessions," p. 551.

14. Of course, there are differences between analysts on the likely degree of centralization in ROC and the relative power of the provincial and federal governments. Some insist that legitimacy and support would flow to Ottawa in the crisis, temporarily; others, notably Gibson, expect that the richer western provinces would play a major role in negotiations with Quebec and would insist upon a very substantial decentralization in ROC.

15. Kenneth McRoberts, "After the Referendum: Canada with or without Quebec," in McRoberts (ed.), *Beyond Quebec*, p. 414.

16. For a more subtle treatment of the extant literature, see Douglas M. Brown, "'ROC' Analysts and the Quebec Secession Debate," unpublished paper, March 1995.

17. Pierre Martin, "Association after Sovereignty? Canadian Views on Economic Association with a Sovereign Quebec," *Canadian Public Policy* 21, 1 (March 1995): 53-71.

18. Dion, "The Dynamic of Secessions," p. 550.

19. Suzanne Dansereau, "L'intelligentsia du Canada anglais veut qu'Ottawa fasse 'souffrir le Québec,'" *Le Devoir*, 16 March 1995; Suzanne Dansereau, "Jean Chrétien invité à 'faire souffrir' un Québec qui dirait Oui," *La Presse*, 16 March 1995.

20. Philippe Cantin, "Parizeau dénonce l'idée de 'faire souffrir' un Québec qui dirait Oui," *La Presse*, 17 March 1995; Rhéal Séguin, "Parizeau bristles at suggestions of retaliation," *The Globe and Mail*, 17 March 1995.

21.   Jean-V. Dufresne, "Faites-les souffrir!" *Le Journal de Montréal*, 17 March 1995; Daniel Latouche, "Parler vrai, mais lentement," *Le Devoir*, 18-19 March 1995.

22.   Paul Cauchon, "Johnson laisse le palabres à l'Institut C.D. Howe," *Le Devoir*, 18-19 March 1995; Mario Fontaine, "Johnson et Bélanger refuseraient de pénaliser un Québec souverain," *La Presse*, 18 March 1995.

23.   For an account of the Toronto discussion, see Robert A. Young, "Qui joue les prophètes de malheur?" *Le Devoir*, 4 April 1995.

24.   See Robert A. Young, "Le Canada hors Québec: Voudra-t-il coopérer avec un Québec souverain?" in Alain-G. Gagnon and François Rocher (eds.), *Répliques aux détracteurs de la souveraineté du Québec* (Montréal: VLB éditeur, 1992), 392-407; and Robert A. Young, "The Political Economy of Secession: The Case of Quebec," *Constitutional Political Economy* 5, 2 (1994): 221-45.

25.   Derriennic, *Nationalisme et Démocratie*, p. 70.

26.   Young, *The Secession of Quebec*, pp. 208-44.

27.   Monahan, *Cooler Heads Shall Prevail*, Figure 1 ["The Road to Quebec Sovereignty: Options and Critical Path"], p. 6.

28.   Dion, "The Dynamic of Secessions," p. 549. See also p. 551.

III

Evolving
Fiscal
Federalism

4

The Canada Health and Social Transfer: Fiscal Federalism in Search of a Vision

Susan D. Phillips

La création du transfert canadien en matière de santé et de programmes sociaux et le retrait de 6 $ milliards en argent du nouveau transfert dans le budget 1995 est un point tournant dans l'évolution du fédéralisme fiscal qui aura des effets dramatiques sur les politiques publiques au Canada. Cet article évalue les conséquences du transfert sous trois angles : son efficacité comme instrument du fédéralisme fiscal, son effet sur la prestation de l'aide sociale, des soins de santé et de l'éducation postsecondaire et son influence sur le fédéralisme. Il soutient que le nouveau transfert est déficient à la base puisqu'il ne remédie aucunement aux problèmes fondamentaux des transferts actuels et n'offre aucune vision cohérente du fédéralisme qui pourrait guider les politiques publiques. Alors que le gouvernement Chrétien a fait la promotion du transfert comme un mécanisme qui permet une plus grande flexibilité aux provinces, il a tergiversé — en promettant de redessiner la formule du transfert pour garantir le maintien de standards nationaux — lorsque confronté à la critique. Les coupures considérables que le transfert signifie seront probablement effectuées de façon disproportionnée dans l'aide sociale, même si l'augmentation des frais de scolarité pour l'éducation postsecondaire et un accroissement des pressions financières sur les systèmes de services de santé provinciaux en résulteront probablement aussi. À court terme, le transfert empêchera toute nouvelle tentative de coordination d'une réforme de la politique sociale et, à long terme, il nous forcera à nous redéfinir comme communauté politique et inscrira le fédéralisme dans un sens unique vers une plus grande décentralisation.

INTRODUCTION

The creation of the Canada Health and Social Transfer (CHST) in the 1995 budget will alter the dynamics of Canadian federalism and produce significant changes in the provincial delivery of social programs. The CHST is a super block-funded transfer which will replace both the Canada Assistance

Plan (CAP) that cost-shares welfare and Established Programs Financing (EPF) that provides support for health care and postsecondary education.[1] The concomitant withdrawal of $6 billion in cash over two years from the new transfer represents a significant retraction of the federal spending power and marks the end of the postwar era of an activist federal stance towards intervention in social programs. In essence, the federal government appears to be renouncing its national interest in ensuring equity across individuals by providing income redistribution from richer to poorer citizens. The underlying logic of the transfer directly pits the aspirations of middle-class Canadians, keen on assuring affordable, quality health care and postsecondary education for their children, against the interests of lower income Canadians who might need support from social assistance. In a zero sum game played with significantly fewer resources, this will exacerbate class tensions in a way that has been uncharacteristic of this country. Ultimately, the CHST is likely to force a redefinition of ourselves as a political community and contribute to making Canada not only a leaner, but a meaner nation.

The CHST is born of deficit-cutting. It was conceived within the Department of Finance in the near crisis atmosphere of finding ways to produce major reductions in federal spending in the months leading up to the February 1995 budget. In preparation of the Liberal government's second budget, Finance Minister Paul Martin had little room to manoeuvre. Business leaders had been strongly advocating deep cuts to social and other program spending and international bond-rating agencies had been keeping a vigilant watch on the country with well-timed threats of downgrading Canada's credit rating if the federal government did not seriously and quickly begin to reduce our $37.9 billion deficit and $546 billion debt. Thus it was critical for Canada's credibility with international capital markets that the finance minister meet his deficit reduction targets of $32.7 billion in 1995-96 and $24.3 billion, or 3 percent of GDP, in 1996-97. With a domestic tax revolt being fomented with the aid of the Reform Party, there was little scope for raising taxes so that deficit reduction had to be achieved through cuts in program spending. The magnitude of the cuts demanded by this political climate could not be realized through minor tinkering with departmental operating budgets. Because the provincial transfers are big ticket items, comprising 16 percent of federal spending, they were natural targets for cost-cutting.

The idea of the CHST was also supported by the Liberal Cabinet, especially the members from Quebec, on the argument of promoting flexible federalism. The principle of limiting the federal presence so that provinces can fully exercise their rightful jurisdiction over social policy design and spending plays well in the politics of national unity during a critical period in the run-up to the Quebec referendum on sovereignty. However, the CHST is not the product of a careful reconception of federalism by the Chrétien government. As a result of the inherent tensions within the Liberal caucus between hard-line proponents of cost-cutting and those favouring the maintenance of a federal policy role, no consistent vision of federalism to which the federal government is willing to commit itself — and live with all of the consequences — has been articulated, instead producing equivocal behaviour in response to criticism of the new transfer. On the one hand, the Liberal government has touted the CHST as providing greater flexibility to the provinces, but when confronted with the likelihood that it would also diminish the federal ability to enforce the provisions of the *Canada Health Act,* a promise was made to redesign the formula so that national standards could be maintained. Due to the exigencies of deficit reduction, however, the finance minister has been reluctant to make a firm commitment to a stable level of funding for a cash transfer over the long term, but he simultaneously has tried to downplay the enormous impact that reduced funding will have on provincial policymaking.

Consequently, the way in which the major changes in social policy implied by the CHST have been presented to the Canadian public has been profoundly undemocratic.[2] Although the CHST was proposed to Cabinet shortly before the completion of the extensive year-long public consultation on the review of the social security system, no opportunity was afforded for public debate over its implications until it was introduced in the House of Commons as part of Bill C-76, the omnibus bill providing for implementation of the broad sweep of budget measures. Instead of addressing the impact of the changes to funding, the budget papers attempt to disguise the actual magnitude of the cuts entailed by the CHST and in a clever, but confusing statement during Question Period, Minister Martin contended that "The fact is that the Canada Social Transfer as such will not involve any cuts in transfers to the provinces."[3] Because the 1995 budget is designed to be "time-released" so that most of its massive reductions to social spending will not kick in until 1996-97 (after the expected date of the Quebec sovereignty referendum), immediate reaction by Canadians has been subdued and so far the federal government has not encouraged public debate over the impact of the new transfer.

The purpose of this chapter is to examine the implications of the CHST for fiscal federalism and social policy in Canada. The CHST must be understood not only in light of the Liberals' commitment to deficit reduction, but in the context of social policy reform. The chapter begins by setting this context with a brief overview of the existing instruments of fiscal federalism and the history of social policy reform under the Liberal government. The CHST is then assessed on three dimensions: its effectiveness as an instrument of fiscal federalism; its impact on the delivery of social assistance, health care, and postsecondary education; and its influence on federalism. My thesis is that the CHST is fundamentally flawed. Even if one takes a fiscally conservative position supporting deep cuts to social policy spending or a decentralist position supporting the withdrawal of the federal presence in provincial jurisdiction, the CHST cannot be viewed as an effective instrument of fiscal federalism because it does not remedy the basic problems with the existing transfers — from either a federal or a provincial perspective.

THE FISCAL FEDERALISM CONTEXT

The CHST is a landmark in the evolution of fiscal federalism and public policy in Canada. To appreciate the significance of this new transfer, it is useful to provide a brief background on the existing set of federal-provincial transfers and the impetus for change derived from the problems inherent in these transfers.[4]

A basic rationale for federal-provincial fiscal transfers is rooted in social policy: that is, in policy directed towards providing a more equitable distribution of the well-being of citizens. One principle of federalism, referred to as *horizontal* equity, is that Canadians should be able to enjoy access to comparable levels of health care, education, and other public services regardless of where in the country they live. This premise implies a redistribution among individuals — from richer to poorer citizens — and among regions as well. A commitment to horizontal equity was reaffirmed by the Liberal Party in its election Red Book: "Liberals will work towards a greater equality of social conditions among Canadians."[5] Horizontal equity is closely related to a second principle of *vertical* equity, the notion that the governments charged with the responsibility for providing public services should have the financial resources to be able to discharge these responsibilities. Because there is a vertical fiscal imbalance in the federation — the federal government collects revenues in excess of its own constitutionally-defined expenditures — it transfers money to the provinces so that they can meet their policy responsibilities.

A distinctive feature of Canadian federalism, argues Simeon, is that concerns about the distribution of costs and benefits among regions tend to take primacy over issues of distribution among individuals: regions "trump" class in Canada.[6] The Equalization program, begun in 1957-58 and now entrenched in the constitution, is the main transfer dedicated to interregional equity. This federal transfer provides payments to the "have-not" provinces (all provinces except Ontario, Alberta, and British Columbia) whose tax capacities are below a national average so that they have sufficient revenues to provide more or less the same levels of services that residents of the wealthier provinces enjoy. The formula for calculating the tax capacity of the provinces includes a wide variety of revenue sources and is set out in federal legislation, although it has been altered a number of times over the years. The per capita Equalization payments are unconditional, meaning that the provinces can spend the dollars on any programs, services or projects that they chose. In 1995-96, $8.9 billion will flow from the federal government in Equalization contributions: by virtue of its population, Quebec is the largest recipient in absolute dollar terms while Newfoundland has the highest per capita entitlement.[7] Although the provincial political will supporting the Equalization program may have wavered somewhat in recent years, especially as Ontario has asserted a demand for its "fair share" of federalism, Equalization undoubtedly has been the most stable — and from a federal perspective, increasingly the most important — of the fiscal transfers.[8] The federal government's continuing commitment to the Equalization program is evident in the 1995 budget because it is the only major transfer that was left intact and, in fact, federal contributions to Equalization are increased by $1.3 billion from 1994-95 to 1997-98.[9]

Established Programs Financing was created in 1977 by consolidating a number of existing cost-shared programs supporting medicare, hospital insurance and postsecondary education. Roughly two-thirds of this block fund are nominally intended to support insured and extended health care and one-third is directed towards postsecondary education. Although the federal government sends out two separate cheques to each province, this is merely a nominal division because EPF, like Equalization, has virtually no conditions attached to it: the dollars flow into the general revenue funds of the provinces and, in reality, they can spend the money on anything they chose. The only limitation is that EPF monies could be withheld if the provinces fail to comply with any of the five principles of the *Canada Health Act*; in particular, if provinces obtain revenues by charging user fees on health-care services, the amount of revenues will be taken back, dollar for dollar, from EPF cash. In 1991, the Conservatives enacted provisions that would allow the federal government to withhold funds from other transfers as well in cases of such violation, although the ability of the federal government to exercise this power has not been put to the test. Under EPF, as modified in 1982, each province has a per capita entitlement (accelerated annually by economic and population growth). From this entitlement, a tax portion (revenues raised from 13.5 points of personal and one point of corporate income taxes transferred to the provinces in 1977) is subtracted, leaving a residual cash portion that the federal government pays to the province. This means that under conditions of economic growth and progressive tax systems, the revenues generated from the tax portion have been growing, leaving the amount of the residual cash transfer to diminish gradually. This erosion of the cash transfer has been greatly accelerated over the past decade by a number of changes imposed unilaterally by the federal government. As part of the "Six and Five" anti-inflation program, the escalator for the postsecondary component was reduced to 6 and 5 percent for 1983-84 and 1984-85 respectively. Under Conservative Finance Minister Michael Wilson, the EPF escalator was reduced by two percentage points beginning in 1986-87 and in the 1990 budget, provincial entitlements were frozen completely for two years and reduced to GNP minus 3 percent thereafter. The federal government claims that it "transfers" $26.9 billion annually under EPF because it calculates the entire entitlement, including both the cash and the tax portion as federal expenditures. This creative arithmetic has been called the "Big Lie of Canadian public finance" by Stefan Dupré because the tax points are rightly provincial revenues, not federal expenditures, and could not readily be retrieved by the federal government.[10] In reality, the actual amount of the annual EPF cash transfer is $8.4 billion.

There are a number of serious flaws in the design of EPF that have rendered it so unworkable that both the federal and provincial governments have been anxious for some time to see it replaced.[11] The first problem lies in the lack of financial stability and security for the provinces that has resulted from the federal government's unilateral freezes on entitlements. As a result, the provincial governments have experienced considerable financial strain and have no security from one federal budget to the next as to Ottawa's plans for the transfer. Second, there is a lack of accountability and transparency in EPF that confuses the public as to which level of government supports and is ultimately accountable for funding health care and postsecondary education. This has allowed both spheres of government to blame the other for program cutbacks. Another consequence of the federal actions has been a problem of equity (which is greatly exacerbated by the federal limits on CAP discussed below). The freeze on entitlements means that provinces that have experienced population and economic growth have been hit relatively harder than those provinces with stable or declining populations and economies.[12] Finally, it is questionable that EPF has been serving its nominal social policy ends well at all. There had been little logic to blending health care and postsecondary education into a single transfer in the first place — other than the convenience of winding up the existing cost-shared programs. Postsecondary education regularly has come up short in the allocation because, with the exception of Quebec, provinces have not put the portion earmarked for education towards universities and colleges, instead spending it in other areas.[13] When the cash portion would have run out — predicted to occur for most provinces in about 2006, but diminishing substantially for several years before that — the federal government would have lost both its financial and its political clout to enforce the provisions of the *Canada Health Act*.[14] Thus, by 1995 it was widely agreed that on social policy as well as on fiscal grounds, EPF had ceased to be a viable instrument of fiscal federalism.

The third major transfer, the Canada Assistance Plan (CAP), was established by federal legislation in 1966 to pay for up to one-half of the cost of provincial welfare and social services. CAP is quite different from either Equalization or EPF because it is a cost-shared program and thus is more targeted with somewhat more specific conditions. It is important to note that, in contrast to funding for health care and postsecondary education which have relatively stable levels of demand from one year to the next, funding for social assistance by its very nature is counter-cyclical: as the economy declines and people run out of Unemployment Insurance benefits without being able to secure a job, they turn to welfare. Thus, governments' expenditures for social assistance generally rise in reverse proportion to economic growth. Although, as constitutionally-defined provincial jurisdiction, provinces set their own regulations and benefit rates for welfare, four broad national standards have been established by the federal government. The CAP conditions are: (i) assistance must be provided to all people in need, regardless of the cause of the need (e.g., assistance must be provided to the disabled, single parents or single employables in need); (ii) no minimum residency requirements can be imposed; (iii) recipients must have access to an appeals process; and (iv) public records regarding the programs and services cost-shared under the Act must be maintained.[15] These parameters, however, have not restricted the provinces from developing individually distinctive welfare systems with varying benefit levels and mixes of social services.[16] In recent years, several specific CAP rules have obstructed innovative social policy reform by limiting the ability of governments to supplement the incomes of the working poor and by preventing workfare programs.[17]

The main complaints about CAP have come from the federal government over its lack of control over spending and from provinces concerned about the inequities created by Ottawa's unilateral restraints on CAP. Because CAP as a cost-shared program is demand-driven, the federal government's expenditures for its share have been rising steadily over the past two decades and would have skyrocketed during the recession of the early 1990s in the absence of federally-imposed ceilings. From 1981 to 1994, the number of social assistance recipients doubled from 1.4 million to slightly more than 3 million and annual federal CAP spending increased from $2.6 billion to $8.2 billion in current dollars.[18] The need to gain control over spending prompted Conservative Finance Minister Wilson to introduce in the 1990 budget a 5-percent ceiling or "cap" on annual increases in federal CAP expenditures for Ontario, British Columbia, and Alberta. This hurt Ontario the most because the cap on CAP coincided with burgeoning welfare rolls due to the economic restructuring taking place during the recession.[19] As a result of the ceiling, Ontario estimates that by 1995 the federal government cost-shared only 29 percent of the province's social assistance expenditures; while the average federal expenditure per social assistant recipient in Ontario in 1993-94 was $1,900, the average federal spending per recipient in the other provinces was $3,200.[20]

Federalism, David R. Cameron suggests, is suited to good times, but is not well equipped to cope with the tough times of economic restraint.[21] In the good times, the federal government enticed the provinces into various social programs with generous use of its spending power; the transfers became integral parts of provincial budgets and the programs they supported garnered widespread public support. But in the tough times of the last decade, the provinces have been reminded that the federal spending power also implies the

Susan D. Phillips

power not to spend — the power of "dis-spending" as Simeon calls it.[22] The transfers are, in fact, based in federal legislation and the federal government could — and did — unilaterally cut back. While substantive public policy discussion about the goals and ends of the programs that the transfers were to support occurred on the "way up," the discourse shifted on the way down to focus on fiscal restraint, losing sight of social policy goals for the most part.[23] During the Mulroney years, the Department of Finance rose to become the dominant institutional player in not only the fiscal, but the social policy realm as well.[24]

THE SOCIAL POLICY CONTEXT

Social policy under the Conservative government of Brian Mulroney has been characterized as "social policy by stealth" because reductions in program spending were attempted through arcane and poorly understood technical changes to programs, mainly through de-indexing and clawbacks in the tax system.[25] While the Liberals did not give details of their plans for social policy in the Red Book, comprehensive social policy reform, along with deficit reduction, quickly came to dominate the political agenda during their first year in office. In his 1994 budget speech, which promised an end to the tactics of stealth, Finance Minister Martin set strict fiscal parameters for the process of social security reform that was about to be launched by Human Resources Development Minister Lloyd Axworthy, taking $1.5 billion out of the "social security" transfer by 1996 (but without making any changes to the structures of the existing transfers).[26] In January 1994, the Standing Committee on Human Resources Development was charged with the task of holding public consultations and presenting recommendations to the government for restructuring Canada's social security system. As part of this process, Axworthy released a discussion paper entitled, *Improving Social Security in Canada* (commonly called the Green Paper), in October 1994 that set out some concerns and possibilities for reform. Some of the alternatives mentioned were: to create a universal guaranteed annual income; convert CAP to a block fund, either with or without conditions; or to reallocate some of the CAP monies to an enhanced Child Tax Benefit. The Green Paper also acknowledged the problems inherent in the decline of the cash portion of EPF and recommended a clever scheme that would replace the postsecondary education portion of EPF with an income-contingent repayment student loan program to assist in paying what inevitably would be higher tuition fees.[27]

In November 1994, the standing committee began travelling the country to consult Canadians about various options; and what it heard from the over 100,000 people who participated is that Canada's social security system is a valued national institution, but that reform to remove inequities and disincentives to work is also supported.[28] In its final report, which was released in early February 1995, the committee embraced the idea of converting CAP to a block fund and making the CAP conditions more flexible in allowing measures such as income supplements for working parents.[29] It also endorsed the Green Paper's ideas of an enhanced, income-contingent repayment student loan program for postsecondary education, although it urged measures to ensure continued accessibility to higher education. These recommendations, like those of the Green Paper, would have the effect of breaking EPF into its two components while maintaining distinct funding for CAP, thus further separating funding for the three policy fields. No mention was made of amalgamating EPF and CAP.

In the end, the standing committee's report went nowhere and comprehensive reform was immobilized by the two basic problems that had never been resolved during the entire social security review process: the fiscal parameters for social policy reform had never been clearly established and the federal government had never undertaken the discussions with the provinces that were originally announced as an integral part of the process. This meant that the standing committee's final report received little political support and, indeed, both the Bloc Québécois (BQ) and the Reform parties issued dissenting opinions. Ultimately, the minister of finance took complete control of the reform process with his 1995 budget.

The idea of a single super block-fund had been developed within the Department of Finance in late 1994, although it was kept secret from both the pre-budget consultation process and provincial officials.[30] The first hint of the super transfer was leaked to the media in mid-January 1995, at the same time that the proposal was being presented to Cabinet, but government ministers and public servants officially refused to discuss it. Unofficially, one senior official was quoted as saying that the Department of Finance could not wait for the politics of the social security review to sort themselves out: "They've decided that Axworthy isn't moving fast enough. The budget has to be prepared."[31] The plan for the new amalgamated transfer was unveiled by the minister of finance in the 1995 budget, putting the social policy review process on hold indefinitely and probably effectively ending the possibilities for comprehensive reform.

THE CANADA HEALTH AND SOCIAL TRANSFER

The CHST has been coined the "Mother of All Transfers."[32] It rolls together funding for social assistance currently provided under CAP with funding for health care and postsecondary education into a super block-fund of $12.8 billion (in 1996-97) that is closely modelled after EPF. Almost half of the cash portion of CHST comes from folding the federal government's spending under

CAP into this block fund. According to Bill C-76, which brought the CHST into effect as part of the package of budget measures, CAP will be repealed formally on 31 March 2000, but all cost-sharing will end on 1 April 1996. The primary objective of this new transfer, according to the finance minister, is first of all to keep the federal government's fiscal burden under control by ensuring that Ottawa's expenditures will no longer be driven by provincial spending decisions for social services.[33] A second objective is to provide the provinces with greater flexibility and scope for pursuing innovative approaches to social policy reform and to end the intrusiveness and administrative expense of cost-sharing under CAP.[34] The conditions of the *Canada Health Act* are to continue to apply, but the only condition that will be preserved from CAP is that provinces cannot apply minimum residency requirements to receipt of social assistance. In addition, Bill C-76 leaves the door open to developing further national principles by stating that the minister of human resources development "shall invite the provinces to consult and work together the develop, through mutual consent, a set of shared principles and objectives."[35]

The original structure of the CHST follows that of EPF with provincial entitlements composed of provincial tax revenues (still being claimed as federal dollars) and a residual cash portion; the initial formula set out in Bill C-76 does not specify the extent to which the growth rate of entitlements will be escalated in relation to GDP. As with EPF, the cash portion of the transfer would still have eroded, probably running out completely between 2006-7 and 2011-12, depending on what growth rate is applied.[36] At least initially, the amount of the entitlement for each province is determined by combining its existing share under EPF (for fiscal year 1995) with the contributions under CAP (for fiscal 1994); a longer term allocation formula is still in question.

In response to widespread concerns that the erosion of the cash portion would subvert the possibility of enforcing the *Canada Health Act*, the federal government made a commitment in late June 1995 to ensure that the cash transfer of the CHST is stabilized at an, as yet, unspecified level.[37] This could be accomplished in several ways. One possibility is not to restrict growth on entitlements, but to allow them to increase at the same rate as or in excess of GDP growth. Given the federal government's extended efforts over the last decade to restrain growth of the EPF and CAP entitlements, however, it seems unlikely that this would be an attractive option to the finance minister. A second possibility is to separate the tax and cash portions of the CHST so that the cash transfer can be stabilized, rather than being a diminishing residual of entitlements minus tax points. A critical question is at what level the cash transfer will be stabilized because if it is set too low the federal government may still have insufficient economic and political leverage to ensure compliance with the *Canada Health Act*. Agreeing upon an appropriate level of the transfer will be a real test for Chrétien's Cabinet because it will pit those who are willing to exercise the spending power to ensure maintenance of federal standards against the more hard-line fiscal conservatives.

As significant as the restructuring of EPF and CAP into a single block fund is the amount of federal money cut from these transfers. The budget sets the CHST entitlements for 1996-97 at $26.9 billion, a reduction of $2.5 billion from 1995-96 levels (this is on top of the $1.5 billion in cuts announced in the 1994 budget) and at $25.1 billion for 1997-98. But the federal government's presentation of the figures masks the real magnitude of the cuts because the entitlement figures include the tax portion of EPF which cannot rightly be counted as federal expenditures. When the budget cuts are calculated from the actual federal *cash* grants under the CHST, they constitute a reduction of $6 billion or 37 percent from 1995-96 to 1997-98. This is a different reality from the statements made in the budget that federal transfers to the provinces are being cut by only 4.4 percent.[38]

Cuts to the CHST, however, are not the only means through which money is taken out of social programs in the 1995 budget. Indeed, the Liberals' second budget makes much deeper cuts to social programs than the Tories ever attempted. First, the Unemployment Insurance (UI) fund will be reduced by $700 million in 1996-97, $200 million of which will be derived from reducing abuse, the remainder from reducing benefits and improving administration. These reductions are in addition to the major tightening of UI benefits and qualifying periods for eligibility that were brought about by the 1994 budget that projected savings of $5.5 billion over three years. Further overhaul of the UI system is scheduled for the fall of 1995 with the introduction of new legislation which will cut benefits by 10 percent or $1.6 billion. The savings will be achieved by raising the thresholds to qualify, reducing the benefits to frequent users and cutting the maximum number of weeks on UI from 50 to 40.[39]

Another major change in social policy delivery is the creation of the Human Resources Investment Fund which consolidates all of the programs of the Department of Human Resources Development, now funded from general tax revenues, into a unified "fund" similar in concept and perhaps eventually integrated with the UI fund. The stated goal of this restructuring is to provide greater flexibility in how training money is used and to fight child poverty. Roughly half — $800 million — of the money saved from the proposed cuts to UI in the fall of 1995 will be redirected to the Human Resources Investment Fund to pay for job counselling, daycare subsidies and the working income supplement (an incentive for the working poor to remain in the labour force which was mentioned in Axworthy's Green Paper and strongly endorsed in the standing committee's report).[40] Battle and Torjman argue, however, that the real purpose of the new entity is creative de-funding: "[t]he Human Resources Investment Fund may simply act as a vehicle for combining the developmental uses of Unemployment Insurance (training and other employment programs funded by employer and employee premiums) and the Canadian

Jobs Strategy or CJS (funded through general tax revenues) under one roof — and then shrinking the size of the house by reducing the CJS monies."[41] In fact, the 1995 budget already makes hefty cuts to the Canadian Jobs Strategy with $600 million removed in 1995-96 and $1.1 billion in 1996-97. In Ontario alone, 500 federal staff involved in employment counselling will be cut in 1995-96 and an additional 750 in 1996-97.[42] The Strategic Initiative, designed to help provinces develop and test innovative pilot projects for social policy that was announced with great fanfare in the 1994 budget, has also been cut in half.

Finally, the budget announces major changes to the pension system. Although the Canada Pension Plan (CPP) was not altered at this time, the budget signals that both the contribution and benefit levels will be examined in the federal-provincial review of CPP scheduled for the fall of 1995. In addition, a review paper on Old Age Security (OAS) and the Guaranteed Income Supplement is to be released in late 1995, but its basic parameters are established in the budget. One specific parameter is that OAS will shift to being determined on the basis of family rather than individual income. In the interim, the OAS benefits will begin to be paid out net of income taxes, rather than being paid out in full and then taxed back from high income recipients. Ultimately, these reforms will evolve into a geared-to-income pension system, an idea that is supported by many social policy advocates, but undoubtedly will produce considerable political heat for the Chrétien government in the last part of its mandate.

IMPLICATIONS OF THE CHST

In this section, we evaluate the implications of the new transfer on three dimensions: its effectiveness as an instrument of fiscal federalism; its impact on services and programs in the three areas nominally funded by the transfer; and its legacy for federalism and political community.

THE CHST AS AN INSTRUMENT OF FISCAL FEDERALISM

Federal-provincial transfers could be designed in several different ways: as conditional or unconditional; as cash or tax room; as equalized and indexed to growth or not. Ideally, the design of a transfer should fit both federal and provincial needs, as well as being properly suited to the policy ends it is supposed to support. Will the CHST meet the test of being an effective instrument of Canadian fiscal federalism?

Three main problems have long been identified with the existing transfers: a lack of financial stability for the provinces; confusing accountability and inadequate transparency; and increasing inequities across the provinces. The

CHST not only suffers from these same problems, but it exacerbates them. Although the CHST provides greater financial stability for the federal government (because the demand-driven CAP is now part of a block fund), it creates greater insecurity for the provinces. First, the CHST is no more protected from unilateral federal cuts and changes to the formula than were EPF and CAP, so that provinces may suddenly find their budgets and long-term plans in upheaval on federal budget day. Second, as originally outlined in Bill C-76, the cash portion of the CHST would erode and eventually disappear, as it would have under EPF, but this time taking CAP money with it. In a short 10 to 15 years, the provinces may pick up the entire tab for health care, postsecondary education and social assistance. Until the form and funding of the cash component is clarified, however, the questions of whether it will in fact diminish or whether it will be stabilized at a sufficient level to give the federal government the requisite leverage to enforce the medicare standards remains in question.[43]

The lack of accountability and transparency are as much a concern under the CHST as they were under EPF. In fact, as Allan Maslove notes, "rather than have ambiguous messages about Ottawa's participation in two provincial program areas, we will have ambiguity about three."[44] Although the CHST is a federal transfer, there will be no accountability to the federal Parliament as to how the dollars are spent. As provinces make cuts to social and other programs, they will probably blame the federal government which, in turn, is likely to shirk responsibility by claiming that these are matters of provincial jurisdiction. This built-in "buck passing" will work to the detriment of democracy as voters will be confused about who should ultimately be held responsible. These concerns are perhaps most acute in the area of health care because the federal government's commitment is not very transparent, and this is a critical time in the reevaluation of the field. As the cash portion of the CHST dwindles — or if it is stabilized at an insufficiently low level — the federal government will lose its economic clout to enforce the provisions of the *Canada Health Act* by withholding money for non-compliance. More importantly, the federal government will also lose its political clout: why should the provinces abide by national standards when the federal government has renounced its claim of a national interest by retracting its spending power? Banting and Boadway are unequivocal about the reaction of the public to the federal withdrawal from medicare if this withdrawal were presented openly, rather than being accomplished covertly: "The Canadian people would not tolerate the open repeal of the Canada Health Act. Yet the slow quiet erosion of the federal cash transfer has the same effect. In our view, declaring the inviolability of the *Canada Health Act* but then slowly abandoning the means of sustaining it is simply not a credible position."[45] The fact that the Chrétien government got itself into such a prevaricating position in the first place over its intentions for the CHST relative to the *Canada Health Act* is reflective of its lack of a consistent underlying vision of federalism and its failure to grapple with the trade-offs between retracting the spending power and enforcing national standards.

The third problem relates to interprovincial inequities. Although some transfers, such as those for regional economic development, are not intended to benefit all provinces equally, the underlying logic of both EPF and the CHST is that the programs they support should be funded on a roughly equal per capita basis. But interprovincial equity has been distorted under CAP and EPF due to the freeze on entitlements and will be further skewed under the CHST. By using an initial allocation arrangement based on the status quo, rather than equal per capita entitlements, the CHST — at least for the first year — will entrench the existing losses for the richest provinces that were created as a result of the earlier federal freezes. Ontario will be the big loser, bearing 54 percent of the cuts — $3.6 billion over two years — which is more than the losses of all of the other provinces combined.[46] Because Quebec also had a large number of people receiving social assistance in 1994-95, however, it will also have large decreases in funding under the CHST. Table 1, which is based on Department of Finance estimates, shows the distribution of gains and losses across the provinces under the CHST as compared to the funding levels under the three existing transfers. A fairer system of distribution will need to be implemented for the longer term and Ottawa has invited the provinces to negotiate a different allocation formula for 1997-98; a more equitable distribution based on per capita entitlements or cash grants may emerge from this process.[47] This possibility notwithstanding, the CHST fails the first test of being a sound instrument of fiscal federalism because it does not fix what is wrong with the existing transfers.

Table 1: Changes in Federal-Provincial Transfers (including the CHST and Equalization)

	1994-95 $ millions	1996-97 $ millions	Change $ millions
Newfoundland	1,484	1,512	+ 28
Prince Edward Island	316	323	+ 7
Nova Scotia	1,932	1,949	+ 17
New Brunswick	1,610	1,632	+ 22
Quebec	11,446	11,096	− 350
Ontario	10,530	9,653	− 877
Manitoba	2,039	2,032	− 7
Saskatchewan	1,411	1,450	+ 39
Alberta	2,525	2,313	− 212
British Columbia	3,573	3,291	− 282
Northwest Territories	74	68	− 6
Yukon	34	32	− 2
TOTAL	36,974[a]	35,351[b]	−1,623

[a]Comprised of EPF, CAP and Equalization
[b]Comprised of CHST and Equalization
Source: Canada, Department of Finance, *Budget 1995* (Ottawa: 27 February 1995).

IMPACT ON SOCIAL PROGRAMS, EDUCATION, AND HEALTH CARE

The impact of the CHST on specific programs and services will depend on what choices the provinces make, but the choices available to them are extremely limited: they will need to cut programs or, if they want to maintain existing levels of services, will need to deficit finance or raise additional revenues. For most, there will be only one option. There is little public support in the country for raising taxes and many provinces have limited tax bases from which to raise substanial additional revenues, even it they wanted to do so. International bond-rating agencies have become as watchful of provincial governments as of the federal government and any indication that the provinces will turn to deficit financing is likely to meet with a quick response in the form of a credit downgrade. In particular, Nova Scotia, Quebec, Newfound-

land, and Ontario which carry the highest per capita debt loads will be under
considerable pressure from international agencies to cut spending — a process
that has already begun in most provinces.[48]

Social Assistance

The logic of the transfer directly pits funding for the universal, popular medicare against postsecondary education with its middle-class constituency and
against welfare, a program that directly benefits a minority of low-income,
politically less powerful citizens. To most observers, the outcome of this cal-
culus is obvious: cuts are likely to come disproportionately out of welfare. In
addition, the creation of the CHST has produced new incentives to cut welfare in relation to the EPF-funded programs: whereas a dollar taken from social
assistance under the cost-shared CAP netted a province only 50 cents, a dollar
from the CHST yields a full dollar. Moreover, in several provinces, notably in
Ralph Klein's Alberta and Mike Harris' Ontario where his government was
elected in June 1995 in part on a promise to cut welfare by 20 percent, there is
political leadership from the top in favour of severe cuts to welfare.[49]

In an instructive comparative analysis of various scenarios for funding,
James Rice has demonstrated the probable impact of cuts to welfare under the
CHST.[50] The top line of Figure 1, which Rice calls "The Next Recession,"
predicts what the costs of welfare demand would be in the face of another
recession. The second line, "Normal Demand," charts the expected costs of
welfare (at an annual growth rate of 5.3 percent) in the absence of another
recession in the immediate future. The third line represents funding for welfare under the CHST, assuming that the provinces made the CHST allocations
in direct proportion to their previous funding under CAP and EPF. The bottom line reflects what would happen to welfare if the provinces chose to leave
funding for health care and postsecondary education at their existing levels,
but to take the required cuts out of welfare. Under the latter scenario, Rice
estimates that funding for social assistance would plummet by $2.8 billion in
1996-97 and by $3.2 billion in 1997-98.

But, would it be so wrong to cut welfare funding by this amount when the
polls indicate that welfare does not have a high public approval rating among
many Canadians? If we value a tolerant and compassionate society and do not
wish to create a permanent underclass of people, the answer is an emphatic
yes. While there undoubtedly are savings and efficiencies that could be
achieved and some cuts that will need to be made to provincial welfare systems, it should be recognized that the level of cuts entailed under the probable
scenario created by the 1995 budget are massive ones. The road of "letting the
less fortunate fend for themselves" is likely to be a dangerous one, destined to
create enclaves of people, divided by fear and intolerance.

Figure 1: Projected Effect of the CHST on Social Assistance Expenditures, 1992-93 to 1997-98

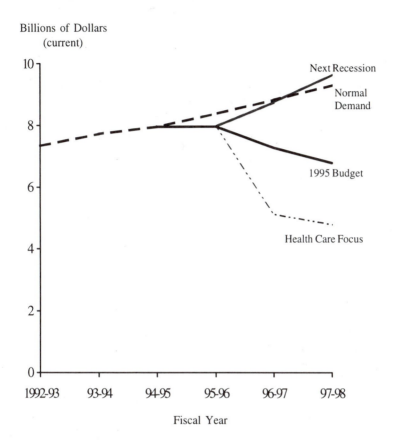

Source: James J. Rice, "Redesigning Welfare: The Abandonment of a National Commitment," in Susan D. Phillips (ed.), *How Ottawa Spends 1995-96: Mid-Life Crises* (Ottawa: Carleton University Press, 1995), p. 195.

In assuming that trimming welfare will merely force reluctant workers into the labour force, it is important to keep in mind that the main beneficiaries of CAP funding are not single employables who could just as easily be working. In fact, 38 percent of people receiving social assistance benefits are children and a further 15 percent are single parents.[51] In addition to providing basic assistance, CAP also funds a wide variety of other services, including adoption and child welfare services, help for abused children, home support and equipment to encourage independent living for the elderly and people with disabilities, and subsidized childcare for low-income earners and recipients in training programs. As Battle and Torjman note, "welfare systems play a quasi-health role by paying for and supplying many of the goods and services that are not supported under medicare."[52] Although many provinces may continue to fund these services, there is no requirement under the CHST that they be supported; indeed, there is no requirement that people in need be assisted at all. The savings that would result from cutting such services, however, would be illusory because a poorer population is likely to result in higher costs for health care and institutional care for the elderly and people with disabilities.[53] Contrary to the image of Canada as a lavish spender on welfare that has been perpetuated by some conservative commentators in recent years, Canada actually spends slightly below the average of the OECD countries on social programs. Yet, we are second only to the United States in total spending on health care (10 percent of GDP compared to 13.4); one of the major reasons for such high health-care spending, argues the Canadian Health Coalition, is our low investment in social programs.[54] There is little doubt that cuts to welfare of the magnitude forecast by Rice, without compensatory initiatives targeted at children, would make the Liberal government's repeated commitment to reducing child poverty laughable.

Postsecondary Education

Although there are no existing national standards governing postsecondary education — and education is a highly guarded provincial jurisdiction — there are few differences in higher education systems across the provinces. Such harmonization is due to provincial regulation, university tuition levels do not vary wildly across the country; higher out-of-province fees have not been charged; as standard practice, degrees from Canadian universities are recognized by each other; and institutions enjoy a great deal of autonomy. The scale of withdrawal of funds entailed by the CHST, however, is likely to produce a much more uneven system.

Proposals for cuts to postsecondary education have been sustained on the premise that the burden could be shifted to the users — students and their parents — in the form of higher tuition fees. Because subsidized tuition is argued to benefit primarily the middle-class, this idea has gained considerable support outside student circles. But, when the idea of withdrawing federal funding from postsecondary education first emerged in Axworthy's Green Plan, it was accompanied by an income-contingent repayment scheme designed to help students meet the inevitably higher tuition fees. The CHST offers no additional loan funds to soften the blow; on the contrary, in August 1995

Axworthy announced that the existing $1 billion Canada Student Loan Program will be contracted out to the commercial banks which will assume responsibility for collecting on loans, although Ottawa will continue to set the qualifying criteria.[55] Predictions, based on the Green Paper proposals, are that college and university tuition will rise by at least $2,000 to $2,500 a year which would bring the average debt for a student graduating from a four-year program to $32,676.[56] It is also possible that universities and colleges will initiate differential out-of-province fees on the rationale that if the provinces are picking up the entire tab for postsecondary education, students who are not provincial taxpayers should pay more.

Although the debate about requiring students to pay the real cost of their education has cast education as a private good, the public benefits derived from a well-educated society should not be overlooked. The Conservative government spent years and millions of dollars trying to convince us that a well-educated population is an essential component in enhancing the nation's international competitiveness and the Liberals reinforced this perspective in their Red Book commitment that the federal government "can and should support and facilitate the national effort to prepare Canadians to compete in the world."[57]

Funding cuts for postsecondary education affect not only accessibility, however, but the research capacity of universities. While the federal government provides $657 million annually in support to research through the three granting councils (also cut in the 1995 budget), this covers only the direct costs of research, based on the premise that the indirect costs are subsidized through EPF.[58] David M. Cameron argues that the loss to universities' research capacity under the CHST will be enormous: higher fees will put pressure on universities to direct tuition revenue to the costs of instruction, draining money from research. The provinces have shown little interest in supporting research, in part because the benefits of research are often exported out of province. In Cameron's view, the CHST cuts will result in fewer universities being able to afford a serious research effort and research activities increasingly will be concentrated in three universities — the University of Toronto, University of British Columbia, and McGill — which already account for a third of all research grants awarded to Canadian universities. Such a scenario would quickly undermine the Chrétien government's strategy of building an innovative economy that was outlined in the Red Book. While I agree with Judith Maxwell who makes the excellent point that universities and colleges are in need of reform to become more accountable and innovative, such reform needs to occur as planned change, and there is no evidence so far that the federal government or the provinces have any strategic plans for postsecondary education other than transfer cuts.[59]

Health Care

The changes to funding health care come at a time when the sector and the federal government's role in it are at a crossroads. Medicare is an enormously popular program, consistently identified in the polls as the most important public service provided to Canadians, and is soon to be the country's only universal program — now that Family Allowances have disappeared and the OAS will become a geared-to-income pension. But the federal government's commitment to medicare is contradictory: it claims a strong public commitment to the *Canada Health Act* while shedding its financial stake in it. Many scholars argue that it is time for the federal government to clarify its interest in and commitment to health care. As Maslove suggests, "it is time for Ottawa either to recognize that it no longer wishes to or is not prepared to play the game and to fold, or to revive and reassert its role and up the ante."[60] In other words, either the federal government should decide that it will allow the provinces to continue to develop their own systems and individual responses to health-care rationalization and repeal the *Canada Health Act*, or firmly declare its national interest and reinforce the provisions of the Act. In either case, Maslove argues that it is simply not feasible to remove federal funding for medicare without replacing it with either tax room in the first scenario or direct funding in the second. All of the provinces have taken extensive, albeit different measures in recent years to contain health-care costs with the result that public sector health-care costs are now in decline.[61] There has been growing disparity, however, between the ability of the richer and the poorer provinces to offer comparable services and, as funding is increasingly shifted onto the provinces under the CHST, these disparities are likely to increase. In 1994, the Chrétien government announced the creation of a National Forum on Health, chaired by the prime minister himself, that is to develop a new vision and identify priorities for our health-care system. But, the implementation of the CHST may undermine the work of the National Forum because it casts the federal government's long-term role in doubt.

IMPLICATIONS FOR FEDERALISM AND POLITICAL COMMUNITY

One goal of the CHST is to provide the provinces with greater flexibility in designing programs to meet their individual needs and in integrating social services with support for the working poor. Thus, few national standards are applied to the CHST; while the existing standards for health care will continue to apply, there are, at least initially, minimal standards for social assistance and none for post-secondary education.[62] The federal government's decentralization stance is undoubtedly designed for popularity in Quebec at a crucial time in referendum and national unity politics. In my view, however, the CHST is not underpinned by a coherent vision of a new federalism, but is primarily a quick and easy way to produce large reductions in spending. An ambivalence over the national government's role in the federation, fed by basic divisions within the Liberal caucus between the social Liberals and the right-wing, non-interventionist members, has produced a ridiculous kind of double-speak over its ability and willingness to enforce national standards. In particular, Minister of Health Marleau asserts that the "decision to cut transfer payments actually will make it easier to ensure that medical standards are maintained."[63]

The Liberals' attachment to flexibility as a primary objective of the CHST is suspect for two reasons. First, flexibility could have been built into the existing transfer system by relaxing some of the CAP conditions — which would have been equally possible if CAP had been converted to a separate block fund, as recommended by the Human Resources Standing Committee. In fact, there is considerable flexibility and diversity in the system already and the existence of national standards has not created uniform systems of welfare and health care or unduly fettered the provinces in developing idiosyncratic responses to fiscal pressures. For example, notwithstanding the provisions of the *Canada Health Act*, provinces have taken quite different approaches to rationalizing their health-care systems and containing costs: Quebec has chosen to close major hospitals; Saskatchewan and British Columbia have engaged in regionalization while other provinces have preferred to de-insure certain services.[64] This experimentation is both highly adaptive for individual provinces and likely to produce a more innovative health-care system overall. My point is simply that experimentation is taking place already and, without repealing the *Canada Health Act*, the only difference that the CHST will make is to exert greater financial pressure on the provinces.

Second, if a more decentralized federation, in fact, had been its primary objective, the federal government could have transferred tax room to the provinces. But, this would have exposed Ottawa's shrinking commitment from health care because national standards would have been impossible to maintain, and medicare is too politically popular to publicly abandon. The transfer of tax room would also have been a more expensive option because the lost revenues would have exceeded a diminishing or limited cash transfer.

In its present form, the CHST does little to please provincial governments, including Quebec which has a strong preference for the transfer of tax room. In the House of Commons debates over Bill C-76, the BQ harshly criticized the CHST on two counts: the magnitude of the cuts imposed and the attachment of conditions to the transfer. In addition, Quebec politicians are concerned that the open-ended clause in the legislation which allows further standards to be developed by "mutual consent" might mean the same kind of agreement that produced the 1982 constitution, leaving Quebec with even less flexibility than it has under current fiscal arrangements.[65] The reaction to the CHST from other provinces has been equally negative: as one provincial official put it, "These guys are brain-dead. It's pure and simple off-loading."[66]

In spite of its inconsistent position that the CHST implies both more flexibility and more easily enforced national standards, there is little question that the federal government is giving up some of its leverage to influence the direction of provincial policy in health care, postsecondary education, and social assistance. This is due as much to the magnitude of the cuts as it is to the limited national standards developed to accompany the new transfer. Depending on the level at which the CHST cash is stabilized, there may be few incentives for the provinces to work collaboratively together to develop additional national standards or principles. Decentralization will be almost irreversible. The policy levers given up at this point will not be readily reclaimed once deficit reduction is less of a priority and the federal government again wishes to exercise the positive use of its spending power — if we can imagine such a scenario ever again being a likely possibility. While many observers of federalism argue that greater decentralization would be an extremely positive outcome for the federation — a debate that is beyond the scope of this chapter — it is much too important a decision to deliver *fait accompli* in a budget with limited public debate.

The role of the provinces will also be altered in at least two important respects. First, they will take on a more significant role as stabilizers in the economy. Under CAP, the federal government assisted in meeting the costs of rising welfare caseloads that usually occur during periods of high unemployment and structural adjustment. Under the CHST, the provinces will increasingly be left to fend for themselves during recessions. This may mean reducing social assistance eligibility or benefits during the periods in which such assistance is most needed or, less likely, raising taxes during recessionary periods when the economy and the public can least tolerate them. Alternatively, some of these costs may be passed on to municipalities (which in several provinces cost-share the provincial portion of CAP) where they will be paid for mainly by increases in property taxes which are less progressive modes of taxation than are income taxes. Second, over the long term as the use of the federal spending power shrinks and provinces have to pay for social, education, and health services primarily out of own-source revenues, they will assume more important roles relative to the federal government as revenue-raisers. The implication is that the provinces will need to find ever more creative ways of raising money and of beating their neighbours in attracting potential sources of revenue. The danger, as Boadway argues, is that a more aggressive stance by the provinces as revenue raisers may threaten the viability of the Tax Collection Agreements that are critical in maintaining the efficiency of the economic union.[67]

The CHST in combination with other dimensions of the 1995 budget is also likely to force a redefinition of the core values of Canada as a political community. Banting makes a compelling case that the symbolic message of the budget is that Equalization is our most important social program — more important than medicare, assistance for poor Canadians or postsecondary education. Although a vigorous Equalization program is essential in the Canadian federation, the changes set in motion by the budget, Banting argues, say that "[w]e are a people who reject greater inter-regional inequality but accept greater inter-personal inequality."[68] Debates over the distribution of income and the differential well-being across classes may be destined to become matters of significance only at the local level. But, would a loss of a sense of political community at the national level be so bad? Surely this has been the central defining question of the federation for the past century. It is not a debate that should be settled silently and irrevocably through the relatively invisible workings of an instrument of fiscal federalism.

A final question relates directly to the CHST as an means of federal fiscal policy. At this point, the fiscal conservative reader may be asking: While cuts to social programs, education and health care may be unfortunate, are they not a necessary step toward getting the federal government's deficit under control? Obviously, deficit reduction is a serious concern for the federal government and because provincial transfers are major components of the federal budget, they are unlikely to be spared completely. As Boadway notes, however,"[u]sing transfers to the provinces to address the deficit is not the economic imperative it is sometimes made out to be."[69] While this action may reduce the federal deficit, it may also increase provincial deficits and thus have little or no impact on the *national* (combined federal and provincial) deficit. A strong case can be made that the provincial governments are less equipped to carry a heavy debt load than is the federal government and that shovelling the federal deficit into the backyards of the provinces is not a progressive step for the overall financial health of the federation.

THE PROCESS

The process of intergovernmental relations, David R. Cameron reminds us, should be a trilateral relationship involving a dialogue of the federal and provincial governments and the public. Major social policy reform will not be accomplished, he suggests, as long as public opinion remains "federalized," that is, organized, expressed and understood within the jurisdictional framework of federalism itself.[70] The Chrétien government came to power on promises of making the process of governing more transparent to the public and putting an end to the Tories' practice of social policy by stealth. When faced with restructuring fiscal federalism, a change that will be one of the most lasting actions of their mandate, the Liberals did so in a covert manner.

As noted earlier, the notion of a super block-fund was not part of the 1994-95 debate over social policy reform; it was not mentioned in either Axworthy's Green Paper or the final report of the Standing Committee on Human Resources Development. Nor was the CHST a main topic of discussion during the pre-budget consultations. The only opportunity for public debate came before the Finance Committee when it reviewed Bill C-76, the legislative package that implemented a variety of major changes announced as part of the 1995 budget, of which the CHST was only one small part. The representatives before the committee — including both independent scholars and representatives of education, health care, and social policy groups — were virtually unanimous in their condemnation of the new transfer. But they were also highly constructive in recommending a variety of specific alternatives, including suggestions for alternative sources of revenue, devising ways of maintaining a stable cash transfer and reforming CAP for greater flexibility.[71] Given the far-ranging and long-term implications of the CHST, there was strong support for the idea of separating the CHST from Bill C-76 so that there could be more extended public debate on it. Several group representatives felt that they were swiftly processed with mere defensive courtesy, leaving the impression that the committee would prefer not to discuss the potential problems with the CHST.[72] In spite of their pleas, the Finance Committee refused to hold hearings outside Ottawa and would not extend the debate beyond June when the House rose for the summer recess.

The committee issued a report urging that: the existing CAP standards (that people in need are not denied assistance and that there be a right of appeal) be applied to the CHST; the minister develop in conjunction with the provinces further standards for social assistance and postsecondary education; a cash component be provided into the future sufficient to ensure compliance; and annual reporting to Parliament on the spending of the transfer be required.[73] Naturally with a majority in the House, party discipline strongly enforced and time allocation invoked, the legislative proposal for the CHST emerged from the Commons substantially unchanged from its original form. Subsequent commitments by federal ministers to sustain a stable cash transfer, however, will reopen the debate over the design of the transfer and the extent to which it will provide sufficient leverage for the enforcement of national standards. The round that will begin in the fall of 1995 may also address the broader question of federalism: whether the federal government should try to maintain national standards at all, in which fields and to what ends.

CONCLUSION

As part of the process of rethinking social programs in recent years, scholars of fiscal federalism have proposed an array of different possibilities, including transforming transfers to provinces into transfers to individuals, implementing a guaranteed annual income, replacing the existing cash transfers with greater tax room (possibly with a special fund to cover health care) and separating health care, postsecondary education, and social assistance into three separate transfers.[74] But in suggesting such arrangements, most of these scholars were looking towards achieving social policy ends. The inventors of the CHST, in contrast, appear to have been focused mainly on stabilizing and reducing federal spending. Although its final design is still to be worked out, the CHST will set strict parameters over the possibilities for the fiscal arrangements that follow it, making most of these alternative innovative concepts outmoded. If the present formula is allowed to stand, the CHST will necessarily be a short-lived instrument of fiscal federalism with a life span of only 10 to 15 years. If the CHST is redesigned to provide for a stable cash portion, but the amount of that cash is token, it is unlikely that future transfers will include cash grants at all. Thus, the CHST appears to set the federation on a one-way street of decentralization, involving limited use of the federal spending power and reduced opportunities for renewed federal government activism.

Such decentralization may, in fact, be the best route for encouraging policy innovation and may be the only way to keep the country together. In the short term, however, the CHST may also preempt our ability to address the unresolved issues of social policy reform in a coordinated way and may suffocate the fledgling National Forum on Health before it can produce any lasting results. The most serious concern is that the Chrétien government is not leading Canadians into a more decentralized federation with a coherent vision of purpose and set of desired outcomes. Rather, in promoting the CHST, it has assumed what we might call a "bi-federalist" position which is inherently contradictory: it has asserted to Quebec and the other provinces its willingness to have a more hands-off role in areas of provincial jurisdiction, while simultaneously vowing to the Canadian public that it will protect national standards in certain policy areas. In preparation for the 1996 budget, the Liberal government will need not only to finalize the design and funding allocations for the CHST, but more clearly articulate its underlying vision of federalism. Consequently, the essential debate may be just beginning.

NOTES

Appreciation is expressed to Sandra Bach, Allan Maslove, Jonathan Rose and two anonymous reviewers for their constructive comments. My thanks also to Sandra Bach for research assistance.

1. When first announced in the February 1995 budget, the CHST was labelled the "Canada Social Transfer," but the name was soon changed to include the health aspect as well.

2. For a discussion of the current tensions within the Liberal caucus see, Edward Greenspon, "Grumpy Young Grits," *The Globe and Mail*, 10 June 1995, pp. D1, D5 and "Liberals Facing Own Report Card," *The Globe and Mail*, 26 June 1995, p. A5.

3. Canada, House of Commons, *Debates*, 14 June 1995, p. 13803. This statement may be technically correct in that the CHST is a concept to which various funding levels could be attached. But it is also, at the very least, obfuscatory because in reality the actual allocations attached to the transfer were reduced by $7 billion in entitlements (equivalent to $6 billion in cash) from the transfers it replaces. Not surprisingly, the media also found the minister's statement somewhat confusing; see, Terrance Wills, "Martin's Way with Words Leaves Observers Scratching their Heads," *The Gazette* [Montreal], 15 June 1995, p. A. 18.

4. For more detailed assessments of the transfer system, see Richard M. Bird, "Federal-Provincial Fiscal Arrangements: Is There an Agenda for the 1990s?" in Ronald L. Watts and Douglas M. Brown (eds.), *Canada: The State of the Federation 1990* (Kingston: Institute of Intergovernmental Relations, Queen's University, 1990); Robin Boadway, "Federal-Provincial Fiscal Relations in the Wake of Deficit Reduction," in Ronald L. Watts and Douglas M. Brown (eds.), *Canada: The State of the Federation 1989* (Kingston: Institute of Intergovernmental Relations, Queen's University, 1989), pp. 107-35; Robin Boadway and Frank Flatters, "Fiscal Federalism: Is the System in Crisis?" in Keith G. Banting, Douglas M. Brown and Thomas J. Courchene (eds.), *The Future of Fiscal Federalism* (Kingston: School of Policy Studies, Queen's University, 1994), pp. 25-74; Thomas J. Courchene, "Equalization Payments and the Division of Powers," in R. D. Olling and M. W. Westmacott (eds.), *Perspectives on Canadian Federalism* (Scarborough: Prentice-Hall Canada, 1989), pp. 182-94; Allan M. Maslove, "Reconstructing Fiscal Federalism," in Frances Abele (ed.), *How Ottawa Spends 1992-93: The Politics of Competitiveness* (Ottawa: Carleton University Press, 1992), pp. 57-77; and Kenneth Norrie, "Intergovernmental Transfers in Canada: An Historical Perspective on Some Current Policy Issues," in Peter M. Leslie, Kenneth Norrie and Irene Ip (eds.), *A Partnership in Trouble: Renegotiating Fiscal Federalism* (Toronto: C.D. Howe, 1993).

5. Liberal Party of Canada, *Creating Opportunity* (Ottawa, September 1993), p. 74.

6. Richard Simeon, "The Political Context for Renegotiating Fiscal Federalism" in *The Future of Fiscal Federalism*, p. 140.

7. Canada, Department of Finance, *Budget Plan*, (Ottawa, 27 February 1995), p. 51 and Department of Finance, *The Fiscal Equalization Program* (Ottawa, 1991), Tables 1 and 2.

8. Throughout Bob Rae's leadership, Ontario continued to demonstrate its support for Equalization, but there were signs late in his mandate that this was beginning to waiver. See, "Ontario May Run Out of Altruism, Rae Warns," *The Globe and Mail*, 6 March 1995, p. A6. The Equalization program is not without its problems. Perhaps the most serious is that the level of the transfers is tied to the provinces' willingness and ability to impose taxes, and the effect of this on the formula's "standard." During growth years, this normally has had the effect of raising the Equalization payments, but in the recession years of the early 1990s, it has had a dampening effect. One implication of Premier Harris' plan to cut Ontario's personal income taxes by 30 percent is that it may reduce somewhat the federal Equalization transfers to the seven recipient provinces because Ontario is one of the "standard" provinces used in the Equalization formula.

9. Department of Finance, *Budget Plan*, p. 51.

10. J. Stefan Dupré, "Comment: The Promise of Procurement Federalism," in *The Future of Fiscal Federalism*, p. 250.

11. These problems have been well documented in the literature. See Maslove, "Reconstructing Fiscal Federalism," pp. 57-77.

12. Maslove also makes the interesting point that the freeze on entitlements has meant that Ottawa has taken back some of the tax room that it originally transferred to the provinces because every dollar of provincial tax revenue results in a dollar less in the cash transfer. By Ontario's estimates, the restraint measures have resulted in a cumulative loss for the province of $2.5 billion per year. Allan M. Maslove, "Time to Fold or Up the Ante: The Federal Role in Health Care," 1994-95 John Graham Memorial Lecture (Halifax: Dalhousie University, 1995), p. 3.

13. Canada, House of Commons, Standing Committee on Human Resources Development, *Security, Opportunities and Fairness: Canadians Renewing their Social Programs* (Ottawa, February 1995), p. 84.

14. Informetrica Ltd., *Review of the Established Programs Financing System* (Toronto: Report prepared for the Ontario Ministry of Intergovernmental Affairs, 1993), p. 11. Because Quebec initially received slightly more tax points, the cash portion would have run out first in Quebec.

15. For elaboration of these conditions, see Sherri Torjman and Ken Battle, *Can We Have National Standards?* (Ottawa: Caledon Institute, May 1995).

16. For a comparison of the benefit levels across the provinces, see National Council of Welfare, *Welfare Incomes 1993* (Ottawa: The Council, 1994). (See also chapter by Gerard Boychuk in this volume – ed.)

17. A good discussion of the possibilities for reform of CAP is presented by Sherri Torjman, "Is CAP in Need of Assistance?" in Keith G. Banting and Ken Battle (eds.), *A New Social Vision for Canada?* (Kingston: School of Policy Studies, Queen's University, 1994), pp. 99-113.

18.   Canada, Department of Human Resources Development, *Improving Social Security in Canada* (Ottawa: Minister of Supply and Services, 1994), p. 71.

19.   As one reviewer of this chapter pointed out, the impetus for Ottawa to impose the cap on CAP in 1990 was the rise in Ontario's welfare benefit levels and number of recipients during the late 1980s, before the recession set in.

20.   Ontario, Ministry of Finance, *The 1995 Federal Budget: Impact on Ontario* (Toronto: Government Printers, March 1995), p. 7. British Columbia has also expressed concerns about its "fair share." See Norman J. Ruff, "Pacific Perspectives on the Canadian Confederation: British Columbia's Shadows and Symbols," in Douglas M. Brown (ed.), *Canada: The State of the Federation 1991* (Kingston: Institute of Intergovernmental Relations, Queen's University, 1991), pp. 190-93.

21.   David Robertson Cameron, "Half-Eaten Carrot, Bent Stick: Decentralization in an Era of Fiscal Restraint," *Canadian Public Administration* 37 (Fall 1994): 436-41. See also Simeon, "The Political Context for Renegotiating Fiscal Federalism," pp. 143-44.

22.   Ibid., p. 146.

23.   Cameron,"Half-Eaten Carrot, Bent Stick," p. 439.

24.   Ken Battle and Sherri Torjman, *How Finance Re-Formed Social Policy* (Ottawa: Caledon Institute of Social Policy, 1995), pp. 5-6.

25.   Grattan Gray (a pseudonym for Ken Battle), "Social Policy by Stealth," *Policy Options*, 11, 2 (1990); James J. Rice and Michael J. Prince, "Lowering the Safety Net and Weakening the Bonds of Nationhood: Social Policy in the Mulroney Years," in Susan D. Phillips (ed.), *How Ottawa Spends 1993-94: A More Democratic Canada . . . ?* (Ottawa: Carleton University Press, 1993), pp. 381-416.

26.   The grouping together of CAP and EPF as the "social security" transfer in the 1994 budget suggests that the Department of Finance may have had plans as early as 1994 to amalgamate the two transfers into a block fund or, at least, was planning changes for both CAP and EPF. See Susan D. Phillips, "Making Change: The Potential for Innovation Under the Liberals," in Susan D. Phillips (ed.), *How Ottawa Spends 1994-95: Making Change* (Ottawa: Carleton University Press, 1994), p. 26.

27.   The proposal laid out in the Green Paper was that EPF would be scrapped, thereby saving $2 billion in cash transfers to the provinces. It was assumed that the provinces would pass on this loss to students who would pay on average $2,000 more per year in higher tuition fees. The federal government would assist students in meeting this rise in fees with an enhanced student loan program that would offer a total of $2 billion in loans outstanding at any time. This allowed the federal government to claim that it was not, in fact, withdrawing any funding from education. As David M. Cameron notes, however, the cleverness of the scheme was that $2 billion in loans could be supported at an annual cost of $500 million—leaving $1.5 billion annually for deficit reduction. David M. Cameron, "Shifting the Burden: Liberal Policy for Post-Secondary Education," in Susan

D. Phillips (ed.), *How Ottawa Spends 1995-96: Mid-Life Crises* (Ottawa: Carleton University Press, 1995), p. 167.

28. Standing Committee on Human Resources Development, *Security, Opportunities and Fairness*, pp. 21-55.

29. Ibid., pp. 94-5.

30. Edward Greenspon, "Ottawa Plans Lump Payments," *The Globe and Mail*, January 20, pp. A1-2. Pre-budget consultations were conducted by the Finance Committee of the House of Commons between mid-October and the end of November 1994. The Bloc Québécois issued a dissenting opinion to the committee's report on the consultation, in part because the Chrétien government was violating its promise not to reduce transfer payments further. House of Commons, Finance Committee, *Confronting Canada's Deficit Crisis: Building Our Next Budget through Consultation* (Ottawa, December 1994), pp. 89-90.

31. Greenspon, "Ottawa Plans Lump Payment," p. A1.

32. Ibid., p. A1. The phrase was actually coined as a joke within the Department of Finance during the period of the Gulf War when officials were studying a variety of options for changing the fiscal arrangements. Some of the possibilities included melding components of EPF with CAP and Equalization, but details of these proposals were never made public. Personal communication with Finance official.

33. The budget speech lists the first priority as providing greater flexibility to the provinces and the second to create a system that is financially sustainable. Department of Finance, *Budget Speech*, p. 17. In response to a question by a BQ member during Question Period, however, Finance Minister Martin gives top priority to controlling federal spending. House of Commons, *Debates*, 14 June 1995, p. 13806.

34. Department of Finance, *Budget Plan*, p. 53.

35. Canada, House of Commons, *Bill C-76, An Act to Implement Certain Provisions of the Budget*, June 1995, s. 13 (c).

36. Battle and Torjman, *How Finance Re-Formed Social Policy*, pp. 7-8.

37. Coinciding with the end of the federal-provincial conference of health ministers in late June 1995, federal Health Minister Marleau announced that, "There will be stable, on-going cash in the system. The federal cash will not disappear." Although she said that she had to "fight like hell" for the idea in Cabinet, she apparently has the support of both Martin and Chrétien. The finance minister is to work out the specification of what constitutes an "adequate" level of the cash transfer in meetings with his provincial counterparts in the fall of 1995. See Tu Thanh Ha, "Marleau Tries to Ease Worries about Medicare," *The Globe and Mail*, 5 July 1995, p. A4; Mark Kennedy, "Preserving Medicare," *The Ottawa Citizen*, 30 June 1995, pp. A1, A2.

38. Department of Finance, *Budget Plan*, p. 54. The estimate of only a 4.4 percent cut is based on inclusion of all federal transfers, including Equalization (which

will experience an increase from 1995-96 to 1997-98) and the tax portion of EPF.

39. Edward Greenspon and Susan Delacourt, "Liberals Lay Groundwork for UI Overhaul," *The Globe and Mail*, 10 August 1995, pp. A1, A6.

40. Ibid. Although Axworthy has also claimed that the money promised for childcare will come out of the new fund, it appears unlikely that a national system of childcare as envisioned in the Red Book or the Green Paper will be funded.The Red Book promised to dedicate $720 million over three years for the creation of up to 150,000 new childcare spaces if growth exceeds 3 percent (which it has). The Green Paper also made a compelling case that access to affordable, quality childcare is a critical support for helping people move into the labour force and is a "priority for the reform of social security programs." Human Resources Development, *Improving Social Security in Canada*, p. 53.

41. Battle and Torjman, *How Finance Re-Formed Social Policy*, p. 11.

42. Ontario, *The 1995 Budget: Impact on Ontario*, p. 5.

43. Apparently in the initial presentation of the idea of the CHST to Cabinet, many federal ministers assumed that there would be a guarantee of a continuing cash component; the implicit trade-off for cutting transfers so radically was a promise that they would be stabilized at this lower level. The implementing legislation, however, did not guarantee a stable cash portion. The serious concerns raised about the future of the *Canada Health Act* as a result of the House of Commons debates on Bill C-76 forced the finance minister to revisit the original design. Edward Greenspon, "Liberals Facing Own Report Card," *The Globe and Mail*, 26 June 1995, p. A5.

44. Maslove, "Time to Fold or Up the Ante," p. 13.

45. Keith G. Banting and Robin Boadway, "Presentation to the Standing Committee on Finance" (Ottawa, 9 May 1995), p. 7.

46. Ontario, *The 1995 Budget: Impact on Ontario*, p. 1.

47. Boadway suggests the idea of including an additional allotment for welfare caseloads in addition to the basic per capita transfer. This would provide for differential needs without requiring that need be based on provincial expenditure as it is under CAP. It is unreasonable, he suggests, to expect the provinces to negotiate the allocation of funds among themselves. This is a federal responsibility and ought to be done according to national objectives. Robin Boadway, "The Canada Health and Social Transfer," Presentation to the House of Commons Finance Committee (May 1995), p. 4.

48. Statistics Canada, *Public Sector Finance* (Ottawa: April 1995), cat. 68-212, Table 1.1, p. 2 divided by the population figures. As of 31 March 1995, the estimated net per capita debt for the top four provinces was: Nova Scotia $8,350; Quebec $8,339; Newfoundland $7,683; Ontario $7,324. Alberta has the lowest per capita debt at $1,386.

49. Harris has supported the federal cuts to transfers, as long as the money saved is earmarked for deficit reduction. Martin Mittelstaedt, "Harris Supports Cutting Federal Transfer Payments," *The Globe and Mail*, 29 June 1995, p. A1.

50. James J. Rice, "Redesigning Welfare: The Abandonment of a National Commitment," *How Ottawa Spends 1995-96: Mid-Life Crises,* pp. 190-96.

51. National Council of Welfare, *The 1995 Budget and Block Funding* (Ottawa, Spring 1995), p. 4.

52. Battle and Torjman, *How Finance Re-Formed Social Policy*, p. 11.

53. In its brief on Bill C-76 to the Finance Committee, the Canadian Health Coalition makes a case against reducing social assistance on the basis that this would significantly increase the costs of health care. The coalition's brief notes that, "societies which are reasonably prosperous and have an equitable distribution of wealth have the healthiest populations, regardless of the amount they spend on health care." The Canadian Health Coalition, "A Brief on C-76," Presented to the House of Commons Finance Committee (Ottawa, 3 May 1995), p. 2.

54. Ibid., p. 3.

55. Edward Greenspon, "Banks to Collect Student Loans," *The Globe and Mail*, 2 August 1995, pp. A1, A4.

56. The figure of $2,000 comes from the Green Paper and is an estimate shared by the Association of Universities and Colleges of Canada (AUCC), based on Axworthy's original plan, rather than the 1995 Budget. See Canadian Federation of Students, "Missed Opportunities: An Analysis of Bill C-76," Presentation to the House of Commons Finance Committee (Ottawa, May 1995), p. 8. Cameron suggests that this estimate is low because university tuition is higher than college fees and that there would be enormous variation across provinces and across individual institutions. Cameron, "Shifting the Burden," p. 176.

57. The Liberal Party, *Creating Opportunity*, p. 30.

58. Cameron, "Shifting the Burden," p. 174.

59. Judith Maxwell, "More Carrots, Please: Education, Training, and Fiscal Federalism," in *The Future of Fiscal Federalism*, pp. 217-32.

60. Maslove, "Time to Fold or Up the Ante," p. 13.

61. The Health Action Lobby (HEAL), "Submission to the Standing Committee on Finance on Bill C-76, the Budget Implementation Act," (Ottawa: May 1995), p. 3.

62. It is unlikely that mutual consent would ever be reached by the provinces on standards for postsecondary education, nor would standards be imposed by the federal government. Quebec is particularly sensitive about its jurisdiction over education and is not likely to assent to federal intrusion. For a discussion of Quebec's concerns about standards for postsecondary education, see House of Commons, *Debates*, 6 June 1995, pp. 13296-97.

63. Tu Thanh Ha, "Health Standards now Easier to Maintain, Marleau Says," *The Globe and Mail*, 4 March 1995, p. A1.

64. Jeremiah Hurley, Jonathan Lomas and Vandna Bhatia, "When Tinkering is Not Enough: Provincial Reform to Manage Health Care Resources," *Canadian Public Administration* 37 (Fall 1994): 490-514.

65. In response to the concerns raised by the BQ Members, David Walker, the parliamentary secretary to the minister of finance, clarified the meaning of mutual consent: "Mutual consent means that no government in Canada can be subjected to new principles and objectives against its will ... Governments that do not agree would not be bound by those objectives and principles." House of Commons, *Debates*, 6 June 1995, p. 13291.

66. Greenspon, "Ottawa Plans Lump Payments," p. A5.

67. Boadway, "The Canada Health and Social Transfer," p. 5. For further discussion of the tax collection agreements, see Boadway,"Federal-Provincial Fiscal Relations," pp. 107-135;

68. Keith G. Banting, "Who R Us?" Presentation to the Canadian Association of Business Economists (Ottawa, 2 May 1995), p. 10.

69. Boadway, "Canada Health and Social Transfer," p. 5.

70. David R. Cameron, "Half-Eaten Carrot, Bent Stick," p. 443.

71. See National Council of Welfare, "Notes for an Opening Statement to the Commons Standing Committee on Finance," (Ottawa, 11 May 1995); Canadian Hospital Association, "Brief to the House of Commons Standing Committee on Finance," (Ottawa, 4 May 1995); Canadian Federation of Students, "Missed Opportunities;" and Social Planning Council of Metropolitan Toronto, "Re-Writing the Contract with Canada," Submission to the Standing Committee on Finance (Ottawa, 16 May 1995).

72. "CHST—A Liberal Retreat to Meaner Times," *CAUT/ACPPU Bulletin*, June 1995, p. 20.

73. House of Commons, Standing Committee on Finance, *Sixteenth Report*, 19 May 1995.

74. For a discussion of some of these options, see Kenneth Norrie, "Social Policy and Equalization: New Ways to Meet an Old Objective," in *The Future of Fiscal Federalism*, pp. 155-74; François Vaillancourt, "Income Distribution, Income Security, and Fiscal Federalism," in *The Future of Fiscal Federalism*, pp. 255-81; Maslove, "Time to Fold or Up the Ante;" Paul A.R. Hobson and France St-Hilaire, *Reforming Federal Provincial Fiscal Arrangements: Toward Sustainable Federalism* (Montreal: Institute for Research on Public Policy, 1993).

5

Nova Scotia's Fiscal Challenge: Intergovernmental Relations and Structural Adjustment

David M. Cameron

La Nouvelle-Écosse a fait face à la nécessité de procéder à de profondes coupures dans ses dépenses à la suite de l'élection d'un gouvernement libéral mené par le Dr. John Savage en 1993. Pendant plus d'une décennie, les gouvernements conservateurs ont généré des déficits budgétaires annuels qui, cumulativement, ont eu pour effet de faire passer la dette nette directe de la province de 800 $ millions en 1980 à 6,9 $ milliards en 1993, avec des frais d'intérêt annuels qui ont augmenté pendant la même période de 142 $ millions à 804 $ millions. Le gouvernement Savage a entrepris une importante révision de ses postes de dépenses. Le résultat de cette révision peut être décrit assez adéquatement comme une adaptation des structures. Entre temps, les coupures dans les transferts intergouvernementaux annoncés par Ottawa dans son budget 1995 forcera une adaptation encore plus importante dans les provinces, même si l'effet final de ces compressions sur la province reste encore à déterminer.

L'adaptation structurelle en Nouvelle-Écosse a porté jusqu'à maintenant sur trois principaux programmes : la santé, les gouvernements municipaux et l'éducation. Dans le cas de la santé, la réforme a porté sur le transfert de la prestation des services des hôpitaux vers des mécanismes communautaires gérés par quatre conseils régionaux établis récemment alors que le gouvernement provincial continue d'établir les politiques et de distribuer les ressources disponibles. Dans le cas des gouvernements municipaux, la réaffectation des responsabilités en matière de services a été conjuguée à un programme de consolidation municipale dont le premier élément fut la dissolution des huit unités gouvernementales du Cap Breton ainsi que les quatre unités du Halifax métropolitain pour établir des gouvernements régionaux à un seul palier. On envisage aussi la consolidation pour le système scolaire public. C'est toutefois au niveau postsecondaire que la compression budgétaire la plus dramatique a été effectuée, jusqu'à 30 % sur cinq ans. La nature et l'étendue de la rationalisation des institutions comme des programmes, nécessaire pour implanter ces coupures, restent encore à déterminer.

INTRODUCTION

The federal government has for some time now engaged in the practice of off-loading a portion of its deficit problem onto the provinces. Just as the chronic surpluses of an earlier day yielded federal shared-cost and conditional grant programs in areas of provincial jurisdiction, so it seems that tough times in Ottawa bequeath reduced and "deconditionalized" transfers to the provinces.

Up to a point, a similar phenomenon can be observed as between provincial governments and their municipal governments and other agencies. In the initial phases of expenditure control, provinces frequently resort to freezing or reducing their own transfers. But there is a limit to how far this process can go at the provincial-local level. Municipal governments have very restricted revenue bases, and some other local authorities, like hospital boards, may have virtually none at all. Cuts in provincial transfers quickly translate into cuts in services or service levels. Moreover, constitutional jurisdictions do not blur the lines of authority and responsibility within a province. It may fall to municipalities, school or hospital boards, or universities to administer program cuts, but the public is likely to identify the true locus of responsibility at the provincial level.

It is not surprising, then, that a number of provincial governments came to the realization earlier than did the federal government, that deficit reduction required real cuts in program expenditures. What is particularly interesting is the way in which different provinces have dealt with the implications of that realization. Nova Scotia's experience warrants attention because of the lengths to which it has gone, and may yet have to go, in restructuring or rationalizing the institutional infrastructure through which many provincial program expenditures are actually chanelled. Nova Scotia has had to "reinvent" a variety of institutions in order to prepare or equip them to manage change.

This process was underway before the 1995 federal budget gave such dramatic warning of the magnitude of cuts yet to come in federal expenditures generally, and federal transfers to the provinces particularly. And it is still too early to state with clarity or certainty what the consequences of those cuts will be. But it is interesting to observe the extent to which the prospect of declining funds from the federal government has galvanized Nova Scotia's determination to prepare itself for a future of reduced discretionary resources at all levels of government. This is structural adjustment, domestic style.

This chapter examines the interplay of federal and provincial deficit-reduction strategies, as they affect a number of policy areas. It begins with a summary of Nova Scotia's expenditure reduction strategy, and the political background to its formation. It then addresses the potential implications of the 1995 federal budget, both in terms of direct transfers to provincial governments, and in terms of departmental spending, upon which Nova Scotia is also very dependent. Finally, it examines the efforts of the province to restructure its own institutions, particularly its municipalities, school boards, health authorities, and universities, in order to create the capacity to operate with substantially fewer public resources.

The story of Nova Scotia's struggle with expenditure reduction really began in 1990, and has an almost eerie parallel with the pattern of events at the federal level. Two things make the provincial experience different. The first is timing: Nova Scotia came to grips with the structural nature of the deficit earlier than the federal government. The second is the bizarre political context in which restructuring has thus far unfolded.

THE POLITICAL CONTEXT

Nova Scotia's political culture reflects two characteristics: the commitment of its politicians to the art of patronage, and the dependence of its governments on federal transfer payments. Both of these are now under attack, the first by its current and immediate past premier, and the second by the federal government. The cumulative effect may be to change dramatically the way Nova Scotians do their political business.

In the 1980s the government of John Buchanan dissipated the relative financial strength it had inherited. It was not, however, fiscal distress but various scandals that created the semi-disgrace in which the premier moved to the safe haven of the Senate in 1990. After a short interim regime, he was succeeded in February 1991 by Donald Cameron.

Despite some seemingly harsh restraint measures, the reconstituted Conservative government could not break the pattern of overly optimistic revenue projections and underestimated expenditures. The 1991-92 budget forecast an increased deficit of $192 million. It turned out to be $345 million. Donald Cameron's studied opposition to the traditional practice of patronage led to a rapid decline in his popularity within the Conservative party. His popularity with the general public remained untested, as he played out the electoral mandate of his predecessors. But what kept him securely in office for the better part of two years was the disarray of the opposition Liberals. Vince MacLean was forced to resign after a leadership vote in March 1992 (which he technically won, but by the slimmest of majorities). He was replace in June by Dr. John Savage. The leadership vote was conducted by telephone, enabling all registered party members to participate. This enthusiasm for grass-roots democracy led the party to institute regular leadership reviews. This planted the seeds of a governmental and party crisis in 1994-95, after angry trade unionists had taken out party memberships for the specific purpose of voting down Dr. Savage.

Meanwhile, the Conservatives had been roundly trounced in the election of 25 May 1993. The Savage government's first speech from the throne outlined its intention to introduce radical reform in health, education, and municipal government, and these we shall return to shortly as instruments of provincial structural adjustment. But what drove the reform agenda was the crushing burden of the province's runaway deficit and debt. Savage and his ministers decided to set aside their good-news election promises and face the fiscal challenge head-on. The magnitude of that challenge was revealed in their first budget, tabled on 30 September 1993.

THE FISCAL CONTEXT

Nova Scotia was in virtual free-fall as far as its deficit was concerned. The situation reflected two fundamental weaknesses in the province's revenue base. On the one hand, economic recession kept eating away at the projected level of revenues, especially from income taxes. On the other hand, Nova Scotia's dependence on federal fiscal transfers (37 percent of total ordinary revenues) compounded the problem as cash receipts were reduced by virtue of both federal policy (in the case of Established Programs Financing — EPF), and poor economic performance in other provinces (in the case of equalization).

Throughout the 1970s, the provincial government ran deficits in two years only, although they were substantial ones and left the province with a net operating deficit of $73.3 million over the decade. The province entered the 1980s with an accumulated net direct debt of just under $800 million, approximately $900 per capita.[1] By the time the Savage government took office in 1993, the government had run deficits for 12 consecutive years, and was well on its way to a record deficit for 1993-94. The consequence of this for the public debt was obvious and serious. By 1990, the total net direct debt had risen to $4.5 billion, almost six times the 1980 level, and representing almost $5,000 per capita. It continued to climb at an escalating rate through the early 1990s, hitting $5.4 billion in 1992 and jumping to $6.9 billion in 1993 (almost $7,500 per capita). The principle of compound interest was at work with a vengeance, promising ever more dramatic increases in debt if the habit of deficit financing was not broken quickly. Already, the annual costs of interest on the debt were reaching near crisis proportions.

In 1980, interest charges on the provincial debt amounted to $142 million, 9.4 percent of total operating expenditures. By 1990, they had risen to $571 million, or 15 percent of total expenditures. Three years later, in 1993, that proportion had jumped to 18.25 percent, with interest payments at $804 million. Interest payments now constituted the third largest expenditure item in the provincial accounts, exceeded only by health and education.

The deficit for 1992-93 had been projected at $153 million but had actually come in at $471 million. And things were looking even worse for 1993-94, which was already half over when the budget was tabled. And so, the new

Liberal finance minister, Bernie Boudreau, erected his budget plan on "two realities":

> First, we did not get into this fiscal mess overnight, and neither will the solution be implemented in one year. Secondly, any debt and deficit management program must be active on both sides of the ledger — on the expenditure and on the revenue-side — to hold any promise of success.[2]

The detailed steps that followed represented an enormous about-face for the Savage government. "No new taxes," one of the principal promises of the election campaign, yielded to a 1 percent hike in the retail sales tax to 11 percent, plus a surtax on higher personal incomes. Investment in jobs gave way to a host of specific expenditure reductions. But two elements lay at the heart of the Liberal's new found aggressiveness in attacking the debt and deficit. First, and for the short term, all public sector employees would be required to take five unpaid days off, or forfeit the equivalent pay, during the remainder of 1993-94. These quickly became known as "Savage days." Second, and extending over the life of the government, the budget set forth an expenditure control plan entitled "a blueprint for restructuring." Overall targets for expenditure reduction were set at 3 percent per year for 1994-95 and 1995-96, followed by further reductions of 2 percent for 1996-97 and 1997-98. And because four areas account for over 80 percent of program spending (i.e., excluding interest charges) they were singled out for review and restructuring. The four areas identified were health, education, transportation and communications, and community services. We will return to two of these areas later. The estimated deficit for the current year, 1993-94, was put at $396 million, down a mere $75 million from the previous year. Nonetheless, the Liberals had finally broken the back of the rising deficit-debt spiral. Economic recovery was a big boost, but expenditure control was no small factor either.

All of this was meant to be spelled out in the second budget, scheduled to be tabled on Friday, 29 April 1994. The House never heard the budget speech that day. Instead, a rowdy gang of several hundred construction workers and supporters, angry over the government's decision to reestablish the practice of allowing union and non-union employees to work on the same job sites, filled the public galleries and hallways before the House began its morning sitting, and broke into open riot despite the presence of a hastily called, but hopelessly overpowered police unit. Several members, including the premier, were assaulted by members of the crowd. The House was adjourned by the speaker, without sitting. This would not be the last of the premier's problems with union members.

The 1994 budget was deemed to have been presented on 29 April, but was read to the House the following Monday, 2 May. In it, the minister of finance reported on a fiscal year that actually turned out slightly better than forecast, the first time this had happened for some time. The deficit for 1993-94 came in at $372 million, down $24 million from the level forecast in September. A further reduction, to $297.5 million, was forcast for 1994-95. Debt charges continued to escalate, however. For example, they were $16 million higher than forecast for 1993-94. As the finance minister observed:

> The province is financially strapped. Debt and debt-servicing payments have severely eroded our ability to pay for public programs and services. For example, debt-servicing costs now exceed expenditures on public education.[3]

To deal with this continuing crisis, the four-year fiscal recovery plan would continue. No new taxes were added for 1994-95 (indeed, a few minor reductions were announced), but a number of user charges were introduced or increased. The key addition to the plan was the decision to replace the one-time unpaid leave provision of the September budget with a 3 percent roll back of public sector wages and salaries, beginning 1 November 1994, and extending to 1997, collective agreements notwithstanding. This provision extended to politicians, provincial and municipal employees, and employees of crown corporations, school boards, hospitals, community colleges, and universities. Total payments to doctors were reduced by $10 million, in addition to the effect of the 3 percent roll back for individual payments. The government also proposed to shed employees, and therefore salary costs, through an early-retirement package. An estimated 755 provincial civil servants were expected to take advantage of this option during 1994-95, and the government used the opportunity of the budget to announce its intention to extend a similar offer to school teachers.This fiscal strategy roused inevitable resentment. To those affected, it looked like a concerted attack on public sector employees and collective bargaining generally. Resentment by organized labour increased. Meanwhile, Savage's resistance to traditional practices of patronage yielded growing opposition to his leadership within the Liberal party.

So real was the prospect of his defeat, that as the scheduled October 1994 leadership review approached, the party executive decided to postpone the meeting rather than face the anticipated outcome. The vote was rescheduled for June 1995, with the results to be announced at an annual meeting in July. And to avoid the controversy which had led to Vince MacLean's resignation, the tally of votes would be treated as confidential. Only the result — win or lose — would be announced to the membership.

1994-95 turned out to be a year of solid economic growth. The year ended with a deficit of only $99 million, down dramatically from the $297.5 million forecast a year earlier. Moreover, growth was expected to continue through 1995-96, yielding a projected deficit of only $28 million, and allowing the finance minister to state confidently:

> This year will see the last operating deficit in our government's mandate. 1996-97 will bring an operating surplus — Nova Scotia's first since 1979.[4]

Nova Scotia had virtually succeeded, in just three years, in resolving its fiscal crisis. Or had it? For one thing, the cost of servicing the public debt is enormous, and increasing; it is the fastest growing expenditure item in the public accounts. For the second year in a row, interest charges exceeded budget projections, this time by some $18 million. As Jeffrey Simpson observed in a column devoted to Nova Scotia's fiscal battle:

> For all the spending restraint the government has imposed on its operations and programs, debt servicing is wiping out many of the gains ... Running a surplus on operating costs for Nova Scotia ... isn't good enough. They need huge operating surpluses to reduce debt-service costs. And that means fewer government services and perhaps higher taxes for many years just to escape from the deficit-debt trap.[5]

Second, most of the savings that had been effected in program expenditures were general in nature. If not across-the-board from a total government perspective, they often had this effect when off-loaded on other institutions. The most dramatic reductions, of course, were achieved through wage roll backs and early retirements. Real and lasting savings would require structural adjustments, and while the process of rationalization was underway in several sectors, few concrete results were yet visible, and certainly they were not delivering substantial cost reductions. More on this later.

The greatest immediate cause of concern was the federal budget, brought down on 27 February 1995, just 12 days before Nova Scotia's, and promising a very uncertain future for federal transfers to the provinces, upon which Nova Scotia is inordinately dependent. Just as the province was within sight of turning the fiscal corner, the federal budget put almost any long-term provincial plan into jeopardy.

THE FEDERAL BUDGET

Nova Scotia is deeply dependent on the federal government for its fiscal well-being. Thirty-seven percent of its operating revenues come in the form of federal transfers. Equalization, the major vehicle in this regard, accounts for about the same revenue as do provincial income taxes. It is small wonder, then, that Nova Scotia takes a keen interest in federal fiscal policy generally and federal budgets in particular. The budget of 1995 was certainly no exception, with interest focused on two issues: the outcome of the federal review of social security programs, and the expenditure-reduction decisions that were to flow from the more extensive exercise in program review, both of which had been set in motion by the 1994 budget, and were products of the federal Liberal government commitment to get the deficit down to not more than 3 percent of GDP by 1997-98.

In the case of social security, the 1994 budget set the target of savings for the federal government in transfers to the provinces for social assistance (under the Canada Assistance Plan) and postsecondary education (under Established Programs Financing) at $1.5 billion for 1996-97. The Minister of Human Resources Development, Lloyd Axworthy, proposed in his October 1994 discussion paper that the whole amount come from postsecondary education, but in a quite ingenious fashion.[6] Cash transfers to the provinces, running at about $2 billion annually, would be terminated, with about $500 million put into an income-contingent repayment loan fund. Under the proposed scenario, provinces would be expected to pass on the cuts in transfers via increased tuition fees, leaving the students to obtain relief via federal loans. What was so clever was that the $500 million a year could sustain total outstanding loans of about $2 billion, meaning that the same total amount would be available to the postsecondary system, but federal expenditures would be reduced by $1.5 billion annually. The scheme was harshly criticized by student groups, but perhaps even more telling was the enormity of its intergovernmental consequences. Not only would a major transfer program be terminated, but the net benefits of the substitute arrangement to each province, measured in terms of university revenues obtained from higher fees, would vary widely, because of wide variations in the proportion of the population actually attending college or university. Nova Scotia, with a very high participation rate, especially in its universities and resulting largely from a net in-migration of students from other provinces, might actually have gained from Axworthy's scheme, at least in comparison with most other provinces.

The 1995 federal budget, delivered just days before Nova Scotia's, killed the Axworthy proposal. Instead, it indicated that a new transfer arrangement would be put in place, bringing CAP within EPF and retitling the whole thing the "Canada Health and Social Transfer." The amount of money to be transferred is to increase in the first year, 1995-96, but thereafter will be reduced dramatically, by $6 to $7 billion by 1997-98, and eventually disappearing altogether.[7] Moreover, the basis for distributing the cuts to individual provinces after 1996-97 remains to be negotiated, as does the future of equalization. The upshot for Nova Scotia has been to surround the entire expenditure reduction plan with a thick cloud of uncertainty, given the province's dependence on federal transfers. Cuts in federal transfers seem certain, but the magnitude of the cuts remains a mystery.

This uncertainty was compounded by the second major focus of the 1995 federal budget: program review. After an extensive inquiry into a very wide range of federal departments and individual programs, the government announced in the budget that a staggering $29 billion in cumulative savings would be achieved over three years. 45,000 public servants would lose their jobs, and departmental spending would be reduced by as much as 50 percent. The list of casualties was extensive, from transportation systems and subsidies, including the *Maritime Freight Rates Act* and the *Atlantic Region Freight Assistance Act*, to defence, to regional development assistance under the Atlantic Canada Opportunities Agency.[8]

Once again, the precise consequences of these cuts for individual provinces were not, for the most part, spelled out, but they will almost certainly be substantial, and will make further cuts in provincial government spending even harder to achieve.

But that is precisely what seems now to be in the cards for Nova Scotia. How successful the province will be, not simply in spending less but in minimizing the negative consequences of reduced spending, will depend largely on how successful it is in effecting what I have called structural adjustment. That is, can it redesign its public institutions so that they are able to deliver what programs remain more efficiently and more effectively, so that all of the cuts in program spending are not merely translated, dollar for dollar, into reduced levels of service?

Nova Scotia has been at this exercise for several years, and the federal budget has unquestionably injected a new sense of urgency into its successful completion. Three examples will be explored, in order to illustrate something of the scope of the undertakings and their attendant problems. The three case studies deal respectively with health reform, municipal reorganization, and university rationalization.

HEALTH REFORM

Reform of the health delivery system, and especially hospitals, is a priority for virtually all provinces. It has become a necessary precondition for reducing public expenditures on health, which is itself essential if provinces are to live within their means. Federal restrictions under the *Canada Health Act* make this difficult, especially when combined with shrinking transfers under EPF and the new CHST.

Nova Scotia has been at the task of restructuring its health system for a long time, but contemporary efforts date from the 1989 Gallant Royal Commission. Noting that spending on health was not only the largest single item in the provincial budget, but was rising as a proportion of total spending, the commission determined that expenditure control was the single most important issue facing the government. It concluded that the province had too many doctors and too many hospitals, and that a fundamental change was required in the way the system is funded. Expenditures should reflect the health needs of Nova Scotians, and not the demands of health professionals.

The commission offered two principal recommendations. First, a provincial health council should be established, advisory to the minister but responsible for the formulation of a provincial health policy, and the establishment of public health goals. Management of the system should then be decentralized, to four regional authorities and a network of community boards. The budgets of these bodies should be set by the provincial government, but paid as a block grant calculated on a weighted per-capita basis. The regional authorities, in turn, would not actually operate the health system, but would contract for specific services and facilities as required.[9] Responding to demands from local communities for their own hospital had been an important aspect of Nova Scotia politics, and shifting this power to just four appointed bodies represented a dramatic change. The government moved with appropriate caution. It established the provincial health council in the 1990 legislative session, and launched a number of studies and task forces on specific issues raised in the report. The council began functioning in 1991, and by the end of 1992 had prepared a set of health goals, which the government accepted.

The pace of reform began to quicken, albeit somewhat erratically, with the change of government and the appointment as minister of health of Ronald Stewart, a physician with an international reputation in certain areas of health management. Stewart is an enigmatic character. He has succeeded in attracting the anger of many groups in the health field, including fellow physicians, while pursuing objectives with which most of them seem to agree. His first major move in terms of system reform was to appoint a minister's action committee on health system reform, the so-called "blueprint committee," which got down to work in late 1993 and reported in April 1994.[10]

The "blueprint" presented by the committee was very similar to that recommended by the royal commission five years earlier: a community-based delivery system with four regional management boards and funding decisions made at the centre. Five years is a long time in politics, however, and the difference this time was the enormous pressure generated by the government's expenditure reduction plan. The "blueprint" offered the prospect of actually shifting health-care costs from hospitals to communities, and the government embraced it almost immediately. The four regional boards were established by legislation in the 1994 session, and their membership announced in September. Their first tasks will be to devise plans for their regions and establish networks of community health boards. Meanwhile, four small hospitals have been closed.

The amazing outcome is that the new, and decentralized structure is actually in place. It is too early to judge its success in revamping the delivery system, but it represents a major reform in the design of government. It also enjoys general public support, although health-care workers have not been equally enamoured of the wage roll backs and terminations which have so far accounted for much of the expenditure reduction that has been achieved. But structural adjustment now represents the best alternative to the continuation of such short-term measures, and it is in place just in time to deal with the consequences of federal off-loading of a portion of its fiscal problem onto the provinces. Part of the political problem for the government has arisen from the fact that structural change has been presented in a fashion that looks like service reduction, despite promises to the effect that it is a necessary precondition for what is really intended: a shift in health care from high-cost institutions to less costly home and community services. And that component was finally fleshed out in some detail in June 1995, with the announcement of a major expansion of home-care services. Once the regional boards are fully up and running, they will assume responsibility for hiring the personnel or contracting for the services, for the home-care component.

MUNICIPAL CONSOLIDATION

Proposals for the consolidation of Nova Scotia's 65 municipalities go back even further than those relating to regional health authorities. The current action plan dates from the 1992 report of a ministerial task force on local government composed of senior provincial and municipal officials. The report called for municipal consolidation, but not according to a single, provincewide plan. Instead, priority should be given to establishing single municipal units out of contiguous urban areas, with five areas requiring immediate attention, including Sydney and the surrounding Cape Breton County, and Halifax-Dartmouth-Bedford and its Halifax County hinterland. The report also recommended a major reallocation of service responsibilities, shifting welfare wholly to the provincial level, standardizing municipal responsibilities over police and roads, and terminating a number of shared-cost programs.[11]

The Cameron government moved to implement the first part of the proposal, appointing commissioners to design plans for municipal amalgamation in the Sydney and Halifax urban areas. But in uncoupling this from the reform of service responsibilities, he prompted a bitter attack by the then mayor of Dartmouth, Dr. John Savage. Savage vowed to reverse the process, putting service exchange before consolidation. And he did. A discussion paper was released in December 1993. It conceded that several municipal units, mostly towns, were "to all intents and purposes insolvent."[12] Without a major reorganization of responsibilities, it predicted a chaotic future, with several towns forced to dissolve their municipal governments, cities trying to raid their surrounding rural municipalities for additional land in order to expand their tax bases, and rural municipalities shirking their responsibilities for expenditures in such areas as social welfare. The proposed scheme would operate in both directions. The provincial government proposed to relieve municipalities of their current responsibilities for social welfare, the administration of justice (courts and registries, but not their financial contribution to correctional facilities), and local boards of health (regulatory bodies and not part of the proposed decentralized health delivery system). Conversely, all municipalities would be assessed a local road levy (the original proposal was that local roads be transferred to municipal jurisdiction, but it proved impossible to distinguish between local and other roads), while rural municipalities would be required to provide for local policing on the same basis as towns and cities. Meanwhile, virtually all shared-cost grants would be eliminated and a self-financed, intermunicipal equalization scheme introduced. Legislation was duly introduced and passed in the 1994-95 legislative session, implementing the service exchange program, effective 1 April 1995. Then the other shoe fell.

The government had indicated that municipal consolidation would follow the implementation of the service exchange program, but it decided to move virtually simultaneously on the two fronts. This was partly due to the weakness of several municipalities in industrialized Cape Breton, and partly to the fiscal consequences of the service exchange itself, which was expected to cost rural municipalities substantially, to the comparative disadvantage of cities and towns. Amalgamation, at least in the two major urban centres, would mask the distributional effects of service exchange. And, despite ample evidence to the contrary, the reports of the two commissioners established by the Cameron government to study the two target regions had concluded in virtually identical arguments that substantial savings would attend larger municipal units.[13]

With that, the government moved quickly. Legislation to amalgamate the eight municipalities constituting Cape Breton County (the county itself, plus the City of Sydney and six towns) into a single unit was announced in May 1994. Elections were scheduled for 13 May 1995, with the new council to take office the following August first. A powerful coordinator was appointed to determine the details of the new structure, and to hire the city manager and department heads.

An identical approach was taken in the case of Halifax, Dartmouth, Bedford and Halifax County a year later. This time, however, the government's capacity for self-inflicted political damage intervened. The minister of municipal affairs appointed an implementation commissioner without tender, contravening the government's own rules. But what was even more damaging was the fact that the individual named turned out to be the accounting partner of the deputy minister's wife. Both survived the ensuing controversy, but the government backtracked on the appointment process and held a competition. This time, the commissioner who originally recommended amalgamation was hired to coordinate its implementation. Legislation passed in the spring session of 1995, providing for elections in December 1995 and a new 24-member metro council to take office on 9 January 1996.

Once again, the Savage government had managed to execute a restructuring project that had been variously proposed, discussed, and shelved for years, in this case for at least 45 years. And once again, it was designed to strengthen the capacity of regional authorities to exercise delegated legislative powers, including in this case the power to tax. Piece by piece, the government has been putting in place a radical restructuring and strengthening of the agencies of program delivery. Stronger delivery mechanisms were clearly becoming key elements in the longer term strategy of expenditure reduction. One more example is worthy of consideration, partly because it is proving to be considerably more difficult to implement.

POSTSECONDARY EDUCATION

The Savage government is actually moving on at least three fronts in restructuring education in the province. One involves community colleges, an area which the province entered long after most provinces. In 1988 it had cobbled together an assortment of technical institutes and vocational high schools to create a single provincewide community college with 19 campuses. The term college, however, was more a product of wishful thinking than a description of reality. The Savage government determined to modernize and expand the system, and once again to restructure its governance. By April 1996, the Nova Scotia Community College will operate at arms length from government, under its own board.

The public school system is also slated for radical restructuring. The current 22 school boards are to be reduced in number to either four or six, the largest enrolling nearly 60,000 students, plus a provincewide Conseil Scolaire Acadien to coordinate and deliver French-language programs. Like health reform, this is to be a two-tier arrangement, with individual school councils reporting to regional boards. The councils will be composed of parents, teachers, students (in the case of junior and senior high schools) and community representatives.[14]

The third element of reform involves the universities, all 13. This highly distributed system of relatively small institutions dates from the eighteenth and nineteenth centuries, and is the product, both positively and negatively, of religious denominationalism. The saga began with the founding of King's College in Windsor in 1789, and its royal charter of 1802 which limited its degrees to those of the Anglican persuasion. That led the governor, the Earl of Dalhousie to push for a non-denominational, public institution, which he founded in 1818 with funds confiscated in customs duties from Americans during the War of 1812. But when Dalhousie finally got going, at least briefly, in 1838, the decision not to hire a Baptist professor led directly to the founding of Acadia, and thereafter Saint Mary's, St. Francis Xavier, and Mount Allison (just across the boundary in New Brunswick). Mount Saint Vincent and Université Ste. Anne would follow. On the opposite side of the religious ledger, a number of professional schools were created as independent institutions precisely because they did not fit the denominational mould. Many of them, including law, social work, medicine and related health professions subsequently merged into Dalhousie, as it grew beyond its Presbyterian roots, but

a number remained independent as well. These include engineering and architecture in the Technical University of Nova Scotia, the Nova Scotia Teachers
College, the Nova Scotia Agricultural College, and the Nova Scotia College
of Art and Design. The two most recent additions, bringing the total to 13, are
the University College of Cape Breton (formed of a merger of a junior college
and a technical institute) and the Atlantic School of Theology.

The failure to persuade King's to merge with Dalhousie in 1818 marked the
beginning of a long history of failed attempts at "rationalization" of the university system in Nova Scotia. The two most outstanding involved the
establishment of a University of Halifax in 1876, which came to nothing, and
the proposal by the Carnegie Foundation to assist in consolidating all the universities and colleges of the three maritime provinces in Halifax. This scheme
came the closest of any so far to succeeding, but ended up with only King's
and Dalhousie agreeing to a formal association.

The current effort dates from the 1985 report of the MacLennan royal
commission, which recommended the establishment of a provincial council,
exercising "executive authority" with respect to the allocation of government
grants or, if that were unsuccessful, a full-fledged University of Nova Scotia.[15]
Establishing a provincial council ran head-on into the existing buffer agency,
the three-province Maritime Provinces Higher Education Commission. A compromise was eventually reached, by which Nova Scotia would indeed form its
own council, but the members of the provincial body would simultaneously
constitute the province's membership on the regional body.

Out of this came a call for each university to submit a planned role and
capacity statement, intended to inform subsequent decisions on program "rationalization." The statements were less than precise, but did allow the council
to draw up a list of programs where substantial overlap or duplication was
apparent and which became candidates for change. Teacher training, business
education, computer science, and graduate programs were among the primary
targets.

The task of addressing the rationalization of these programs was turned
over to the university presidents, through their formal association known as
the Committee of Nova Scotia University Presidents, or CONSUP. Unable to
rise above their individual institutional interests, they could reach no agreement and admitted as much. With that, and on the advice of an advisory
committee chaired by Stefan Dupré of the University of Toronto, the government moved to strengthen the hand of the Council on Higher Education. A
national search for a full-time chair was launched, and a year later Janet
Halliwell, former chair of the Science Council of Canada, was appointed.
Systemwide reviews on teacher education, engineering, and computing science
were launched.

It was at this point that the government changed and John MacEachern was
named minister of education. He had to work within the expenditure restraint

program initiated in the September 1993 budget. That plan called for a reduction in spending on universities of nearly 13 percent between 1993-94 and 1997-98.[16] MacEachern decided to move quickly, at least to demonstrate the seriousness of the government's commitment to institutional change. The opportunity was provided by the report on teacher education. It recommended closing four of the seven programs, including those at Dalhousie, Saint Mary's, and St. Francis Xavier, and the entire Teachers College in Truro. MacEachern bought this proposal, with the single exception of St.Francis Xavier, which happened to be his *alma mater.*

Closing university programs at Dalhousie and Saint Mary's turned out to be difficult enough, but closing an entire institution was unprecedented. The government stuck to its decision, but mitigated the intended savings by agreeing to turn the facility into a community college and refurbish it as a "state-of-the-art" institution. There would be one fewer university in the province — now an even dozen — but also one more college.

Meanwhile, the prospect of a four-year program of annual cuts spurred the Nova Scotia Council on in its mandate to "rationalize" the university system. In this, the universities began to form their own views on what was desirable or acceptable. Dalhousie and the Technical University favour some form of merger or federation. The other universities in Halifax — five in number — want almost anything *but* this, advocating a partnership of existing institutions. And the five outside the Halifax area seem to want nothing so much as to be left alone, told what funding they can expect and allowed to adjust their activities to available resources.

This is the context in which the proposed cut in federal transfers must very shortly be accommodated. And while no one knows the precise size of that cut, nor the proportion that will be allocated to university funding, participants are openly discussing a figure for total funding of as little as $150 million. This would constitute a reduction of almost 30 percent compared with 1993-94, and would represent the equivalent of eliminating entirely provincial operating support for nine of the thirteen degree-granting institutions operating in that year. Needless to say, such a prospect has added urgency to the deliberations of the council, which is expected to report its recommendations to government this summer. Some very substantial rationalization seems virtually certain if a viable university system is to survive. But no one seems prepared to offer up any concessions from their particular bailiwick.

CONCLUSION

Nova Scotia's fiscal crisis has forced it to take radical measures that previous governments have variously contemplated, attempted, or rejected. In particular, municipal amalgamation is in place in the province's two metropolitan centres, and a four-region system of boards in in place to oversee the decentral-ization of health-care delivery. More is obviously to come, especially in education.

If the trials and tribulations of Nova Scotia's political leaders have pro-vided a humourous backdrop to the process of structural adjustment, it may have served unintentionally to divert attention from the seriousness of the fiscal crisis. The province may have dug itself out of the immediate swamp of chronic deficits, but it has a long way to go to escape the quagmire of accu-mulated debt and rising interest charges. And just as it could appropriately lay claim to having begun to put its fiscal affairs in order, the province has been dealt a fierce blow by the federal government, the erstwhile "sugar daddy" of the eastern "have-not" provinces. Reducing its dependence on federal trans-fers will be as difficult for Nova Scotia as it appears likely to be necessary. The federal budget has bequeathed more than expenditure reductions for Ot-tawa. It has virtually guaranteed that structural adjustment will continue and cut more deeply than anything witnessed to date. At least the Liberals will no longer have to look over their shoulders in fear of losing their leader in a party revolt; Dr. Savage survived the leadership review.

NOTES

1. Data taken from *Public Accounts of the Province of Nova Scotia* (Halifax: Queen's Printer, various years).

2. Nova Scotia, *Budget Address*, 30 September 1993, p. 7.

3. Nova Scotia, *Hansard*, 2 May 1994, p. 808.

4. Nova Scotia, *Hansard*, 11 April 1995, p. 411.

5. Jeffrey Simpson, "Nova Scotia's Deficit-Debt Struggle is a Cautionary Tale for All," *The Globe and Mail*, 16 May 1995, p. A20.

6. Canada, Department of Human Resources Development, *Improving Social Se-curity in Canada: A Discussion Paper* (Ottawa: Minister of Supply and Services, 1994).

7. The reductions come in part from actually cuts, and in part from the way the EPF-CHST formula works. With respect to the latter, EPF is based on a formula that involves equal per-capita provincial entitlements, from which are subtracted equalized provincial revenues derived from income tax points transferred to the provinces in stages going as far back as 1960. The amount remaining after subtracting the tax point revenue is paid as an actual cash grant. But the per-capita entitlements are designed to grow more slowly than tax revenues, at least in most years, with the result that cash payments actually decline year over year, and will disappear altogether in a decade or so. The same basic formula will continue under the CHST, with CAP thrown in, except that the per capita base of the provincial entitlements is up for negotiation. The consequences for

individual provinces of using a different base, such as prorating the previous year's allocation, could be enormous, and this adds considerable uncertainty to provincial revenue forecasts. For the specifics of the federal proposal, see Canada, Department of Finance, *Budget Plan* (Ottawa: H.M. the Queen in Right of Canada, 1995), pp. 51-4.

8.   Ibid., pp. 32-51.

9.   Nova Scotia, Royal Commission on Health Care, *Report: Towards a New Strategy,* J. Camille Gallant, Chair (Halifax: Government Printing, 1989).

10.   Nova Scotia, Minister's Action Committee on Health System Reform, *Nova Scotia's Blueprint for Health System Reform*, April 1994.

11.   Nova Scotia, Task Force on Local Government, *Report to the Government of Nova Scotia*, April 1992.

12.   Nova Scotia, *Provincial-Municipal Service Exchange: A Discussion Paper.* December 1993, p. 1.

13.   See *Interim Report of the Municipal Reform Commissioner, Halifax County (Halifax Metropolitan Area)*, C. Willian Hayward, Commissioner, 8 July 1993, and *Interim Report of the Municipal Reform Commissioner, Cape Breton County (Industrial Cape Breton)*, Charles A. Campbell, Commissioner, 8 July 1993.

14.   Nova Scotia Department of Education, *Education Horizons: White Paper on Restructuring the Education System*, 1995.

15.   Nova Scotia, Royal Commission on Post-Secondary Education, *Report*, 1985.

16.   The base level of funding for 1993-94 was $208.1 million. This would drop to $199.6 million for 1994-95, $194.8 for 1995-96, $183.8 for 1996-97, and $181.5 for 1997-98. See Nova Scotia, *Government By Design: An Action Plan for Reform and Fiscal Recovery in Nova Scotia*, p. 28.

6

Reforming the Canadian Social Assistance Complex: The Provincial Welfare States and Canadian Federalism

Gerard Boychuk

La réforme des politiques sociales au Canada est embrouillée dans l'enchevêtrement intergouvernemental du fédéralisme canadien. L'enjeu soulève non seulement la question du type d'État-providence que les Canadiennes et Canadiens veulent, mais également celle quant à savoir si l'État-providence canadien devrait se rapprocher davantage d'un système national relativement standardisé ou d'un ensemble plus disparate de systèmes provinciaux. C'est cette dernière direction que la politique fédérale semble privilégier à l'heure actuelle. Des critiques affirment que ceci constitue une menace pour l'uniformité nationale et pour les standards d'aide sociale qui existaient sous le Régime d'assistance publique du Canada. Cet article conclut que ces critiques tendent non seulement à exagérer le niveau d'uniformité nationale qui existe à l'heure actuelle mais aussi à surestimer le rôle que joue le partage conditionnel des coûts dans l'uniformisation nationale. Les modalités actuelles des divers régimes provinciaux d'aide sociale démontrent clairement qu'il existe d'importantes différences entre les dispositions relatives à l'aide sociale. À plusieurs égards, fondamentaux, le Canada n'a pas un seul État-providence mais bien un amalgame de dix variantes provinciales. Il semble que le partage des coûts sous le Régime d'assistance publique n'a pas contribué de façon significative à réduire les distinctions inter-provinciales.

Cet article examine les possibilités que le recours à des outils fiscaux permette d'atteindre des niveaux mêmes minimaux d'uniformité nationale. À l'heure actuelle, même en arrivant à surmonter tous les autres obstacles pratiques et les objections philosophiques qui s'élèvent contre la poursuite de standards nationaux en matière de dispositions d'aide sociale, il est tout simplement improbable que le gouvernement fédéral puisse allouer les ressources fiscales nécessaires à cet objectif. La stratégie politique de promotion du bien-être social et d'un filet de sécurité sociale adéquat par le recours à des exhortations pour des standards nationaux n'est tout simplement pas réaliste.

INTRODUCTION

There are mounting pressures in Canada, as elsewhere, for the reform of the welfare state. Social policy reform in Canada, however, is confronted by the fact that reform is embroiled in the intergovernmental entanglement of Canadian federalism. Thus, the issue of social policy reform raises not only the question of what kind of welfare state we want, but it also implicates the question of whether this Canadian welfare state should approximate, to some extent, a relatively uniform national system or a more disparate set of provincial systems.

The latter question is both implicitly and explicitly raised in the federal government's discussion paper, *Improving Social Security in Canada,* released in the fall of 1994 under the aegis of the federal Minister of Human Resources Development Lloyd Axworthy. Possible directions for reform identified in the paper include devolving more latitude to provincial governments in the area of social assistance by replacing conditional matching cost-sharing under the Canada Assistance Plan (CAP) with block-funding. Alternatively, the paper notes the possibility of attaching national standards to federal transfers to the provinces for social assistance. The announcement in the 1995 federal budget of the replacement of CAP with block-funding for social assistance under the Canada Health and Social Transfer (CHST) to be implemented in 1996 has made the move to block-funding an imminent reality.[1]

In comparison to CAP, current federal policy is moving more explicitly towards accepting diversity in provincial program design and delivery if not actually encouraging provincial variation. Unlike CAP, under the CHST, it seems apparent that there will not even be federal pretensions of ensuring some minimum standards of uniformity in provincial assistance provision with the exception of the restriction against provincial residency requirements. Critics claim that this change poses a threat to national uniformity and the standards in social assistance that exist under CAP. However, the uniformity that currently exists among provincial social assistance systems is minimal and is generally overstated by critics of the move to block-funding. Significant differences in assistance provision are currently evident in the contemporary design of the various provincial social assistance regimes. In some fundamental sense, Canada has not one welfare state but an amalgam of ten provincial variants.

Critics of the move to block-funding not only tend to overstate the level of national uniformity which currently exists but also explicitly or implicitly tend to overestimate the role of conditional cost-sharing in fostering such uniformity. It appears that cost-sharing under CAP and its attendant conditions has not contributed significantly to diminishing interprovincial distinctiveness. In fact, CAP's performance in imposing even the most minimal standards in provincial assistance provision appears relatively dismal. It seems likely that meaningful national standards constituting even a minimal level of national uniformity in this field would be extremely difficult to achieve through fiscal means alone.

This chapter begins by presenting a brief exposition of current provincial differences in social assistance provision. After establishing that significant interprovincial differences in social assistance exist, we then turn to a consideration of the philosophic underpinnings of arguments both for and against encouraging or discouraging the continuation of such provincial variation. This, in turn, is linked to much larger issues about the type of country that Canada is and will be. These debates, which raise all of the broader issues of federalism, are examined, although left unresolved. In turning to the practical dimensions of the issue, this chapter examines the feasibility of using fiscal means to pursue even minimal levels of national uniformity. This includes a discussion of CAP and the extent to which it was unable to impose even a modest measure of national uniformity in provincial assistance provision. Even if all the other practical obstacles and philosophic objections to pursuing national standards in social assistance provision could be overcome, it is simply unlikely that the federal government would devote the fiscal resources required. The political strategy of promoting social welfare and an adequate social safety net through recourse to calls for national standards is simply not a realistic political strategy.

COMPONENTS OF PROVINCIAL SOCIAL ASSISTANCE SYSTEMS

Social assistance is central to determining the nature of any particular welfare state because it is a program of last resort. The social assistance system represents the outer boundaries of the welfare state's intrusion into other social spheres such as the market and family. Those who are unable to secure adequate income in the market, do not have sufficient family support to maintain themselves, or are ineligible for or have depleted benefits from all other government programs have, as a last-resort, social assistance. Even the most social democratic systems (with a commitment to full employment and generous government programs) still face the question of how to provide for the people who "fall through the cracks" and at what standard. Social assistance is a critical element of the welfare state and is crucial to the question of what kind of welfare state we want. Yet, while much of the larger Canadian welfare state edifice has been constructed at the federal level, this crucial component remains a provincial responsibility.

Not only is social assistance a provincial responsibility, the provinces differ considerably in the goals that they pursue through social assistance policy. The welfare state is a response to conditions caused by economic and social changes but, in turn, contributes to shaping economic and social development.

This is the central focus of the current debates on the welfare state — what should be the ends of social policy in its interaction with the economy and society? There are, broadly defined, at least three possible answers to this question: social policy may attempt to reinforce the market distribution of status and well-being; reinforce a non-market status hierarchy; or attempt to erode both market- or non-market-based status differentials. In pursuing the first goal, the welfare state may stigmatize recipients and actively contribute to creating status differentials between those dependent upon the state and those who are not. Alternatively, the welfare state may stratify assistance recipients into a hierarchy of deservedness by identifying certain categories of beneficiaries as more or less deserving and, in so doing, may serve to reinforce traditional family and gender roles. Finally, the welfare state may undermine the market and traditional family by providing a level of well-being such that individuals are not forced by absolute need to participate in either the labour market or family.

The tension among these broad aims of social policy and the extent to which provincial social assistance serves these different ends is evident in the nuts and bolts of the various social assistance delivery systems. Provincial answers to the broad question of the appropriate ends of social policy are encoded in the actual components of provincial assistance delivery: eligibility requirements, asset exemptions, tax-back rates, benefit levels, employment/training programs, and verification/enforcement mechanisms.

Eligibility requirements can be either categorical, specifying particular groups as eligible or ineligible for assistance, or non-categorical — specifying the level of well-being at which people are considered to be in need. The broad issue which is raised in a consideration of categorical eligibility requirements is whether there are some individuals that are considered sufficiently undeserving that, regardless of their level of need, the system would deny them assistance. This is in contrast to the conception that some minimal level of social provision is an inherent right of citizenship.

Asset exemptions are the levels of assets that recipients may possess and still qualify as being in need. The issue here is how poor people have to be to qualify for benefits. A major dilemma is ensuring that benefits are targeted to those most in need while making sure that asset exemptions are not so low that it is difficult for recipients to re-enter the labour market or normal family life (for example, having to dispose of vehicles or tools in order to be eligible for assistance).

Tax-back rates are the rates at which benefits are reduced for employment earnings. Overall tax-back rates are determined by a combination of earnings exemptions and tax-back rates assessed against non-exempt earnings. *Earnings exemptions* are the amounts that applicants may earn that do not result in a reduction of assistance benefits. In addition, benefits are generally reduced at a specified rate for earnings above this exempted level. The issue regarding overall tax-back rates is identifying the adequate trade-off between limiting the number of people on assistance and ensuring that there are incentives to work. Lower overall tax-back rates provide a greater incentive for recipients to seek employment but, concomitantly, define a wider range of individuals as eligible for assistance.[2]

Benefit levels raise the question of the appropriate balance between providing adequate support and ensuring that benefits are not so high that they discourage participation in the labour market.[3]

Employment/training programs and requirements may be punitive or beneficial. In the case of the former, the policy issue is balancing work requirements which discourage voluntary assistance dependence against creating impediments to labour market entry (e.g., work requirements that displace job search in the private labour market). In the case of the latter, the policy question is identifying the appropriate balance between providing training and employment opportunities that give recipients some real chance of leaving assistance and ensuring that these opportunities are not so attractive that they draw people into the assistance system.

Verification and enforcement mechanisms include such aspects of assistance provision as fraud investigation and mandatory home visits. In part, the stringency of these mechanisms are determined by the nature of the assistance system. More complex rule systems and categorization schemes require higher levels of verification and enforcement. One policy concern is ensuring that the system is well-policed. Another is limiting the extent to which the system erodes the self-respect of recipients and contributes to the persistence of negative stereotypes of assistance recipients among the broader public — both of which may contribute to fostering dependence. The policy problem is to strike an appropriate balance between these two ends.

MODELS OF SOCIAL ASSISTANCE PROVISION

The components of assistance provision outlined above comprise the standard set of tools that provincial assistance systems have at their disposal. Comparisons of provincial systems must consider how provinces employ this range of instruments. The author has devised the following typology[4] of five distinct ideal-types of sets of policy instruments (as further described in Table 1):

- the *residual* assistance regime which provides some minimal social protection, but not at the expense of the operation of the market;

Table 1: Assistance Regime Type and Program Design

Regime Type	Eligibility	Benefits	Asset Exemptions	Tax-Back Rates	Employment/Training	Verification/Control
Residual	• no categorical restrictions • restricted definition of need	Low – Standardized	Low – Standardized	High – Standardized	No	Low – Standardized
Market/Family Enforcement	• no categorical restrictions • restricted definition of need	N/A – Standardized	Low – Standardized	High – Standardized	May enforce work requirements and/or training	High – Standardized
Market Performance	• no categorical restrictions • may include generous definition of need	N/A – If differential – higher for market and training participants	Medium – may be differential (must not be so low as to impede market entrance)	Low – (if differential – lower for employable recipients	Employment and training programs with significant participation incentives	N/A
Conservative	• categorical restrictions • differential (generous definition of need for deserving recipients, restricted definition for undeserving recipients)	N/A – Differential (dependent upon status of recipient)	N/A – Differential (dependent upon status of recipient)	N/A – Differential (used to create status distinction or discourage market entrance)	Differential (may enforce work requirements for undeserving recipients or provide beneficial training and employment for deserving recipients)	Differential (higher for undeserving recipients)
Redistributive	• no categorical restrictions • generous definition of need	High – Standardized	High – Standardized (must not be so low as to impede market entrance)	High – Standardized (actual market wage must provide incentives for market entrance)	May enhance employability of recipients but strictly voluntary	Low – Standardized

- the *market-family enforcement* system which enforces market and famly discipline by actively stigmatizing recipients so that those who are participating in the market or family are provided with a visible reminder of the fate that awaits them should they come to require state assistance;

- the *market performance* model which is designed to provide positive rewards for assistance recipients participating in or preparing to participate in the market;

- the *conservative* assistance model which is aimed at reinforcing an existing status hierarchy (based on class, race, gender) which recognizes some recipients as deserving and some as undeserving; and

- the *redistributive* model which treats all recipients equally and provides assistance at a level that constitutes a viable option to working, thus making participation in the market or family a matter of choice.

DIFFERENCES AMONG PROVINCIAL ASSISTANCE SYSTEMS

In reality, assistance regimes mix elements of each of the models outlined above. However, on the basis of the extent to which the various provincial systems appear to be pursuing the different ends implicit in these models, provincial regimes can be grouped into four of our regime types described above: conservative assistance regimes (Ontario, Manitoba, Nova Scotia, and Newfoundland), market-family enforcement regimes (Saskatchewan, Alberta, and Quebec), market performance regimes (New Brunswick and British Columbia), and redistributive regimes (P.E.I.). The following section outlines some general characteristics of each group (in order of its prevalence in the Canadian assistance complex). The section emphasizes the aspects of the relevant provincial systems unique to that particular category, and identifies specific provinces as illustrations of the particular regime-types.

CONSERVATIVE REGIMES

Conservative assistance regimes (Ontario, Manitoba, Nova Scotia, and Newfoundland) are characterized by the strong categorization of recipients. This model is best represented by the three two-tiered systems (Ontario, Manitoba, Nova Scotia). These regimes designate some recipients as deserving provincial-level recipients while undeserving recipients are left to the vagaries of municipal assistance provision which is often particularly harsh in comparison to provincial assistance. Because they are not primarily concerned with reinforcing the market, these systems define a wide range of recipients as unemployable or, alternatively, as legitimately relying on the assistance system.

The provision of work incentives is subordinate to reinforcing this status hierarchy of deserving and undeserving recipients. As a result, employment incentives tend to be more generous and overall tax-back rates lower for unemployable than employable recipients.

Nova Scotia is the best example of the conservative approach to assistance provision. Its two-tiered system provides assistance for deserving recipients that is relatively standardized. Undeserving recipients rely on municipal provision which varies widely from municipality to municipality. Municipal provision of assistance to undeserving recipients includes the denial or reduction of benefits during particular fruit seasons, the practice of relying solely on food vouchers, and surprisingly stringent job search requirements which may require the recipient to make up to three contacts with prospective employers per day.[5]

Despite stringent job search requirements, tax-back rates are considerably higher for employable recipients in comparison to unemployable recipients.

MARKET-FAMILY ENFORCEMENT REGIMES

The primary aim of the market-family enforcement systems (Saskatchewan, Alberta, and Quebec) is to make assistance relatively unattractive for all recipients through active stigmatization. Participation in the labour market or family becomes a relatively attractive alternative in comparison to receipt of assistance.

Of the current provincial assistance regimes, Saskatchewan's system incorporates a measure of stigmatization of all recipients that is not evident in any other province. This stigmatization includes mandatory home visits on application and then yearly for all recipients; denying assistance to appellants during the appeal process; issuing rental cheques jointly payable to the recipient and the landlord, and requiring all recipients to pick up their monthly cheques in person or have their files frozen.[6]

MARKET PERFORMANCE REGIMES

The primary aim of the market performance systems (New Brunswick and British Columbia) is to promote labour market participation through positive employment and incentive programs. These programs include the provision of certain benefits for a period after the recipient has left assistance for employment. In addition to the provision of such programs, tax-back rates decrease according to employability, employability is defined widely, and recipients may find themselves better off being classified as employable rather than unemployable.

New Brunswick demonstrates these characteristics. New Brunswick offers several employment and training programs including N.B. Works and N.B. Job Corps. As a result of these programs and the tax-back rate structure, recipients may be better off if categorized as employable — in stark contrast to provinces such as Nova Scotia or Ontario. Although earnings exemptions are time-limited, employable recipients may be allowed to keep their full earnings. In addition, the New Brunswick system is not intrusive or stigmatizing; for example, there are no mandatory home visits.[7]

REDISTRIBUTIVE REGIMES

P.E.I. is the closest of the provinces to providing an example of a redistributive regime. The assumption underlying this regime is that employable recipients will seek employment voluntarily:

> The policy is that applicants are to be presumed unemployable. Destitution itself should be sufficient evidence of severe unemployment problems ... [The system] ... operat[es] on the assumption that the vast majority of recipients will actively seek any work which is available, and for which they are capable.[8]

As a result of this philosophy, benefits in P.E.I. are based solely on need and not employability or length of time on welfare. As well, benefits are high relative to other provinces. Tax-back rates are relatively high such that recipients are only modestly rewarded for choosing to work at wages below the level of assistance. In addition, the system incorporates relatively lax job-search requirements (for example, three job contacts per month in comparison to three job contacts per day in Nova Scotia). As well, the system is not intrusive and there is no evidence of stringent verification techniques.

In contrast to regimes that require single mothers to attempt to secure employment, P.E.I. allows the choice about her role in the market and/or family to fall to the single parent: "single parents with children under school age are given the option of remaining at home with their children or of being assisted ... to pursue employment."[9] This is contrary to the practice in other provinces: "[u]nlike a few other provinces, welfare assistance policy on Prince Edward Island does not clearly identify a preference for working or stay-at-home mothers, thus allowing both options."[10]

THE FUTURE OF PROVINCIAL DIVERSITY

The provincial differences outlined above highlight the fact that there is no consensus among provinces about the most appropriate goals of social assistance policy. The question is whether these differences among provincial systems can reasonably be expected to continue. If one expects convergence among provinces arising from factors other than federal involvement, turning to federal policy in order to foster national uniformity becomes unnecessary.

One line of reasoning in the current debates regarding social policy focuses on external constraints on governments — fiscal constraints, constraints imposed by changing world conditions including globalization, changing technology, and other external forces. The argument is that these forces are increasingly limiting the range of policy responses open to governments. Policymakers across political units are forced to adopt similar solutions in response to these forces and the result is (or will be) convergence.

There are powerful arguments for convergence among welfare states which might also be expected to apply to provincial social assistance regimes. The external constraints imposed by changing economic conditions such as globalization will be felt most powerfully where welfare states are most generous and present the greatest impingement upon efficient market performance. Fiscal pressure will be most onerous where the welfare state presents the largest fiscal burden relative to fiscal capacity. Ideological backlash against the welfare state will be most significant where the burden of the welfare state is most visible and has exceeded the level of generosity deemed acceptable by a significant segment of the population.

However, there are compelling reasons not to expect these forces to apply to provincial assistance regimes. First, provinces currently do not share the same predispositions towards providing assistance; and changing external conditions do not appear to have lessened these differences. External economic constraints such as changing global market conditions and the fiscal crisis do not directly alter government policy; rather, they alter the relative cost (or opportunity cost) of adopting particular public policies. Changes in these external factors can be expected to have different effects in the various provinces. Provinces do not share identical preferences regarding social assistance. The effects of changes in the relative costs of providing social assistance in any particular province depends on the policy preferences unique to that province.

Second, convergence arguments often assume that technical solutions to the policy issues raised by poverty are obvious and that economic imperatives point clearly in a particular policy direction. The difficulty with this line of reasoning (evident in the complex trade-offs identified above in the section on components of assistance systems) is that there are no self-evidently superior solutions to the questions raised by the issue of social assistance and no particularly compelling reason to believe that regimes will develop inexorably in the direction of one particular solution. The optimal form of assistance provision cannot be reduced to a technical problem. Solutions depend on how the problem is defined. The question of the model that assistance systems *should* adopt remains in essence a political one. Expert opinion seems widely divided on the particular policy direction mandated by current economic imperatives and there does not appear to be convergence around a social policy consensus about the causes of poverty and the appropriate ways of alleviating it.

Another more immediate argument for convergence is related to the issue of the mobility of assistance recipients. It is argued that mobility of recipients will exert downward pressure on levels of support across provinces as recipients move to provinces providing more generous benefits. The expected result is convergence among provinces upon a lowered level of assistance. However, the mobility of recipients is often accepted as axiomatic or supported by anecdotal evidence rather than rigorous cohort analysis which traces the movements of assistance recipients across provinces over time. Recent data suggests that the mobility of assistance recipients is often overstated.[11] Most simply, assistance recipients are probably the least likely portion of the population to have the financial means to move interprovincially and establish a new residence while facing a certain (perhaps lengthy) interruption of benefits. Second, the intricacies of the various components of assistance systems (especially eligibility requirements) may discourage recipients from moving and attempting to re-establish eligibility in another jurisdiction. Due to a variety of factors, including the existence of special benefits and discretionary benefits, recipients may also not easily be able to compare rates across jurisdictions. Finally, for recipients who do relocate, such mobility is most likely to be based on consideration of the relative employment opportunities in the various provinces rather than on consideration of the relative generosity of the various assistance regimes.

Distinctiveness among provincial systems may also be sufficiently robust to withstand pressures towards convergence. There are at least two ways in which assistance regimes may be self-reinforcing. First, they may be self-reinforcing as a result of the views about poverty and its causes that particular forms of assistance provision instill in the broader public. Second, they may be self-reinforcing as a result of the behaviour that various approaches to assistance provision encourage among individual assistance recipients.

There are many ways in which assistance provision may have significant effects on the beliefs of the broader public about the causes of poverty and the appropriate methods of alleviating it. For example, high levels of fraud may undermine public support for the assistance system. However, complex and intrusive rules or stringent verification techniques will lead to a significantly higher incidence of fraud in any given system. This may undermine public support for the assistance system as well as reinforce stereotypes of assistance recipients as dishonest. Certain aspects of provision such as mandatory work requirements can also be expected to reinforce stereotypes of recipients as lazy and the perception of indigence as resulting from the personal failure of the recipient. In both cases, poverty may increasingly be seen as related to individual moral failure. Considering the significant differences in provincial program design, it would not be surprising if different forms of assistance provision have resulted in provincial differences in public perceptions about poverty and assistance policy. An adequate, let alone conclusive, examination of the similarities and differences in provincial distributions of public opinion regarding poverty and social assistance remains to be undertaken.

There are also several ways in which the specifics of program design may condition the behaviour of individual recipients. The most familiar examples are systems in which the combination of benefit levels and tax-back rates discourage recipients from pursuing employment. There are also many more subtle ways in which the provision of assistance may shape the behaviour of assistance recipients. Regimes that provide substantially better treatment for particular categories encourage recipients to declare and consider themselves as belonging to those favoured groups. For example, in many systems there is an advantage for recipients to be classified as unemployable and recipients may be encouraged to think of themselves as such. Assistance regimes which are highly intrusive in determining the consumption patterns of recipients encourage them to see individual life choices as determined by the system and not as matters of personal responsibility. Thus, as a result of their interaction with the assistance system, these recipients may become ill-prepared to enter the market where prevailing norms are those of individual choice. A related argument is that assistance provision often punishes the exercise of skills that are rewarded in the market and that certain approaches to assistance provision discourage innovation and adaptation.[12]

These effects on public perceptions as well as the behaviour of individual recipients suggest ways in which differences in provincial assistance systems may be significantly self-reinforcing. These self-reinforcing effects may make national uniformity more difficult to achieve, but, depending on one's point of view, perhaps also more necessary. In the absence of some mechanism to enforce national uniformity, there are good reasons to expect that provincial assistance regimes will not naturally develop in a uniform direction. It is in light of this line of reasoning, that we now turn to the question of appropriate policy responses to provincial diversity.

THE PHILOSOPHICAL DEBATE: NATIONAL STANDARDS VERSUS PROVINCIAL DIVERSITY

If significant diversity currently exists among provincial social assistance systems and, in the absence of federal intervention, will continue to exist in the foreseeable future, the question is whether the federal government should be encouraging such diversity. This debate takes place on at least two separate planes: philosophical and practical. This section briefly considers some of the philosophical issues regarding the question of whether Canada should have some modicum of federally-enforced national social assistance standards or whether a looser set of provincial systems is more desirable. This question raises all of the traditional issues of federal versus provincial jurisdiction:[13] democratic implications (devolving decision-making responsibility to the level of government closest to the people and ensuring the integrity of the lines of accountability between different orders of government and the people), equity concerns (ensuring that disadvantaged citizens in different parts of the country can expect reasonably similar levels of social protection), efficiency concerns (containing spillovers and preventing provincial exportation of social assistance caseloads to other provinces) and broader concerns about national unity.

At one level, arguments in favour of a national system appear to be rooted in a strong conviction about the substance of the most desirable type of welfare state independent of jurisdictional concerns. The assumption of this line of reasoning is that for a variety of reasons (including ideological differences or factors such as interprovincial spillovers) provinces will not voluntarily adopt the favoured model of assistance provision. One example of these arguments focuses on the issue of spillovers and the reasoning that provinces will attempt to off-load their social assistance burdens on other provinces through a variety of means including residence requirements and meagre levels of assistance. The overall result of this process of provincial levelling will be a very low-level safety net. These arguments shift the focus of debate from the question of the appropriate division of responsibility among orders of government to a consideration of the strengths and weaknesses of the particular models of assistance provision. For example, the levelling effects of interprovincial competition may well be seen in a positive normative light by an observer who favours a minimalist welfare state. This demonstrates the extent to which the debate about the type of welfare state and the appropriate breakdown of jurisdictional responsibility cannot be easily separated.

The case for national uniformity is also often made on the basis of national unity concerns and the expected effects of a patchwork of provincial safety nets in eroding a sense of national community. Typically, this is where interregional equity arguments appear: national citizenship implies a right to reasonably comparable levels of social protection regardless of province of residence. National standards are assumed to encourage perceptions of national citizenship — especially in disadvantaged provinces. These arguments also tend to make assumptions about the ability of provincial governments (especially in advantaged provinces) to create and foster distinct provincial political cultures and attachments to the provincial (as opposed to the national) state. These appeals for national uniformity are often not made distinct from pleas for a minimum level of social protection — implicitly at a level higher than currently furnished by provinces providing assistance at the lowest levels.

A related argument in favour of national standards which appeals more directly to economic concerns rather than nationalist sentiments may be based on the reasoning that different provincial assistance policies fragment the internal common market (and labour market in particular). Where assistance provision varies across provinces, recipients may be unwilling to give up the security of assistance in their home province in order to seek employment in another province. The mobility of surplus labour across the national labour market would be facilitated by a uniform national assistance system especially if interprovincial relocation could be undertaken without the interruption of benefits. Thus, the question of whether social assistance should be a nationally uniform system or a set of provincial systems entails questions of economic efficiency.

However, these arguments in favour of national uniformity are confronted by a range of arguments in favour of provincial variability. One version of these arguments is predicated on a concern with certain principles of democracy. The most democratic government is argued to be that which takes place at as close a level to the people as feasible. Imposing standards ultimately governing the appropriate ends of assistance policy upon a provincial community infringes upon this aspect of democratic governance and provincial autonomy.[14] A further argument, considering the current assignment of jurisdictional responsibilities, is that cost-sharing and other forms of imposing standards of national uniformity in an area of exclusive provincial jurisdiction increase the difficulty of determining which level of government is responsible for particular policy decisions and, thus, blurs the lines of democratic accountability.

Another view favouring provincial variability is that the provincial order of government is more adept than the central order at determining what form of assistance provision is most beneficial. The central order of government may be simply unable to be sufficiently responsive to the varying economic conditions in the provinces. Underlying this approach is a rejection of the assumption that the relationship between assistance provision and market performance is fixed (e.g., higher levels of one necessitating lower levels of the other); rather, this approach stresses that various forms of assistance provision may be differentially beneficial or detrimental to economic performance depending on the economic context of that particular province. According to this logic, there is no model of social assistance provision which is uniformly appropriate to the different provincial economic contexts that make up the Canadian economy.

Finally, another possible benefit of provincial variability is that it allows provinces the necessary flexibility to experiment in the field of social assistance provision. Policy initiatives which are successful may then be adopted by other jurisdictions. This approach encourages innovation and adaptation.

While there are strong arguments to be made on both sides, this debate is impossible to resolve. There is no agreed upon or objective standard against which to weigh the varying concerns such as democracy, efficiency, or national unity when they come into conflict. However, those who favour a national welfare system over one comprised of a set of distinct provincial components are left with the practical problem of how to construct such a national system. The next section turns to a consideration of this issue.

PRACTICAL POLICY RESPONSES TO PROVINCIAL DIVERSITY

If one accepts that significant differences among provincial social assistance systems will persist in the absence of federal initiatives and that the philosophic bases for adopting some standard of national uniformity outweigh arguments for provincial variability, the question becomes how to foster uniformity. Critics of the move to block-funding — often by default — appear to be advocating the continuation of some form of conditional matching cost-sharing. A retrospective examination of conditional cost-sharing under CAP offers some insights into the inability of the federal government to ensure even a modicum of national standards using this tool. Another quite closely related possibility identified by the federal social policy review is attaching national standards to block-funding. The following section reviews both of these policy alternatives with reference to their own implicit policy goal of fostering at least some minimal level of national uniformity.

THE CANADA ASSISTANCE PLAN

The Canada Assistance Plan represented the federal answer — albeit a weak one — to both the question of what kind of welfare state was most desirable as well as the question of whether the social assistance complex should be fashioned as a national system or a set of provincial systems. CAP was more clearly consistent with the national model relative to the situation prior to CAP or the current federal policy direction. Even so, CAP was only a tentative step in the direction of national uniformity in social assistance provision.

Instituted in 1966, CAP allowed for the consolidation of a variety of cost-sharing programs for categorical assistance including Old Age Assistance, Blind Persons Allowances, Disabled Persons Allowances and Unemployment Assistance under one umbrella program.[15] Under CAP, the federal government would continue to match the funds expended by the provinces on these categorical programs dollar for dollar. In addition, cost-sharing would be extended to provincial categorical programs for needy mothers and widows which were not previously cost-shared as well as to a variety of welfare services.[16]

Administration and program delivery legally remained the full responsibility of the provinces.[17] There were federal conditions included in the CAP legislation, although they were not very rigorous.[18] For most of the agreements under the Act, there are five conditions: (i) assistance must be provided to anyone "in need"; (ii) there must be no provincial residency requirement;

(iii) an appeal procedure must exist; (iv) the province must "maintain accounts" regarding funds disbursed; and (v) the province must make available all provincial legislation and regulations concerning the plan.[19] CAP was intended to have, and indeed had, little effect on the administration of provincial assistance programs which it was assumed would continue to be based on existing provincial categories.[20]

An important aspect of CAP in relation to previous categorical programs was that administrative costs were to be covered.[21] This could be expected to lead to the professionalization of assistance provision and an increased reliance on trained social workers. In turn, this professionalization might then lead indirectly to convergence in provincial assistance provision based upon shared professional norms. This professionalized model of assistance provision was inextricably linked with the principle of assistance provision on the basis of a fixed test of need rather than on an ad hoc case by case basis. However, outside of this, flexibility in the cost-sharing arrangements was viewed as an end in itself by the federal government. This is evident, for example, in the fact that, while categorical cost-sharing programs had fixed limits on the level of benefits that would be cost-shared, CAP uncapped these programs by removing such limits. Certainly, to the extent that CAP could be expected to contribute convergence, its effects on benefits would at best be indirect.[22]

CAP remained relatively unchanged from its inception until the early 1990s. The 1990 federal budget announced that the funds transferred to the three richest provinces — Alberta, British Columbia, and Ontario — would be limited to a 5 percent annual increase for the following two fiscal years.[23] This change quite fundamentally altered the open-ended matching cost-sharing nature of CAP. Despite the fact that provincial legal action against the cap was still before the courts, the federal government in the 1991 budget extended the cap for an additional three years.

CAP, CONDITIONAL COST-SHARING, AND CONVERGENCE

Undoubtedly, there are good reasons to expect that this extension of federal cost-sharing would lead to increasing homogeneity in provincial assistance programs. However, cost-sharing may have potentially contradictory effects. On the one hand, cost-sharing is argued to equalize the fiscal capacity of provinces so that they might be expected to provide more similar levels of services.[24] On the other hand, cost-sharing may allow those provinces that already demonstrate a willingness and ability to commit funds to a particular program or service to offer those services at an even higher level relative to other provinces. Thus, there is no *a priori* reason to expect that cost-sharing would lead to convergence in social assistance provision.

For example, the cap on CAP in 1990 may be explained by the fact that Ontario had the highest rate of growth in CAP transfers in the mid- to late-

1980s and expensive plans for social assistance reform. The federal government's move simply indicated its refusal to pay for Ontario's proposed reforms.[25] This demonstrates the ways in which matching cost-sharing can contribute to divergence in provincial assistance provision. Had CAP not been capped, it seems likely that Ontario's already generous assistance provision and benefit levels would have been increased even further relative to other provinces.

Despite the potentially contradictory effects of cost-sharing, others have argued that CAP did lead to convergence in provincial social assistance in terms of overall spending,[26] assistance rates,[27] and standards of assistance provision.[28] The following discussion assesses at least the first two of these claims. While the logical case for a linkage between federal initiatives and convergence is weak, there is also mixed empirical evidence regarding such a link.

The range of difference among provinces (the per capita expenditures of the highest spending province as a multiple of the expenditures of the lowest spending province in any given year) was greater in the early 1980s than it was in the early to mid-1960s.[29] The pattern of convergence and divergence over the CAP period is extremely irregular. (See Figure 1.) Certainly, this index of dispersion does not depict the strong continuous downward trend described by Simeon and Miller.[30]

Using a different data set to extend this analysis into the 1990s,[31] indices of difference in social service expenditures per capita and social service expenditures as a percent of total expenditures also do not reveal strong patterns of convergence. Differences followed a tumultuous path of development although they hardly suggest a pattern of convergence. In the case of social services as a percent of total spending, the range between the highest and lowest spending provinces is greater throughout the CAP period (and currently) than in the immediate pre-CAP period.[32] (See Figures 2 and 3.)

Provincial social assistance rates over the CAP period do not demonstrate significant and continued convergence.[33] Rather, the pattern appears cyclical. Differences among provincial benefit rates for single employables by the mid-1980s were as significant as they were at the inception of CAP. By the early 1990s, differences in provincial assistance rates for single mothers were also as significant as differences at the inception of CAP.[34] Though they had not reached the levels of the mid-1960s, differences in provincial rates for couples with two children increased significantly in the 1980s. (See Figure 4.)

Even using these aggregate-level indicators, it appears that a patchwork of different programs rather than a more uniform set of programs continued to exist over the course of CAP's tenure. This raises the question of the extent that the federal government has the ability to fashion something akin to a relatively uniform national system solely through fiscal means.

The three substantive conditions regarding the qualitative aspects of assistance provision were that assistance be provided to anyone "in need," that there be no provincial residency requirement, and that an appeal procedure exist.

Figure 1:   *Dispersion in Provincial Assistance Expenditures, 1945-1984*

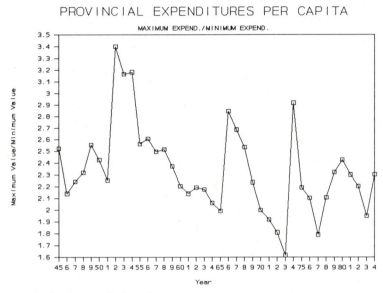

Source: Author's compilation.

Figure 2:   *Dispersion in Provincial Social Service Expenditures, 1965-1991*

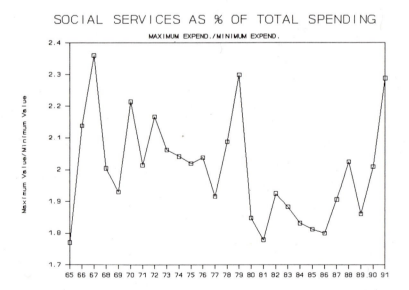

Source: Author's compilation.

Figure 3:   *Dispersion in Provincial Social Service Expenditures, 1965-1991*

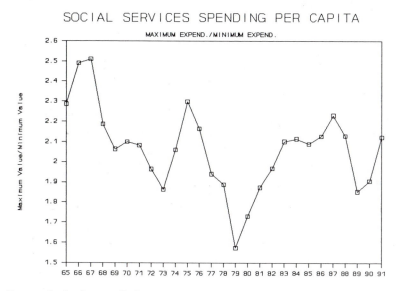

Source: Author's compilation.

Figure 4:   *Dispersion in Provincial Assistance Rates, 1966-1991*

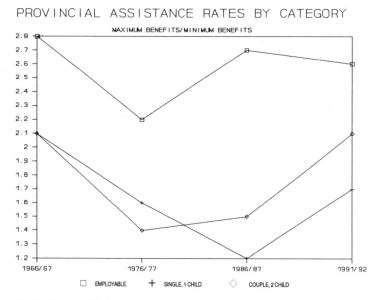

Source: Author's compilation.

There is considerable debate about the implications of the stipulation that assistance be provided to anyone "in need." This is the condition of CAP which is both the subject of the most significant errors in interpretation and apparently the basis for most objections to the move to block-funding. Assistance must be provided to anyone in need; however, need *is defined by the province.* Thus, there is a wide range of grounds on which assistance may be denied to recipients who, by any common-sense definition, could be considered to be in need.[35] More importantly, the federal requirement of a needs-test appears to have been primarily designed not to identify assistance that provinces were *obliged* to provide but to identify those costs *that the federal government would not share.* For example, the needs-test criteria renders provincial income supplementation schemes ineligible for cost-sharing if they are income-tested rather than needs-tested.

Even accepting that federal aspirations of ensuring some level of national uniformity were extremely low, it is reasonable to wonder why such a low level of national uniformity was achieved under CAP even regarding its explicit conditions.[36] The root of this problem appears to lie most clearly in the absence of any effective enforcement mechanism. The only option open to the federal government to deal with provinces not abiding by the conditions of CAP was to withhold CAP funding completely. Unlike provisions in the *Canada Health Act* of 1984, there was no inclusion in CAP of a mechanism for the partial withholding of transfers to provinces. Thus, the penalty for non-compliance was much too severe to ever be invoked — which it never was. Cost-sharing provides an automatic disincentive for providing services in a manner or at a level that exceeds allowable cost-shareable limits. Attaching conditions to cost-sharing is a mechanism much less well-suited to ensuring minimum standards of assistance provision.

POLICY ALTERNATIVES: NATIONAL STANDARDS AND BLOCK-FUNDING

Certainly, examining the significant differences among provinces suggests that designing some minimal standards of national uniformity might be a much more difficult challenge than may be recognized. A consideration of the complex interaction of the individual components of provincial assistance provision demonstrates the difficulty faced in specifying national standards. For example, minimum benefit levels do not mean much if they do not stipulate the eligibility requirements placed upon recipients. Specifying minimum benefit levels for everyone deemed to be in need does not mean much if provinces determine the definition of need. It is difficult to imagine specifying national standards in adequate detail to ensure that such standards could not be easily avoided by recalcitrant provinces.

Another important point in a consideration of attaching national standards to financial transfers is Ottawa's fiscal position. It simply does not seem plausible that the federal government would be able to enforce national uniformity at a higher level than currently exists while decreasing fiscal commitment in the field of social assistance. For better or worse, the Axworthy review and the 1995 budget demonstrate quite clearly that it is unlikely that the federal government will increase its financial commitment in this area in the foreseeable future. Thus, the debate is bounded by this fiscal constraint and ranges between attempting to ensure that the very minimal national uniformity now in place continues to exist, or, possibly, the complete abnegation of a federal role in this policy area.

The federal view of its own policy role in social assistance is evident in the commitment in the 1995 budget to ensuring only that provincial residency requirements do not again become part of the social assistance policy landscape. Perhaps this is a reasonable assessment of the limits on the type of conditions which the federal government can realistically impose on provinces using fiscal means. In the absence of even this minimal requirement, it would be difficult to justify the implementation of block-funding for social assistance rather than a move to tax transfers and complete federal withdrawal from the field.[37] At any rate, it is not evident why provinces would agree to conditions even as minimal as those included in CAP while being denied the financial protection offered by matching cost-sharing against unexpected increases in the social assistance caseload and expenditures.

CONCLUSIONS

There are two major questions raised by a consideration of the appropriate direction for social policy in Canada. First, there is the issue of what kind of welfare state we want. The second, albeit highly related question, is whether the social assistance component of the Canadian welfare state should consist of a national system with some modicum of federally-enforced national standards or a set of provincial systems.

The question as to what type of welfare state Canadians want is a valid one in the sense that the answer is not a foregone conclusion. Significant differences among provincial social assistance systems demonstrate that there is no consensus about the type of system we should have. Existing provincial variations outline a menu of possibilities. It is not clear that any of these alternatives is either inherently superior or commands more public or elite support than others. Social assistance policy is a public policy rubik's cube entailing complex trade-offs. There is a need to be wary of arguments that offer one solution as a panacea for the difficult problems with which social assistance policy must grapple. Perhaps this is reason enough to opt for provincial variability and flexibility rather than national standards. If not, the *real politick* of federal-provincial relations combined with the current emphasis in Ottawa on deficit reduction provide ample reason to suspect that any policy moves in the direction of national uniformity are highly unlikely.

NOTES

I would like to thank Nadine Busmann, Peter Leslie, Jon Rose, Debora VanNijnatten and two anonymous reviewers for their helpful comments on earlier versions of this work. A version of this paper was presented to the Canadian Political Science Annual Meeting 1995 and I would like to thank Alain Noël for his helpful comments there. Any errors in fact or interpretation remain the responsibility of the author.

1. See Susan Phillips, "The 'Heads-Up' Budget: Implications for Fiscal Federalism" in this volume.

2. See Appendix 2 for an overview of provincial differences in tax-back rates.

3. Benefit levels are the most often examined aspect of provincial assistance systems because, in part, they are the most easily quantifiable; however, as regards the extent to which they are indicative of the nature of the assistance regime, they are but one indicator. For an overview of absolute differences in support levels, see Appendix 1.

4. This typology is created from the amalgamation and adaptation of the typologies of welfare states developed by Polanyi, Titmuss, and Esping-Andersen. See Karl Polanyi, *The Great Transformation* (Boston: Beacon Press, 1944); Richard Titmuss, *Social Policy: An Introduction* (London: George Allen and Unwin, 1974); and Gøsta Esping-Andersen, "The Three Political Economies of the Welfare State," *Canadian Review of Sociology and Anthropology* 26 (1989): 10-36. Regarding the development of the typology presented here, see Gerard Boychuk, "Comparative Provincial Assistance Regimes: The Development of the Canadian Welfare States," (Queen's University, PhD dissertation, 1995) especially ch. 2,3.

5. This is drawn from Barbara Blouin, "Below the Bottom Line: The Unemployed and Welfare in Nova Scotia," *Canadian Review of Social Policy*, 29 and 30 (1992): 112-31.

6. Graham Riches and Lorelee Manning, *Welfare Reform and the Canada Assistance Plan: The Breakdown of Public Welfare in Saskatchewan, 1981-1989* (Regina: University of Regina Social Administration Research Unit, 1989).

7. See Roger Levesque, *Income Assistance in New Brunswick: Objective 1990* (Fredericton, 1987) and New Brunswick Advisory Council on the Status of Women, *Women and Financial Assistance in New Brunswick: A Preliminary Study* (Fredericton, 1987).

8. "Welfare Assistance in Prince Edward Island," *Bulletin of Canadian Welfare Law* (Spring 1974): 50. Although this quote refers to the mid-1970s, elements of this philosophy are still evident in assistance provision in P.E.I. today.

9. National Council of Welfare, *Welfare in Canada: The Tangled Safety Net* (Ottawa: Minister of Supply and Services, 1987), p. 19.

10. Prince Edward Island Welfare Assistance Review Committee, *Dignity, Security, Opportunity* (Charlottetown: Department of Health and Social Services, 1989), p. 65.

11. Statistics recently gathered by the British Columbia Social Services Ministry finds no support whatsoever for the claim that differences in assistance rates result in the interprovincial movement of assistance recipients. See "Welfare Cuts Unlikely to Cause Exodus," *The Globe and Mail*, 28 July 1995, A3.

12. For example, where actual shelter costs are paid or where recipients living with others face reduced shelter benefits, adaptation in living arrangements is discouraged because the recipient enjoys no resulting financial benefit.

13. For a good review of these issues, see D.V. Smiley, *The Federal Condition in Canada* (Toronto: McGraw-Hill Ryerson, 1987), esp. ch.1.

14. This is integrally related to the question of whether there are significant provincial differences in public perceptions about poverty and the appropriate means of alleviating it.

15. Government of Canada, *A Study Team Report: Canada Assistance Plan*, (Ottawa: Minister of Supply and Services, 1985), p. 66. See also, Government of Canada, *Fiscal Federalism in Canada: Parliamentary Task Force on Federal-Provincial Fiscal Arrangements* (Ottawa: Minister of Supply and Services, 1981).

16. Allan Moscovitch, "The Canada Assistance Plan: A Twenty-Year Assessment, 1966-1986," in Katherine A. Graham (ed.), *How Ottawa Spends 1988/89: The Conservatives Heading into the Stretch* (Ottawa: Carleton University Press, 1988), p. 288.

17. Government of Canada, *Study Team Report*, p. 45.

18. Keith G. Banting, *The Welfare State and Canadian Federalism* 2d ed. (Kingston and Montreal: McGill-Queen's University Press, 1987), pp. 11, 95; and Moscovitch, p. 293.

19. Moscovitch, "The Canada Assistance Plan," p. 275.

20. Allan Moscovitch, personal correspondence with author, Nov. 1993.

21. The following is drawn from Tom Kent, interview with author, Nov. 1993.

22. Moscovitch, "The Canada Assistance Plan," p. 275.

23. Ronald Watts and Douglas Brown, *Canada: The State of the Federation 1990*, (Kingston: Institute of Intergovernmental Relations, Queen's University, 1990) p. 263. See also Canadian Council on Social Development, *Canada's Social Programs Are in Trouble* (Ottawa: Canadian Council on Social Development, 1990), p. 27.

24. Richard Simeon with E.R. Miller, "Regional Variations in Public Policy," in David Elkins and Richard Simeon (eds.), *Small Worlds: Provinces and Parties in Canadian Political Life* (Methuen: Toronto, 1980), p. 275. See also Banting, *The Welfare State*, pp. 93-94.

25. Thomas J. Courchene, "Canada's Social Policy Deficit: Implications for Fiscal Federalism," inn K.G. Banting, D.M. Brown and T.J. Courchene (eds.), *The Future of Fiscal Federalism* (Kingston: School of Policy Studies, Queen's University, 1994), p. 101.

26. Simeon with Miller, "Regional Variations in Public Policy," p. 259.

27. Canada, Department of National Health and Welfare, Program Audit and Review Directorate, *Evaluation of the Canada Assistance Plan* (1991), p. III-39.

28. Banting, *The Welfare State*, p. 115.

29. The data for Figure 1 are drawn from Statistics Canada, *Provincial Government Income and Expenditures* (Ottawa: Minister of Supply and Services, various years) and Statistics Canada, *Local Government Income and Expenditures* (Ottawa: Minister of Supply and Services, various years). This data set is used to provide a historical overview of the patterns of convergence and divergence in the postwar period as a context in which to situate patterns of convergence and divergence since CAP.

30. Simeon and Miller, pp. 258-59. For their examination of dispersion, Simeon and Miller use standard deviation in per capita spending as a percentage of the weighted Canadian average. However, an examination of this measure in the postwar period reveals only moderate convergence over the entire period. This convergence also occurred in an extremely irregular pattern rather than the smooth trend of convergence outlined by Simeon and Miller. See sources for Figure 1, note 29.

31. Statistics Canada, *Provincial Economic Accounts* (Ottawa: Statistics Canada, various years). The Statistics Canada publication used to create Table 1 was discontinued in 1984. The figures for Tables 2 and 3 are also from Statistics Canada but do not extend back to the immediate postwar period and are not directly comparable with the figures presented in Table 1.

32. An examination of the standard deviation in provincial spending (as a percent of total expenditures) as a percentage of the weighted Canadian average leads to the same conclusion.

33. These rate comparisons are drawn from Canada, *Evaluation of the Canada Assistance Plan* and the National Council of Welfare, *Welfare Incomes 1991* (Ottawa: Minister of Supply and Services, 1992).

34. An examination of dispersion in assistance rates measured as the standard deviation in provincial rates as a percent of the weighted Canadian average reveals an identical picture.

35. To provide one concrete example, in certain provinces, recipients could be denied assistance on the basis that they "quit or were fired from a job." Moscovitch, "The Canada Assistance Plan," p. 285. In certain provinces into the 1990s, in apparent violation of the requirement that assistance be provided to anyone in need, assistance continued to be denied to applicants without a residence.

36. Considering the laxity of these conditions and the general inability of the federal government to enforce them, it is quite astonishing that national anti-poverty groups have argued to the United Nations that these conditions constituted "rights of the poor." "Ottawa Quietly Repealing Health Act, Expert Alleges" *The Globe and Mail*, 03 May 1995, A4.

37. However, with the cash portion of federal transfers decreasing relative to the portion consisting of transfers of tax room, this appears likely to occur anyway.

Appendix 1
Provincial Assistance Rates by Category, 1993

Figure 1.1

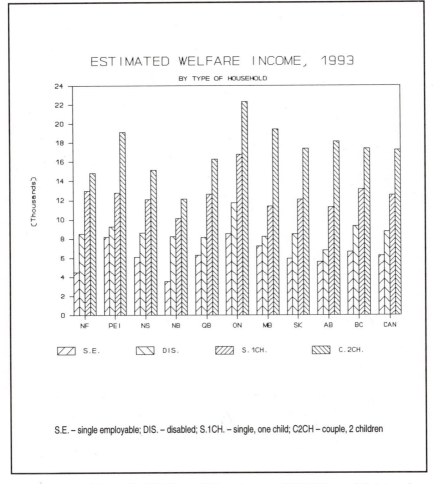

Source: National Council of Welfare, *Welfare Incomes 1993* (Ottawa: Minister of Supply and Services, 1994).

Gerard Boychuk

Figure 1.2

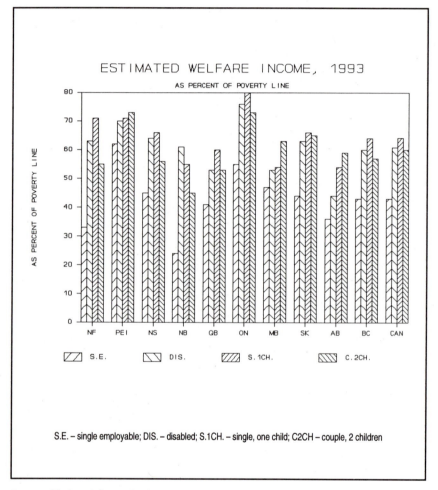

Source: National Council of Welfare, *Welfare Incomes 1993* (Ottawa: Minister of Supply and Services, 1994).

Figure 1.3

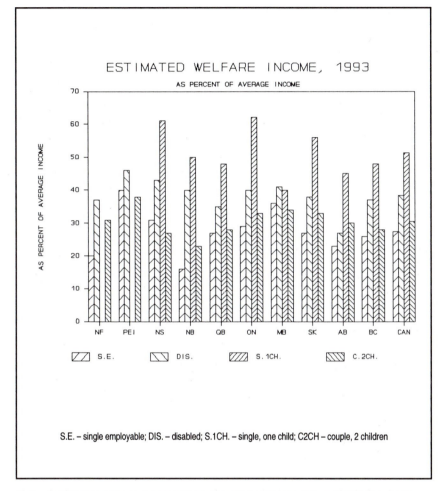

Note: Assistance rates as a percentage of average income not available for single parents with one child in Newfoundland and P.E.I.
Source: National Council of Welfare, *Welfare Incomes 1993* (Ottawa: Minister of Supply and Services, 1994).

Appendix 2
Provincial Tax-Back Rates by Category, 1993

Figure 2.1

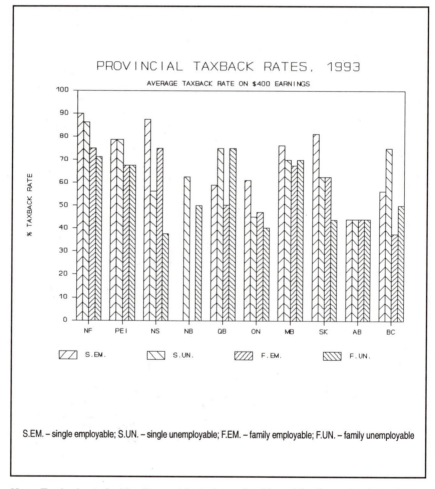

Note: Tax-back rate for New Brunswick single employable and family employable is 0%.
Source: National Council of Welfare, *Welfare Incomes 1993* (Ottawa: Minister of Supply and Services, 1994).

IV

Other Issues

7

Taking Control:
Dismantling Indian Affairs and Recognizing
First Nations Government in Manitoba

Kathy Brock

Ce chapitre examine l'initiative conjointe du gouvernement fédéral et des Premières nations du Manitoba de démanteler les Affaires indiennes pour reconnaître et restaurer la juridiction des gouvernements des Premières nations au Manitoba. Cet accord est sans précédent dans l'histoire des relations entre le Canada et les peuples autochtones. Il servira de modèle autant pour les Premières nations au Canada que pour les peuples autochtones d'autres pays intéressés par un cheminement similaire vers l'autonomie gouvernementale. Pour comprendre cette initiative, on doit analyser l'événement et les facteurs qui ont mené à la signature de cet accord historique, le processus des négociations, de même que le contenu des versions finales des documents. Le démantèlement prête flanc à la controverse et à la critique; il fait également face à des obstacles potentiels. Même si la réussite future de cette entreprise est troublée par ces questions, le projet représente un grand progrès pour la mise en place de l'autonomie gouvernementale autochtone et amène un changement significatif dans la relation entre le Canada et les Premières nations.

INTRODUCTION

On 7 December 1994 representatives of the Manitoba First Nations, including Grand Chief Phil Fontaine of the Assembly of Manitoba Chiefs (AMC), and of the federal government, including the Minister of Indian Affairs, officially signed a framework agreement whose title summarizes its objectives: *The Dismantling of the Department of Indian Affairs and Northern Development, The Restoration of Jurisdictions to First Nations Peoples in Manitoba and Recognition of First Nations Governments in Manitoba.*[1] The historic agreement outlines the rules and framework for the transfer of federal jurisdiction from Indian Affairs to the First Nations. Under this initiative, Manitoba First

Nations governments will assume executive, legislative, judicial, and administrative powers over their communities.

This controversial agreement is without precedent in the history of Canadian-First Nations relations. While some observers decry it as a step backwards from the Charlottetown agreement on aboriginal self-government which promised constitutional entrenchment of the principle of self-government, others praise it for promising what Charlottetown failed to deliver — the achievement and recognition of First Nations' self-government in practice. Supporters of the agreement maintain that it breaks new ground in establishing a process for terminating federal government control over First Nations according to terms jointly defined by the federal government and First Nations and at a pace determined by the First Nations. And the practical implications of the agreement extend beyond the Manitoba border since it may provide a working model for other jurisdictions both within Canada and in other nations with aboriginal populations.[2] Supporters also counter charges that the agreement threatens constitutional recognition of the inherent right to self-government. In their view, and despite disclaimers attached to the agreement, the dismantling initiative and the attendant supporting statements made by the federal government may provide concrete support for the argument advanced by the Royal Commission on Aboriginal Peoples and First Nations spokespersons that section 35 of the *Constitution Act, 1982* already recognizes the inherent right to self-government. However, even the supporters acknowledge that this claim is controversial and rests as a theoretical proposition.

This chapter delves into the controversial agreement by offering a brief description and analysis of the initiative to dismantle Indian Affairs and to recognize and restore jurisdiction to First Nations governments in Manitoba, and of the possible pitfalls. The chapter begins with a short outline of events and factors that generated the historic agreement, followed by a summary of the main features of the negotiations process and the substance of the initiative. The final section examines the prospects for Manitoba First Nations as they travel the road to self-government. The chapter argues that while the future success of the dismantling initiative is marred by some clouds, it represents an important advance in the establishment of First Nations self-government and is bound to yield both positive and negative lessons for Canada and its First Nations in their evolving relationship.

WORDS GIVEN AND TAKEN: THE LIBERAL PLAN

Although the decision to dismantle Indian Affairs, to restore jurisdiction to First Nations, and to recognize First Nations governments, represents a significant departure from past policies, it was a logical result of the push by First Nations for self-government in both the political and constitutional arenas.

Socio-economic conditions spoke to the need for drastic changes in the governance of First Nations communities at the same time as nationalism began a resurgence within First Nations.[3] The 1980-92 constitutional talks among the Canadian governments and representatives of First Nations further empowered the First Nations' leadership and encouraged the drive towards self-government.[4]

The failure of past federal government policies to address the needs and concerns of First Nations was thoroughly documented in numerous studies of the socio-economic conditions affecting First Nations in Canada.[5] As demographic studies indicated that the First Nations population was expanding relative to the larger population, the worsening socio-economic situation in these communities became increasingly problematic.[6] And although the socio-economic conditions of aboriginal communities should not be the sole or even primary justification for self-government, they provide a strong impetus for change.[7]

A brief snapshot of First Nations communities in Manitoba in the 1990s reveals the ongoing problems.[8] While First Nations communities like Opaskwayak (The Pas), and Sagkeeng (Ft. Alexander) are large and relatively wealthy, other Manitoba First Nations experience many of the socio-economic problems of First Nations elsewhere. For example, Manitoba First Nations are among the poorest citizens in the province with 27.2 percent of the aboriginal population making less than $2,000, and only 3.4 percent making in excess of $40,000 in comparison with 11.9 percent of the general Manitoba population. The on-reserve population in Manitoba tends to have the lowest incomes in the province and/or to be among those making $2,000-$9,999. This population is particularly dependent on social assistance in Manitoba (47.4 percent), by comparison with the off-reserve population (30.8 percent) and the Métis (24.3 percent). An estimated 54 percent of the on-reserve population is not in the labour force. The rate of unemployment for aboriginal people in Manitoba is over three times higher than for the general provincial population with this figure reaching into the 90-percent range on some northern reserves. As expected in less advantaged communities, rates for chronic health problems and the incidence of group deaths, suicides, social problems and substance abuse are higher than in the province generally. The lowest education rates in Manitoba occur among the members of First Nations living on-reserve.

A further source of worry to First Nations' leaders is that their cultures and traditions are being eroded through interaction with the dominant culture and lifestyle in Manitoba. This trend is exemplified by patterns of language use in Canada.[9] While 53.4 percent of on-reserve Status Indians in Manitoba speak one of their traditional languages, only 8 percent of off-reserve individuals do. The 1986 census reported that as much as 84 percent of the on-reserve population and 34 percent of the off-reserve population spoke a native language in their homes. The 1991 Census reported that of the population aged 5-14 years 53.4 percent on-reserve and 8 percent off-reserve spoke an aboriginal language, while of the population over 15 years of age, 81.6 percent on-reserve and 36.1 off-reserve spoke an aboriginal language. The trend towards lower levels of traditional language usage is a cause of consternation. Participation rates in traditional economic and cultural activities show a similar decline. Cultural rejuvenation is an important element of the drive towards self-government.

The leaders of the First Nations in Manitoba as elsewhere in Canada have been pursuing means to offset these trends and to reinvigorate their cultures and communities.[10] For the past three decades, First Nations have become increasingly involved in lobbying the federal government for control over programs and services and for a more effective voice in the definition and design of those programs and services. By 1995, Manitoba First Nations directly administered 95 percent of DIAND's regional budget of more than $530 million.[11] However, as the chiefs of Manitoba have pointed out, DIAND still defines the recipients and expenditures of the funds.[12] Control over administration and delivery of programs was not sufficient if First Nations governments were to meet the needs of their communities effectively. To be effective, First Nations governments required the authority to define and priorize problems within their communities and then to design and target the policies and programs that would address those problems without interference from outside jurisdictions. Thus, the First Nations have made a concerted effort to have their powers of self-government restored and constitutionally entrenched.

The First Nations became increasingly frustrated in their pursuit of self-government in the 1980s and 1990s. The 1983 House of Commons Special Committee (Penner) Report recommendations for Indian self-government failed to generate significant changes in the relationship between the federal government and First Nations.[13] Community-based self-government negotiations between the federal government and individual First Nations have been fraught with difficulties and slow to yield results. At the same time, pressures and demands on First Nations governments have increased owing to federal and provincial attempts to off-load expenses for on-reserve and off-reserve populations and to the federal Parliament's Bill C-31 reinstating status for disenfranchised members of First Nations.[14] The sense of frustration and obstruction was heightened by the lack of concrete results in the constitutionally mandated negotiations on aboriginal rights between 1983 and 1987, the failure of the Meech Lake Accord even to address the concerns of Aboriginal Peoples, and the convoluted and opaque provisions on self-government eventually obtained in the Charlottetown Constitutional Accord.[15] Despite this disappointing track record, leaders of the First Nations perceived a window of opportunity with the 1993 federal election and the expected change in the governing party from the Progressive Conservatives to the Liberals.

The prospects for restructuring relations with a Liberal government were signaled in the party's 1993 federal election platform. The Liberal Party announced its intentions to change the direction of aboriginal policy in *Creating Opportunity: The Liberal Plan for Canada*, more popularly called the "Red Book." Liberal party leader, Jean Chrétien expounded upon the plans both in a formal speaking announcement and in a press release on 8 October 1993. First Nations had been alerted to the election platform since it had been derived from the recommendations made in 1990 by the Aboriginal Peoples Commission of the party which included representatives of the aboriginal community, and from the policy resolutions passed unanimously at the 1992 National Liberal Party Convention.

Three aspects of the Liberal plan offered hope to the First Nations communities. First, the Red Book explicitly acknowledged that past policies had failed to rectify the socioe-conomic conditions in aboriginal communities. The Red Book extended to these communities the offer to "define and undertake together creative initiatives designed to achieve fairness, mutual respect, and recognition of rights."[16]

Second, on the level of principle, the Red Book consolidated the gains made in Charlottetown by embracing the position that "the inherent right of self-government is an existing Aboriginal and treaty right."[17] The prime minister designated this as "the cornerstone of our approach" in a news release during the campaign and committed his newly elected government to it in the throne speech.[18] Grand Chief Phil Fontaine described this as "the most important statement in this 'Red Book,'" since it set "the stage, finally, for the First Nations to take control of their own lives and communities."[19]

Third, the principle assumed a more concrete shape in the Red Book promise that "The Liberal government will be committed to gradually winding down the Department of Indian Affairs at a pace agreed upon by First Nations, while maintaining the federal fiduciary responsibility."[20] Dismantling the Department of Indian Affairs meant that powers and control would be transferred to First Nations communities. Together, these three ingredients offered the right mix for the implementation of self-government.

The Manitoba First Nations chiefs took the Liberal plan at its word and began to prepare for the anticipated change in policy direction. The 1 October 1993 general assembly of Manitoba chiefs passed a resolution directing its provincial executive to establish a joint working group to examine the option of dismantling the Manitoba regional office of the Department of Indian Affairs and Northern Development. Operating within this mandate, Grand Chief Fontaine commissioned a former bureaucrat in Indian Affairs to prepare a workplan and costing for the endeavour. This became a prime source of controversy in the project since the former bureaucrat, Don Goodwin, had been one of the federal government negotiators on the Northern Flood Settlements and was distrusted by many of the chiefs. Also, the original workplan was criticized for being written in "bureaucratese" instead of reflecting community values, thus causing community members to question its appropriateness as a base for self-government. Despite the controversy it generated among the First Nations, the workplan became the basis of the subsequent negotiations. By adopting a proactive stance, the chiefs forced the Liberal government to deliver on the election promises. And Minister of Indian Affairs Ron Irwin was only too ready to listen and act.

Why did the dismantling project begin in Manitoba rather than the other provinces? The perspicacity and tenacity of the Manitoba chiefs was certainly one important factor. As if responding to Machiavelli's advice to the Prince, the chiefs took advantage of the opportunity offered by the Liberal promises and prepared themselves to head into negotiations fully armed. Although First Nations from B.C. and Ontario were vying for dismantling of Indian Affairs to begin within their provinces, it was the Manitoba chiefs who acted quickly and effectively, preparing their detailed outline for the transfer of control from Indian Affairs to the First Nations governments and equipping themselves to enter into negotiations with the minister as soon as possible after the Liberals assumed federal office.[21]

The availability of an overarching political structure for Manitoba First Nations facilitated a speedy and coordinated approach to the federal government demanding the transfer of jurisdiction to the 61 reserves in the province.[22] With one exception, Valley River, which is a smaller First Nation adhering to a position of sovereignty, the Manitoba First Nations are all affiliated with the AMC, their provincial political organization.[23] The chiefs collectively direct the AMC through general assemblies and a permanent executive, and elect the grand chief every three years. With few exceptions, the First Nations further belong to seven tribal councils. Three tribal councils of the north comprise the Manitoba Keewatinowi Okimakanak (MKO), and two centre-west tribal councils form the First Nations Confederacy. The individual First Nations communities vary significantly in population, territory, and economic potential.[24] This highly developed political network provides the linkages between First Nations to enable them to assume jurisdiction at the local, regional, and provincewide levels as may be appropriate. While the organizations for dismantling would be different, the structures are in place to begin negotiations.

Strong leadership by the chiefs and the favourable structural arrangements were reflected in and reinforced by a history of political mobilization and consensus necessary for presenting a unified position to Ottawa and for executing the transfer of jurisdiction.[25] For example, then Manitoba Legislative Assembly member, Elijah Harper's decision to obstruct introduction and passage of the Meech Lake Accord was the result of a collective decision by the Assembly of Manitoba Chiefs. Similarly, during the Charlottetown referendum the Manitoba chiefs achieved a consensus position which was reflected in the low turnout and high rate of rejection of the agreement within the First Nation communities.[26] The capacity of the Manitoba First Nations for collective action in policy areas would be indicated by the negotiations such as on the health framework agreement and the education framework agreement.[27]

The scale and character of the population was right in Manitoba. Manitoba is a smaller province with a relatively large First Nations population which makes it an ideal environment for attempting this project. The 1991 Census estimates Manitoba's First Nations population at approximately 34,200 on-reserve Status Indians and 31,960 off-reserve Status Indians, and with the Métis (33,230) and Inuit (465) populations comprising 9.2 percent of the total provincial population. The 1992 Manitoba Native Affairs Secretariat estimates the population at 54,334 on-reserve Status Indians and 23,428 off-reserve Status Indians using Indian and Northern Affairs Community membership lists. The 61 First Nation communities derive from the Chipewyan (Dene) and the Cree in the north, and the Ojibwa in the centre and east, all of whom signed a Treaty with the Crown between 1871 and 1910.[28] The five Dakota First Nations in the south were latecomers (1860s) and not parties to the treatymaking process in Manitoba. Thus, the Manitoba First Nations population was a sufficiently large and cohesive component of the provincial population to allow the province to serve as a working model for the rest of the nation. The right combination of conditions for success were present to a greater extent than in the other provinces.

A final factor should not be underestimated. The right chemistry existed between two key political players, the Minister of Indian Affairs and the Grand Chief of the Assembly of Manitoba Chiefs. Ron Irwin and Phil Fontaine both possessed the degree of commitment and established the mutual trust that were necessary to initiate the discussions and sustain them through strained and difficult periods. When negotiations between representatives of the AMC and Indian Affairs at the bureaucratic level reached an impasse, a phone call or discussion between the two politicians would usually be sufficient to rectify any problems and cause discussions to resume.

The most striking example of the ability of the two men to work together to ensure the success of the negotiations occurred at the critical April 1994 general assembly of chiefs held on Opaskwayak lands adjacent to The Pas when the chiefs had to decide whether to proceed with the negotiations or withdraw. Some chiefs expressed serious reservations over the effect of the agreement on treaties, land claims, and current federal services and programs, among other matters. The chiefs agreed that unless they had an express written guarantee that these rights and entitlements would be protected, they could not pledge their communities to the initiative. Upon his arrival at the assembly, the minister had a private discussion with the grand chief about these concerns. At that point, many of the chiefs and the federal officials attending with the minister expressed doubt that he would sign the guarantee. When the grand chief presented him with the document in question before the chiefs, the minister did not hesitate in signing it. There was a moment of shocked silence and then the assembly rose in applause for the two men. The faces of the federal officials registered surprise if not dismay.[29]

This example should not overshadow the less dramatic ways in which the two men acted and cooperated to see the negotiations through to a successful conclusion. When negotiations reached an impasse over financing and the federal officials threatened to walk out, a call from Fontaine to Irwin rectified the problem. If the federal officials were being intransigent, a visit by the grand chief to the negotiations table would get the negotiations back on track.[30] And the two men conferred regularly on the state of negotiations and had open access to each other regardless of time of day or night. Working within their respective mandates, they drove the issue forward.

TAKING CONTROL

THE NEGOTIATIONS

Negotiations proceeded in a number of distinct phases. In the first phase, beginning in October 1993, the chiefs authorized the AMC executive to proceed by establishing a joint working group with the federal government to examine the idea of dismantling Indian Affairs. The mandate and initiative for the project was the product of collective deliberations among the leadership of the Manitoba First Nations.[31] The second phase began in December 1993 with meetings between the Minister of Indian Affairs and the Chiefs of Manitoba, followed by meetings between the two politicians, staff and the AMC legal adviser.[32] Negotiations did falter as misunderstandings arose between the chiefs and the minister but were subsequently worked out by the AMC team. A political understanding was reached to guide subsequent negotiations. The initiative became a key priority of the grand chief who foresaw the opportunities it could offer his people.[33]

The third phase consisted of negotiations throughout January, February, and March 1994, between officials of the AMC and Indian Affairs. The grand chief and minister withdrew from negotiations by mutual agreement only to intervene when problems arose. Both sides provided formal commitments to the process. In February 1994, the executive of the AMC approved and presented to the minister a tentative "Proposal Regarding the Recognition of Manitoba First Nations Governments." And, on 14 March, the AMC tabled before the AMC/DIAND Joint Co-Ordinating Group their comprehensive discussion paper including the costing entitled "Towards Manitoba First Nations Governments."[34] On 9 March 1994, the Minister of Indian Affairs, Ron Irwin, made a statement in the House of Commons affirming the project in response to a question from Liberal MP Elijah Harper.

As word of the negotiations traveled, First Nations communities desired more direct involvement. So in the fourth phase of negotiations, the process was broadened to include the direct participation of more representatives of the First Nations communities and tribal councils.[35] The national Grand Chief, Ovide Mercredi, began to attend discussions sporadically. More generally, this phase was characterized by the initiation of technical meetings, tribal council consultations, and the landmark AMC general assembly where the minister and the grand chief signed the Memorandum of Understanding to address the chiefs' concerns and whereupon the chiefs passed a resolution to continue the process. During June and September the general assemblies further debated and approved the project.

Negotiations concluded with a series of formal events. At the September 1994 general assembly at Dakota Tipi, the Chiefs authorized the execution of the framework agreement on dismantling in a resolution. While approval was not unanimous and some chiefs expressed serious reservations,[36] support was substantial. The federal Cabinet approved the framework agreement on 22 November 1994 despite cautions expressed by the departments of Justice and Finance. The 7 December 1994 official signing ceremony marked the successful conclusion of negotiations and the commencement of implementation.

WHAT'S IT ALL ABOUT?

The dismantling of Indian Affairs, restoration of jurisdiction and recognition of First Nations governments in Manitoba (FNGM) is a broadly conceived project which lacks a precedent to clarify its meaning. The comprehensive discussion paper on dismantling states:

> While attempts have been made in the past to establish practical examples of Aboriginal self-government, none have been as comprehensive as this. This is not a question of a single First Nation attempting to obtain control over its own affairs but of sixty-one First Nations working in concert. This is not a question of displacing the powers of Indian Affairs alone, but of displacing all federal departments associated with First Nations. And most complex of all, the dismantling of government structures must be accompanied by the creation of fully functioning Manitoba First Nations' Governments.[37]

In a letter to the premier of Manitoba, Grand Chief Fontaine explained that the project broke with past practices and entailed real transfer of jurisdiction to fully constituted governments:

> On the simplest level, self-government means First Nations will possess the powers to determine what our governments should be and how they will exercise power, to define our communities, and to exercise jurisdiction over our

territories.... However, the realization and implementation of that inherent right
is much more complex ... it is neither a continuation of the current process of
devolution nor a divestiture of fiscal responsibility by the federal and provincial
governments. Instead it involves negotiation and cooperation between the federal, provincial and First Nation governments to effect the jurisdiction transfer....
As powers are transferred, First Nations' governing structures will be adapted
to serve the needs of communities.[38]

To illustrate what the concept would mean when implemented in the communities, Grand Chief Fontaine provided concrete examples. He told the chiefs
that under the initiative, he could see:

- how Chief Jerry Fontaine [Sagkeeng] could deal more effectively to
  protect his people from toxic chemical spills by exercising powers
  related to the environment;

- how Chief Alpheus Brass [Chemawawin] could control medical services and finally use the ambulance brought by his people two years
  ago, but sits in a garage because of a squabble between the province
  and medical services branch; and

- how all of the First Nations in Manitoba who have major impacts from
  flooding could negotiate directly with Hydro and the province instead
  of Indian Affairs and Justice telling them how to do it ...

  ... Perhaps the most important changes that we could bring about would
  be the ones that would enable us to deal better with the social problems confronting our people. The suicides, the drug and alcohol abuse,
  and the despair that so many face today.[39]

The effect of the dismantling initiative would be to provide the FNGM with
powers to design and target programs and services for their communities without interference from the federal and provincial governments. To be fully
effective, these governments would have to assume jurisdiction in areas now
controlled by the federal and provincial governments. In the short term, this
would include fire safety, education, and capital management programs; in
the medium term, child welfare; and in the longer term, more complicated
areas of jurisdiction such as natural resources and the environment.

The framework agreement and accompanying workplan provide an overview of the functions, activities, and funding arrangements required to achieve
the objectives of dismantling the existing structures of Indian Affairs, recognizing and legally empowering FNGM "to exercise the authorities required to
meet the needs of the peoples of the First Nations," and to restore to FNGM
"the jurisdictions (including those of other federal departments) ... consistent
with the Inherent Right of Self-Government."[40] The functions, activities and
arrangements are divided into three phases that would run concurrently and
begin immediately. Under Activity A, as it is called in the workplan, the project

team will research all existing DIAND programs and compile an inventory of the existing public sector labour force across First Nations, tribal council, political and other organizations, and DIAND. Activity B involves analyzing the information on programs and services and developing the options for change. Activity C entails considering and recommending the scope of powers to be assumed by FNGM and the broad framework that would become the essential FNGM design.[41]

At this stage, the process is entirely open-ended. The powers that FNGM will assume are yet to be identified, with the exception of the three short-term items of fire safety, education, and capital spending which were already under negotiation. Similarly, the structures of the FNGM have yet to be defined, and what powers will be assigned to which levels of government are yet to be determined. These tasks are largely the substance of Activities B and C. At the conclusion of the three activities, "First Nations in Manitoba will have identified the powers they will exercise, the governmental frameworks they propose to put in place, and the range of programs and services they propose to deliver."[42] To facilitate the process, "DIAND will make ten senior positions available within the department to First Nations representatives to work alongside departmental officials to gain a better understanding of federal practices, procedures and policies."[43]

Once the three initial activities are concluded successfully, three new activities will commence. In Activity D the working group will "design the details of the FNGM structures and institutions of government, as well as operational policies and procedures," and analyze the human and financial resource costs. Under Activity E "detailed implementation plans will be developed to guide the effective transition from DIAND control to FNGM control" with minimum disruption in services to the communities. In Activity F "implementation will proceed within a defined transitional period, with particular attention paid to non-disruption of services and to communications with affected parties."[44] The conclusion will witness fully functioning and empowered FNGM defined in accordance with the needs and cultural and historical practices and principles of First Nations.

The time frame is defined but flexible. Activity A is estimated to take 12 weeks, Activity B 34 weeks, and Activity C 41 weeks. Funding has been calculated to 1995-96, but may be revised. The full transfer of powers is expected to occur over ten years but the time frame may vary according to the needs of the communities as mutually agreed by the federal government and AMC. Progress reviews will occur at the end of the third, sixth, and tenth years.[45] Flexibility is achieved by the agreement in the plan that work on the takeover "will proceed in a timely manner and at a pace that conforms to the needs of First Nations for consultation, deliberation and decision-making."[46] In fact, work under the activities has been delayed over the past year while the First

Nations confer and reach agreement among themselves on the workplan and
framework agreement and on staffing for the initiative. However, the staffing
process is now complete and work is ready to begin in the fall approximately
18 months later than originally projected.

In the negotiations, a complete costing of the process up to phase three was
worked out. The initial cost projections of the federal team were under
$100,000. The AMC initially estimated the project costs at $5 million. Negotiation of the framework agreement and workplan alone cost in excess of
$800,000. The agreement contains an additional commitment on behalf of the
federal government to: a flexible transfer payment agreement providing $3.814
million to cover Activities A, B, C, Consultations, Communications, and Project
Management; $500,000 for the ten positions in DIAND; $500,000 for education; $434,468 for fire safety; and $250,000 for a capital program. The total
exceeds $5 million dollars for the process until 1996. Funding for the subse-
quent phases will be negotiated. The allocation is made within the existing
regional budget in order to avoid affecting adversely other First Nations.[47]
But, perhaps most significantly, the agreement stipulates that "The Assembly
will have flexibility in managing the funds within the context of the detailed
Workplan that focuses on results."[48] The relative decision-making autonomy
of the First Nations is secured within the structure of the agreement.

The organization structure envisioned for the project to oversee the transition is premised upon an equal partnership of the First Nations of Manitoba
represented by the AMC and the federal government represented primarily
but not necessarily exclusively by DIAND (See Figure 1).[49] A Political Overview Committee (POC) consisting of the AMC grand chief and the DIAND
minister will supervise. A Joint Steering Committee answering to the POC
will include AMC senior representatives, AMC legal counsel, AMC senior
technical and policy representatives, and a project director (ex-officio) on the
one side, and senior federal government officials and federal legal counsel on
the other. Below this level will be the joint project office of technicians, the
Consultation Advisory group (to keep the communities informed throughout
the process), and the working groups who will perform the activities.

The framework agreement contains 18 principles intended to allay the concerns expressed by community members and to respect the autonomy of
individual First Nations.[50] The principles ensure that the initiative does not
diminish or adversely affect treaties or release the federal government from
either its fiduciary obligation to First Nations or its liability for past actions.
They render the agreement consistent with constitutional and aboriginal rights
by acknowledging that the inherent right forms the basis of the agreement,
and that FNGM and their powers will be consistent with section 35 of the
Constitution Act, 1982. At once, they protect and empower individual
communities by: placing liabilities and responsibilities for their actions with
FNGM; not impairing the ability of individual First Nations to enter into

Figure 1: Project Organization Structure

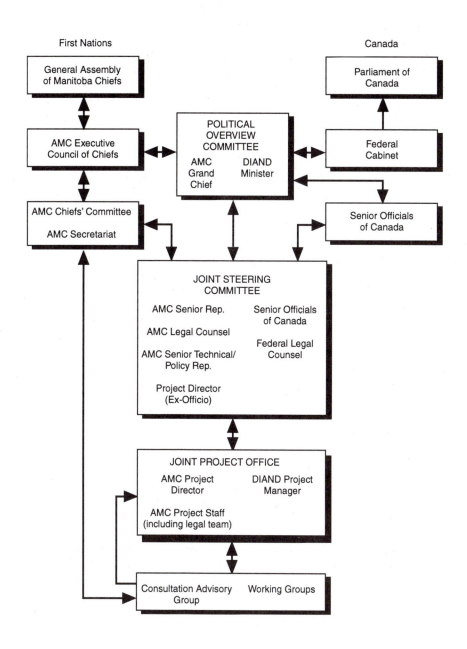

agreements on legislative, executive, administrative, and judicial functions consistent with the right to self-government or other initiatives; providing First Nations with the choice of ratifying or declining new arrangements; making individual First Nations the primary locus of FNGM with the powers to assign designated functions to an aggregate level; and guaranteeing levels of funding.[51] The principle of collective action is secured by the provision that implementation of the agreement is subject to ratification by "a reasonable number" of First Nations.

The framework agreement is at once comprehensive and cautious. It betrays the markings of a carefully conceived and tightly negotiated document which prepares the way for dismantling Indian Affairs and recognizing and re-empowering First Nations governments in Manitoba. However, as with any ground-breaking initiative, the proposed project is by nature evolutionary and captive to both circumstances and the people who execute it. Some cautionary notes should be sounded.

POSSIBLE PITFALLS

The dismantling of Indian Affairs, restoration of jurisdiction to First Nations, and recognition of First Nations governments in Manitoba have been the subject of close scrutiny. Criticisms of the initiative range from theoretical and conceptual to more practical and pragmatic considerations.

One of the leading criticisms of the project is that it is based on a legislative commitment to self-government not a constitutional commitment. In his address to the Opaskwayak Assembly on dismantling, national Grand Chief Ovide Mercredi of the Assembly of First Nations explained that:

> Ultimately, we need constitutional recognition of the inherent right to self-government to protect our jurisdiction. De facto political recognition is not enough. It is not the same thing as legal recognition.... This process that you are considering is important but it is important to pay attention to the larger picture ... Who are you fooling? You can't achieve the inherent right by dismantling.[52]

He observed that the principles for achieving the inherent right are treaties, fiduciary responsibility, and jurisdiction. The approach must be comprehensive and grounded in the constitution to create an enduring structure of government. Under the dismantling approach, future Parliaments could reverse the process and legislate First Nations governments out of existence. Dismantling was dangerous because it fostered the illusion that self-government was being achieved and thus removed the impetus for First Nations to press for constitutional entrenchment of the inherent right. The end result would be that First Nations would not achieve full recognition of their governments in the constitution with a status equal to the federal and provincial governments in Canada, and thus would always be dependent upon the goodwill of the federal government to preserve their rights.

The framework agreement addresses these concerns directly. As seen above, the statement of principles guarantees that the initiative will not derogate from treaty, aboriginal and constitutional rights (5.1, 5.4), and renders dismantling consistent with future negotiations on the inherent right to self-government (5.2, 5.16). It could be argued that the initiative advances the cause for self-government by providing a working model and thus allaying concerns about the definition and shape of self-government of the nature that were expressed during the constitutional negotiations conducted between 1983-87 and 1990-92. However, Mercredi's caution that the project could weaken the will to negotiate the inherent right and set a limiting precedent remains unanswered as yet.

The framework agreement for the dismantling of Indian Affairs and restoration of First nations jurisdiction is also separate from the process to conduct negotiations on the inherent right announced by the federal government on 17 August 1995. Under this proposal, the federal government has recognized the inherent right as an existing right within section 35 of the *Constitution Act, 1982* and has proposed an approach that enables First Nations to negotiate practical arrangements for an enhanced municipal style of government.[53] Prior to the announcement, the minister assured the grand chief that "implementation of the inherent right will be achieved through future agreements which are consistent with the Framework Agreement."[54] Given the limits placed on the powers that First Nations may negotiate in the inherent rights process and the necessity of provincial involvement in negotiations and funding arrangements (in contrast with the openness of the dismantling process and the control over the process secured by the chiefs), the prospects for First Nations governments seem brighter under their own process in Manitoba at this point.

A powerful line of criticism emerged during the general assemblies from the chiefs and community members focusing on the implications of the dismantling initiative for individual First Nations. The project was criticized for raising too many uncertainties. Questions abounded: What structures would replace Indian Affairs? Would the Assembly of Manitoba Chiefs be restructured? If so, how? Would powers and funding be concentrated in the AMC or allocated to communities and tribal councils? Who would be the primary beneficiaries? Who would control the process? Would the initiative be community driven or elite driven? Driven by the First Nations or outside advisers? Would it reflect First Nations practices and traditions? Would current resources and programs provided by Indian Affairs be affected? Would individual First Nations have a veto over the agreement if they did not like the end result or were they limited to opting out? And perhaps most importantly, members of the First Nations asked what would happen if the project to dismantle Indian

Affairs, restore jurisdiction and recognize First Nations governments failed? Would the federal government have a residual responsibility? And, what constitutes failure?

Again, the Manitoba Grand Chief and the Minister of Indian Affairs attempted to alleviate these concerns through guarantees in the Memorandum of Understanding which they signed on 20 April 1994 at the Opaskwayak General Assembly and in the statement of principles in the framework agreement. As described above, the agreement assures First Nations that the primary locus of self-government will be the individual First Nations, their internal powers of self-government remain intact, programs and services will be continued throughout the transition, and they have the power to opt-out. The creation of fully functioning and empowered FNGM, requires the consent of a substantial or reasonable number of First Nations at each stage of the process. When questioned, the grand chief conceded that the project was uncertain and would require faith and courage:

> this opportunity carries with it a very great challenge. It is a great challenge because if we were to be successful in taking control of our lives — which is what this opportunity boils down to — it strikes at the heart of the paternalism of the Indian Act, it strikes at the heart of the self-interests of Indian Affairs, and it strikes at the heart of all others who have controlled our lives for far too long. Many obstacles will be put in front of us. It will be a struggle every step of the way and can only be won if we are united and determined.[55]

Two important areas of concern remain unresolved. First, the implications of the dismantling initiative for urban, non-status, Bill C-31, and off-reserve members of First Nations are unclear. Second, prominent activists such as Kathy Mallet of the Original Women's Network and Winnie Giesbrecht, a leader in the community, have questioned the wisdom of transferring powers to a male-dominated power structure such as exists within the First Nations community without first securing guarantees for the rights and status of women and children.[56] They cite examples of the abuse of women, and political interference by the chiefs in women's shelters and child welfare agencies.[57] With the establishment of autonomous, fully functioning governments, women and children in the communities would not have recourse to external agencies if they felt that their rights and security were threatened. They further fear that the social and economic costs involved in the proposed transition to more accountable and representative institutions within the communities may be intolerable. While some of these concerns may be alleviated through the incorporation of more women into the dismantling project at the decision-making level, others remain unanswered. Even the potential protection provided by the application of the *Canadian Charter of Rights and Freedoms* to the new governments is uncertain since discussions on this matter have been deferred.

The chiefs directed a line of criticism at the AMC during the negotiations. A brief released by the Swampy Cree observed that the process had been elite-driven with limited community input, the time lines were too restrictive, the legal and technical expertise too costly, and the training opportunities were limited.[58] These concerns were more easily settled by opening the process to the tribal councils and communities, increasing the scope of community consultations at each stage of negotiations, and amending the agreement to address individual concerns. The project office is being staffed by some of the people who were the most vocal opponents of the agreement.

A potential area of serious difficulty could reside with the provincial government. First, to this point, the province has not been party to the dismantling negotiations. The negotiations have been bilateral in accordance with the treaty and constitutional relationship between the federal government and First Nations. Provincial support for and cooperation in the initiative has not been secured. This could pose difficulties during implementation of FNGM and negotiation of specific self-government arrangements which affect provincial areas of jurisdiction, provincial laws of general intent that apply on reserves, or involve land transfers, among other areas.

Second, the initiative could strain the relationship between the province and the First Nations. As powers are transferred to First Nations, more flash points could occur with the province. For example, under the agreement, First Nations envisage more control over such areas as resources, gambling, and child welfare — all areas of provincial responsibility. Different visions of management and development would be brought more directly into conflict. Given the existence of First Nations communities within the provincial boundaries, issues of jurisdiction acquire significance. Outstanding land claims in the province only add to these tensions.

Third, the approach adopted towards the achievement of First Nations self-government under the dismantling initiative is inconsistent with the provincial approach towards aboriginal issues at a conceptual level. The dismantling approach is comprehensive and coordinated, which allows for variations among individual communities. The province has repeatedly rejected a more comprehensive strategy in favour of a pragmatic and incremental approach which targets specific initiatives to the specific needs of communities.[59] The provincial government is reluctant to deal with the chiefs as a provincewide force. This could complicate negotiations involving the province.

Fourth, questions of citizenship arise. In private conversations with the author, provincial representatives have questioned whether the province continues to have any obligations to citizens of self-governing First Nations including the off-reserve population. They equate their future obligation to these First Nations citizens with the present status of citizens of other provinces in relation to Manitoba. Ultimately, this line of logic leads to questioning the provincial enfranchisement of First Nations citizens. This is potentially one of the most explosive and profound areas of controversy that will emerge during the course of the development of First Nations government in Manitoba.

Finally, the provincial government has publicly questioned whether the First Nations have the capacity to assume full jurisdiction as proposed under the framework agreement.[60] The result has been further discord between the provincial government, the AMC, and First Nations chiefs. While the chiefs have expressed concerns to varying degrees about the initiative, they are united in viewing the provincial statements as unwarranted interference and as patronizing. The chiefs have been equally adamant in their reluctance to involve the province in negotiations until necessary. They even questioned the need to invite provincial representatives to the official signing ceremony as a courtesy. Upon receiving an invitation, the province was represented by the Minister of Native Affairs. The premier did not attend.

All is not bleak. At a recent meeting between the AMC executive and members of the provincial Cabinet including the premier, the basis for a more positive relationship was laid. The provincial government and the AMC found common ground in the position that all transfers of jurisdiction would have to occur through the federal government and Parliament. The province emphasized that it would be amenable to a transfer of jurisdiction to First Nations if it were clear that residual responsibility (political, legal, and financial) rested exclusively with the federal government in the event that the First Nations governments failed or were challenged by their citizens. The AMC was inclined to accept this position given that it reinforced the bilateral relationship and was potentially less complicated. The federal position is not clear but it has been reluctant to exclude the province and to clarify lines of jurisdiction and responsibility. The position of off-reserve members of First Nations obscures the lines of financial responsibility and jurisdiction alone.[61]

A formidable set of obstacles to the project could be posed from within the federal government. Dismantling Indian Affairs represents a threat to the economic security of federal officials. DIAND and the AMC are firmly committed "to human resource management," but the project proposes the eventual replacement of DIAND personnel with individuals from the First Nations communities as required by the new structures. DIAND officials are placed in the position of negotiating and participating in changes which may be opposed to their self-interest. During the negotiations, the recalcitrance of some officials to accept change was evident to the author. A firm commitment and careful monitoring of the process by the political masters will be necessary to ensure that obstructions do not rise from within the bureaucracy.

A final source of tension could arise within the Canadian public. Taxpayers may view the project with scepticism until they receive assurances that the initiative will not be costly and/or inefficient. Press coverage of the signing ceremony noted that Ottawa spends approximately $1 billion dollars in

Manitoba alone on the Indian Affairs department. "But Irwin would not say whether self-rule means fewer tax dollars will go towards aboriginal bands in future ... Dismantling is costly."[62] This public perception is enhanced by concerns over tax exemptions for members of First Nations and allegations of corruption in band governments. If costs remain high with little visible return, public scepticism could increase while popular support declines. A poll-sensitive federal government might conceivably back away from the project.

This is an important consideration. However, Fontaine does not see it as insurmountable. He believes that "the recognition of the inherent right of self-government, the transfer of jurisdictions to First Nations, the control we would exercise over our own lives — when these things happen — the taxpayer will see that this is not an expense but an investment in the future."[63]

This optimism is founded upon three pillars. First, the transfer of capital management provides a means of leveraging a capital pool into funds that could be used for programs and services targeted at the socio-economic needs of the First Nations. The Royal Bank of Canada and the Toronto Dominion bank have contacted the AMC about plans to facilitate the flow of capital and funds. The Royal Bank has created an office to deal with First Nation governments. Second, First Nations in Canada generally have been investigating the prospects for taxation and revenue raising. There has been speculation about economic redistribution among the First Nations under a system of FNGM. Third, cost savings are envisaged with the transfer of jurisdiction. As an example of this, Grand Chief Fontaine noted that in the 1970s First Nations enrolment in postsecondary institutions was 200 people. With First Nations sponsorship of programs and involvement, that number has increased to 2,200. Education has always been viewed as the most important means of improving the long-term socio-economic conditions of First Nations. Education translates into expertise and jobs in the communities.[64]

CONCLUSION: TOWARDS FIRST NATIONS GOVERNMENT IN MANITOBA

The significance of the endeavour to dismantle the Department of Indian Affairs and Northern Development, to restore jurisdictions to First Nations Peoples in Manitoba, and to recognize First Nations governments in Manitoba should not be underestimated. The scope of the proposal exceeds previous attempts to establish self-government by anticipating the transfer of legislative, executive, and judicial powers as well as administrative controls. The initiative will provide a working model for both a process and the objectives of First Nations self-government. If successful, the model should result in some immediate and tangible benefits and changes in First Nations communities.

The project faces important impediments to its success. The personalities, decisions and actions of the negotiators and project staff will be strong determinants of the end result. Public support within the First Nations communities is crucial for the project to succeed. Support within the larger Canadian community is important for the long-term achievement of self-government. Expectations in both communities must be realistic. The initiative is dependent on the full commitment of DIAND and the federal government, the AMC, and the First Nations communities. Provincial cooperation will be necessary in the transfer of jurisdictions to First Nations governments. Transition costs are likely to be high. As self-government is established and accountability of the new government structures is secured, there will be social and economic costs. If these costs are perceived to exceed both the immediate and future benefits of establishing First Nations governments, the project will likely fail or be terminated.

This elected path to self-government is untraveled, fraught with potential minefields, and uncharted. However, as the Minister of Indian Affairs and the Grand Chief of the Assembly of Manitoba Chiefs assured the chiefs in general assembly, the initiative represents a truly historic undertaking which could result in meaningful changes in the governance of First Nations communities. It provides Manitoba First Nations with the opportunity to take control of their lives and make the decisions necessary to advance towards a brighter future within Canada. But with opportunities come challenges. It remains to be seen whether the First Nations, but also Canada, can respond to the exhortation of Elder Sandy Beardy: "we should not be afraid to face this challenge, to make these changes, and go into the future with confidence as leaders."

NOTES

An earlier version of this paper was presented to the Department of Political Science, McGill University at the suggestion of Antonia Maioni. I am grateful to the Departement de science politique, Université de Montréal, for providing a productive environment which made the writing of this paper possible. I am especially grateful to André Blais and Stéphane Dion for their suggestions, as well as the comments from two anonymous readers.

1. The analysis of the project presented here is largely based on my observations as an adviser and participant in the process of negotiations from January to April 1994, and on the two foundation documents for the project: Assembly of Manitoba Chiefs (AMC) and Department of Indian Affairs and Northern Development (DIAND), *The Dismantling of the Department of Indian Affairs and Northern Development, The Restoration of First Nations Governments in Manitoba: Framework Agreement* (Winnipeg and Ottawa: AMC and DIAND, 22 November 1994);

and AMC and DIAND, *Towards First Nations' Governments in Manitoba: Workplan* (Winnipeg and Ottawa: AMC and DIAND, 26 September 1994).

2. The international relevance of the initiative is already apparent since representatives from Australia and South Africa have contacted the AMC for information on the project and further exchange of information is anticipated according to AMC Grand Chief Phil Fontaine and Intergovernmental Relations Officer Al Torbitt, conversations with the author, August 1995.

3. See for example, Menno Boldt, *Surviving as Indians: The Challenge of Self-Government* (Toronto: University of Toronto Press, 1993); J. Anthony Long, "Political Revitalization in Canadian Native Indian Societies," *Canadian Journal of Political Science* 23,4 (Winter 1990): 751-53; Anne-Marie MaWhinney (ed.), *Rebirth: Political, Economic and Social Development in First Nations* (Toronto: Dundurn Press, 1993); Gerald R. Alfred, *Heeding the Voices of Our Ancestors: Kahnawake Mohawk Politics and the Rise of Native Nationalism* (Toronto: Oxford University Press, 1995).

4. K.L. Brock, "The Politics of Aboriginal Self-Government: A Canadian Paradox," *Canadian Public Administration* 34,2 (Summer 1991): 272-85.

5. See for example, H.B. Hawthorne, *A Survey of the Contemporary Indians of Canada* (Ottawa: Indian Affairs Branch, 1966-67); J.S. Frideres, *Native Peoples in Canada: Contemporary Conflicts*, 3d ed. (Scarborough: Prentice-Hall, 1988); Harold Cardinal, *The Unjust Society: The Tragedy of Canada's Indians* (Edmonton: M.C. Hurtig, 1969); Pauline Comeau and Aldo Santin, *The First Canadians: A Profile of Canada's Native Peoples Today* (Toronto: Lorimer, 1990); Geoffrey York, *Life and Death in Native Canada* (London: Vintage, 1990); and Boldt, *Surviving as Indians.*

6. Andrew Siggner, "The Socio-demographic Conditions of Registered Indians," *Canadian Social Trends* (Winter 1986): 2-9. For an overview of past policies see, John Crossley, *The Making of Canadian Indian Policy to 1946*, unpublished PhD dissertation, University of Toronto, 1987; K. Brock, *The Theory and Practice of Aboriginal Self-Government: Canada in A Comparative Context*, unpublished Ph.D. dissertation, University of Toronto, 1989; Sally Weaver, *Making Indian Policy* (Toronto: University of Toronto Press, 1984); Helen Buckley, *From Wooden Ploughs to Welfare: Why Indian Policy Failed in the Prairie Provinces* (Montreal and Kingston: McGill-Queen's University Press, 1992); and A. Fleras and J.L. Elliott, *The Nations Within: Aboriginal-State Relations in Canada, the United States and New Zealand* (Toronto: Oxford, 1992).

7. Paul Chartrand makes a compelling case for rejecting socio-economic or needs-based justifications for self-government in "Aboriginal Self-Government: The Two Sides of Legitimacy," in Susan D. Phillips (ed.), *How Ottawa Spends 1993-94: A More Democratic Canada...?* (Ottawa: Carleton University Press, 1993), pp. 231-56.

8. Canada, Statistics Canada, *1991 Census of Canada* (Ottawa: Statistics Canada, 1993). See also, Manitoba, Aboriginal Justice Inquiry, *Report: The Justice System and Aboriginal People*, Vol. 1 (Winnipeg: Province of Manitoba, 1991).

9.   Canada, Statistics Canada, *1991 Census of Canada*. See also, Manitoba, Aboriginal Justice Inquiry, *Report,* p. 8.

10.   Alfred argues that many leaders view Aboriginal self-government as a means to reinvigorate nationalism as opposed to a means of integrating with the Canadian political structures (p. 8).

11.   Brenda Kustra, Regional Director General, Indian and Northern Affairs Canada, Manitoba Division, Letter to the editor, *Winnipeg Free Press*, 15 January 1995. At the Opaskwayak (The Pas) general assembly, Grand Chief Fontaine noted that 50 of 61 First Nations in Manitoba have control over programs designed by the federal and provincial governments, and 100 percent control over social services (personal notes, 19 April 1994).

12.   Chiefs of Interlake Reserves Tribal Council, Manitoba, Letter to the editor, *Winnipeg Free Press*, 2 February 1995. At the April general assembly, Fontaine's comments corroborated the chiefs position expressed here. He said "We administer programmes designed by someone else. And we are doing an excellent job of administering programmes. But they were not designed for our people."

13.   Canada, House of Commons, *Report of the Special Comittee on Indian Self-Government in Canada* (Ottawa: Minister of Supply and Services, 1983).

14.   See K. Brock, *Manitoba: A Study of the Relationship Between the Manitoba Government and Aboriginal Peoples*, prepared for the Canadian Domestic Governments Project, Self-Government Branch, Royal Commission on Aboriginal Peoples, forthcoming.

15.   Alan Cairns quite astutely points out that the Charlottetown Accord proposed far-reaching changes in the relationship of Aboriginal Peoples to the federal government beginning with the constitutional recognition of the inherent right to self-government. See Cairns, "Aboriginal Canadians, Citizenship and the Constitution," in Douglas E. Williams (ed.), *Reconfigurations: Canadian Citizenship and Constitutional Change*, (Toronto: McClelland & Stewart, 1995), pp. 238-60, esp. 246-48. However, the Accord generated uncertainty within the First Nations communities because it was disputed whether it secured adequate protection for treaty and aboriginal rights, and to guarantee the fiduciary obligation of the federal government. See, for example, Sharon Venne, "Treaty Indigenous Peoples and the Charlottetown Accord: The Message in the Breeze," *Constitutional Forum* 4,2 (Winter 1993): 43-46. The chiefs believed that there was inadequate time to properly assess the provisions of the Accord, see K. Brock, "Consensual Politics," in M. Mancuso, R. Price and R. Wagenberg (eds.), *Leaders and Leadership in Canada* (Toronto: Oxford University Press, 1994), pp. 236-37.

16.   Liberal Party of Canada, *Creating Opportunity: The Liberal Plan for Canada* (Ottawa: Liberal Party, 1993), p. 93.

17.   Ibid., p. 98.

18.   K. Brock, "Native Peoples and the Politics and Government of Canada: On the Road to Self-Government," in Bob Krause and Ron Wagenberg (eds.), *Introduc-*

tory Readings in Canadian Politics and Government (Toronto: Copp Clark Pitman, 1994), p. 9.

19. Grand Chief Phil Fontaine, AMC, "Notes for Speech to General Assembly of Chiefs," The Pas, Manitoba, 16 April 1994.

20. Liberal Party, *Creating Opportunity*, p. 98.

21. The extent to which their preparedness surprised the federal officials was apparent in the negotiations when the workplan was first tabled. The officials inquired into the origins of the document and criticized it as being too comprehensive. (Personal observations.)

22. Discussions are underway with the federal government to create a 62nd First Nation.

23. The AMC is a political body exclusively. It does not have a mandate for service and program delivery. Brock, *Manitoba*.

24. The First Nation communities vary in size of total population from 90 (Buffalo Point) to 4,870 (Peguis), and of on-reserve population from 36 (Gambler) to 3,235 (Norway House). Twenty-six reserves have populations exceeding 1,000 people.

25. Manitoba First Nations have a long history of mobilization and highly developed political organizations. Under the leadership of David Courchene in the 1960s, the organization and mobilization of the Manitoba First Nations was especially evident. See Brock, *Manitoba*, ch. 2; note the passing comments in Peter McFarlane, *Brotherhood to Nationhood: George Manuel and the Making of the Modern Indian Movement* (Toronto: Between the Lines, 1993), pp. 98, 117, 119, 234; see also, Pauline Comeau, *Elijah: No Ordinary Hero* (Vancouver: Douglas and McIntyre, 1993).

26. According to Elections Canada, "Federal Referendum: Unofficial Results Specific to Aboriginal Communities," 28 October 1992, the average vote against the Charlottetown proposed set of amendments to the constitution was 62.1 percent but on reserves in Manitoba the "no" vote averaged 81.6 percent. Turnout was below average. For a brief discussion of strategy, see Brock, *Consensual Politics*, pp. 236-37.

27. Not only did the fact that the First Nations could negotiate the agreements attest to their capacity for coordinated political action, but also the decision of the chiefs not to accept Ottawa's refusal to accept access to free health care in modern terms as a treaty right — a position that resulted in the federal Minister of Health, Diane Marleau, refusing to sign the agreement in Spring 1995.

28. See Manitoba Aboriginal Justice Inquiry, *Report.* p. 7. Treaties entered included Numbers 1,2,3,4,5,6, and 10 with the majority of Manitoba First Nations signing Treaties Number 1,2, and 5.

29. While drafting the document, we were uncertain of how the minister would react to a written agreement despite the fact that it was consistent with his statements over the course of negotiations. We knew that the DIAND and Justice officials would caution him against signing. The grand chief resolved to

speak to him away from both sets of advisers. Afterwards, the grand chief observed to the author that the key was in explaining to the minister that the long legacy of broken promises by the federal government necessitated a concrete expression of good faith if the trust of the chiefs was to be gained and their support for the project secured. This episode is based on my personal recollection and notes of the meeting. A brief version was told by Dan Lett, "High Drama on Way to History," *Winnipeg Free Press* , 7 December 1994, p. B3.

30. At one point, it was sufficient for Fontaine to call one of the officials who was being most obstinate and ask if DIAND wished to see any future cooperation on any initiatives in the province. The officials returned to the table with a more cooperative attitude.

31. The contingents to the general assemblies where these decisions are taken often include elders, councillors and advisors as well as the chief or her/his designate. If the leadership of a community is in dispute, then it might have two delegations at the table. The AMC does not designate one delegation as the official representative of the community because that would contravene its policy of non-interference in the internal affairs of the First Nations communities. This is consistent with the fact that the AMC is the creation of the First Nations and empowered by them.

32. Throughout the negotiations, Jack London provided legal advice to the grand chief and executive. Again, the use of an advisor from outside the First Nation community generated internal criticism of the process and was the subject of discussion at the general assemblies on dismantling. The chiefs, some more reluctantly than others, have conceded that his expertise was needed for the negotiations and the implementation phase of the project. A compromise occurred with the project legal team drawing on in-house expertise.

33. Fontaine took a risk here since he was heading into unknown territory in an election year. The dismantling initiative did become an election issue but he was returned to office in the fall. It also had an effect on his political career since he was rumored to be the strongest challenger to Ovide Mercredi in the summer 1994 elections for national grand chief. Fontaine was courted vigorously by First Nations in B.C. and Ontario but declined to declare his nomination when the elders and advisors in Manitoba advised him that his responsibility lay in seeing the establishment of First Nations self-government in the province through to completion. He was too central to the project to change offices.

34. This initial draft with appendices exceeded 100 pages and included costings of each phase of the project, time frames with flow charts, organizational structures to oversee dismantling, and a comprehensive workplan with defined tasks and duties.

35. Throughout the entire process, the negotiations were open to any member of the First Nations wishing to attend. The tedious nature of discussions often seemed to discourage people from returning once a break was called.

36. The criticisms, including the national grand chief's concerns, are discussed below in the section on possible pitfalls.

37. AMC and DIAND, *Workplan*, pp. 1-2.

38. Grand Chief Phil Fontaine, Letter to the Honourable Gary Filmon, premier of Manitoba, 10 May 1994.

39. Grand Chief Phil Fontaine, "Notes for Speech to General Assembly of Chiefs," The Pas, Manitoba, 16 April 1994.

40. AMC and DIAND, *Workplan*, 1. Although the objectives state "the peoples of the First Nations," it is still under discussion among the chiefs how and to what extent the off-reserve population will be included and served by FNGM.

41. Ibid., pp. 11-19.

42. Ibid., p. 19.

43. Ibid., p. 23; cf. AMC and DIAND, *Framework Agreement*, p. 9.

44. Ibid., p. 19.

45. AMC and DIAND, *Framework Agreement*, p. 9.

46. AMC and DIAND, *Workplan*, p. 4.

47. This became a source of contention within the negotiations. As the costs of the project were rising above the original forecasts of the federal officials, they noted that there would be no additional appropriation of funds so the costs had to come either from the regional budget or from the budget allocations of other jurisdictions. The AMC team recognized the importance of maintaining the support of First Nations in other jurisdictions and chose to draw upon the regional allocation. However, to ensure that Manitoba First Nations were not adversely affected during the process, they ensured that a clause was inserted in the agreement stipulating that existing programs and services would continue "business as usual" with no disruptions or delays. AMC and DIAND, *Framework Agreement*, p. 9.

48. AMC and DIAND, *Framework Agreement*, p. 10.

49. See Project Organization Structure chart.

50. AMC and DIAND, *Framework Agreement*, pp. 6-8.

51. This is a complex provision which cites the need to balance needs of communities, federal obligations and resources, federal fiscal constraints, historic levels of funding, and the scope of new institutions, structures and responsibilities (Article 5.17).

52. Ovide Mercredi, remarks to the General Assembly of Manitoba Chiefs, The Pas, 20 April 1994, author's notes.

53. Canada, Minister of Indian Affairs and Northern Development, *Aboriginal Self-Government: A Summary of the Government of Canada's Approach to Implementation of the Inherent Right and the Negotiation of Aboriginal Self-Government* (Ottawa: Government Services, 1995). National Grand Chief Ovide Mercredi has expressed dissatisfaction with this arrangement since it involves a piecemeal approach to the inherent right and only offers a limited form of government. The proposal was not endorsed by the Chiefs of First Nations at the annual general assembly held in Ottawa in July 1995.

54. Ron Irwin, Minister of Indian Affairs and Northern Development, letter to Phil Fontaine, Grand Chief of the AMC, 13 June 1995.

55. Grand Chief Phil Fontaine, AMC, "Notes for Speech to General Assembly of Manitoba Chiefs," The Pas, 16 April 1994, pp. 2-3.

56. Paul Samyn, "Natives anticipate their destiny with pride — and trepidation," *Winnipeg Free Press*, 8 December 1994, p. A1. This subject was a non-starter with the chiefs.

57. See also Manitoba, First Nation's Child and Family Task Force, *Children First Our Responsibility* (Winnipeg, 19 November 1993), pp. 60-62.

58. Swampy Cree Tribal Council, "Position Paper on the Dismantling of the Department of Indian Affairs," presented to the AMC Assembly, The Pas, Manitoba, April 1994.

59. See Brock, *Manitoba*, ch. 5.

60. Comments by Premier Gary Filmon, CJOB Radio, Friday, 22 April 1994, 10:20 a.m.; Friday, 29 April 1994, 10:05 a.m.

61. The federal proposal on the inherent right negotiations recognizes the involvement and responsibility of the provincial governments which may indicate the long-term position of the federal government in this area as well.

62. Paul Samyn, "Ottawa Mends Historic Wrong," *Winnipeg Free Press*, 8 December 1994, p. A4.

63. Grand Chief Phil Fontaine, AMC, "Notes for Speech to General Assembly of Manitoba Chiefs," The Pas, 16 April 1994, p. 16.

64. Grand Chief Phil Fontaine, Interview, Toronto, 3 August 1995.

8

The Selling of New Brunswick:
Fibre Optics or Optical Illusion?

Jonathan W. Rose

Le Canada Atlantique a historiquement été une région dépendante de son industrie primaire. Une province de cette région a mis de l'avant d'importantes mesures de diversification de son économie. Ce chapitre examine le Nouveau-Brunswick comme une étude de cas d'une petite province qui a recours à la haute technologie pour diversifier sa base économique. Alors que les mass media ont fait grand cas du «miracle Mckenna», cet article évalue les bénéfices économiques que ces nouvelles technologies ont générés pour la province.

Plus précisément, l'effet qu'ont sur l'économie les nouvelles industries fondées sur l'information comme l'autoroute électronique et les centres d'appels y est évalué. Cet article soutient que bien qu'il y ait des bénéfices au plan de l'emploi, il est trop tôt pour déterminer si ces nouvelles technologies déplaceront de façon significative le moteur principal de la base économique traditionnelle de la province.

INTRODUCTION

In an age where reinventing government seems to be somewhat of a mantra, one province is putting that theory into practice. New Brunswick is undergoing a fascinating social experiment that is literally changing the way citizens communicate with their government and possibly realigning the provincial economy. After his election in 1987 and subsequent victories in 1991 and September 1995, Premier Frank McKenna has taken his Liberal government on a journey which has catapulted the small Atlantic province into the forefront of the technological revolution. In the minds of many in the public and the media, he has turned his back on New Brunswick's traditional natural resource (and labour-intensive) industries, favouring the allure of the high-tech, digital revolution. By doing so, New Brunswick has opened its doors to the world, welcoming business by offering tax deferrals, decreasing employer payroll deductions and offering location assistance to firms willing to locate in the province.

This chapter argues that though there are new innovations occurring in McKenna's New Brunswick, by and large the provincial economy has not changed substantially. New Brunswick continues to rely on primary industry such as pulp and paper, mining, fishing, and agriculture. While there are several innovative programs being undertaken by the provincial government, most notably the call-centre initiative and the information highway, its efforts in the area of high technology may take decades to yield dividends. One thing is certain, what is occurring in the province is a displacement of the low paying, de-skilling jobs in primary industry to low paying service sector jobs in what might be broadly defined as high-tech industries.

The economic profile of New Brunswick has not changed dramatically since McKenna assumed office in 1987. He has slowly managed to reduce unemployment, to eliminate the provincial deficit and to improve the province's Gross Domestic Product (GDP) notwithstanding a recession over that period. Comparing New Brunswick to other Atlantic provinces, New Brunswick has led the Atlantic region in virtually all areas of job creation. The gains it has made on the other provinces are, however, modest. New Brunswick is the only Atlantic province to see a reduction in the unemployment rate since 1987. It has gone from 13.1 percent when McKenna assumed office to 12.4 percent in 1994.[1] Except for PEI, it is the only Atlantic province to see an increase in its labour force participation rate.[2] If 1981 was a base year of 100, New Brunswick's index of employment was 123 in 1994 whereas Newfoundland, PEI and Nova Scotia were 105, 120, and 116 respectively. These data suggest that the gains made over the last several years are modest but not substantially different from those in the region.

The public sector continues to be an important employment source in the province supplying 22 percent of the active labour force, the lowest in the region.[3] Notwithstanding federal cutbacks, the federal government continues to be a significant employer providing 38.7 percent of all public sector employment in the Atlantic region. In New Brunswick the numbers are lower; 28.6 percent of public sector employment comes from the federal government, suggesting that the province gets less than its fair share of federal government jobs.[4] Provincial government employment data paint a different picture. New Brunswick is the only government in the Atlantic provinces to experience an increase in this category. Whereas Nova Scotia decreased 2.8 percent and provinces outside the region, such as Ontario, decreased 1.1 percent, New Brunswick has seen an increase of 3 percent in provincial employment.[5]

Since McKenna has assumed office the reliance on the federal government over that period has virtually remained constant in some areas and changed in others. As Donald Savoie and Maurice Beaudin have written, "[p]rovincial governments in the three Maritime provinces depend heavily on federal transfers."[6] This has not changed since McKenna assumed office. In 1994, 40 percent of provincial revenue came from the federal government; in 1987 it was virtually the same.[7] Of course, federal transfer payments to the provinces have fallen over that period and will likely continue to decrease in the future. The challenge of maintaining the same level of service in the face of the federal government's commitment to reduce the deficit to 3 percent of the GDP has forced New Brunswick, like other provincial economies, to increase provincial revenue by seeking alternative forms of economic development.

While these indicators may suggest that the province has not changed dramatically, they belie a more subtle shift in the province's economic focus. It is here where the so-called McKenna miracle can be seen. Broadly stated, what has changed in New Brunswick is the application of the latest technology to key segments of industry. This is particularly evident in what might be called information industries, or more specifically the information highway and call-centres. If mass media coverage is any indication, these two areas have dramatically transformed the political, economic, and cultural landscape of the province and deserve closer scrutiny.[8]

While the mass media have noted the application of high technology in New Brunswick and the way in which it is realigning the provincial economy, social scientists have been more reticent to explore this new development. There are a few notable exceptions. Dorothy Downing's "High-Tech in Small Towns"[9] sees the benefits of high technology from the vantage point of ten business owners in the Maritimes, three of whom are from New Brunswick. Her article is an attempt to understand the amenities of small Maritime towns for businesses rather than to analyze the role that the technology plays in the local economy. Another chapter in the same book examines the steps taken by Fredericton in competing in the global economy and becoming "an important provider of services for the information economy."[10] Other writers have noted the changes in the relationship between the government and citizens as a result of high technology,[11] or that there needs to be greater public input in technological innovations undertaken by governments.[12] Many of these works are not in main stream political science journals or books despite the important impact of this development on the role of governments generally.

In New Brunswick, the premier has used the rhetoric of business to entice corporations to locate there. Frank McKenna, who speaks of citizens as "customers" and is comfortable being labelled the "CEO of the province,"[13] set out to use his considerable sales skills and a small but mobilized and highly trained bureaucracy[14] to attract large "blue-chip" industries to the province using one of the few endowments of the province as a lure — a state of the art telecommunications infrastructure. Certainly premiers prior to McKenna have courted high technology as a possible addition to economic development. For example, R.A. Young said that Premier Flemming had a "personal faith in

technology and his government's policy encourag[ed] industry to locate in
the province and develop its resource wealth."[15] None, however, have been so
emphatic in their support for it. In Frank McKenna's own words:

> The information highway is so important to us. It is the job driver for New Bruns-
> wick ... Technology really is its own reward. We are investing heavily in
> technology, some of which replaces people, but it creates jobs ... In order to
> have a new, high-growth service sector, we must rely on information technol-
> ogy.[16]

The genesis of establishing New Brunswick as a centre of high technology
may be traced to a report in April of 1993 called *Toward Self-Sufficiency*. The
title reflected the goal of the province's economic development and the theme
that would characterize the province's economic development strategy in
McKenna's second term of office. Continuing the theme of the government's
first-term strategy called *Toward 2000, Toward Self-Sufficiency* provided a
framework for economic development which had more in common with a business plan that stresses profit than it did a government statement stressing
employment to the forty thousand unemployed New Brunswickers. It said that:
To grow in the global economy, we must focus on:

- increasing value, cost-competitiveness, innovation and product quality in niche markets. Investing in and managing the sustainable
  development of the primary resource has to be targeted to these
  objectives.

- moving to competitive excellence through innovation, specialization
  and strategic alliances at the regional, national, and international levels.

- growing and sustaining small business, especially in higher unemployment areas.[17]

The context within which this would occur takes advantage of the province's rich high-tech infrastructure. As the plan stated: "We cannot expect or
afford to do everything. Instead we will focus on our strengths,"[18] Among these
targeted "areas of competitive excellence" were "knowledge-based services,
including communications/information and engineering."[19]

This well-endowed telecommunications infrastructure exists because of a
convergence of decisions taken by NBTel, the provincial telephone company
beginning 20 years ago. What drove this technological revolution was a phone
company that took its universal service mandate seriously. The phone company responded to the demands placed on them by the provincial government
to ensure citizens had equal and cheap access (basic service has not changed
since 1983) and the needs of their larger customers, such as Irving and McCain,
to provide state-of-the-art service. Along the way, NBTel installed digital
switches, which compress and digitalize signals, making multimedia a reality. Fibre optic cable was made accessible with no home being farther than six

kilometers away from fibre optic access, giving New Brunswickers an array of services unknown in other provinces. An interactive broadband network will allow homes and businesses in New Brunswick to access health care, entertainment, education or retail services using the phone, television or personal computer.

While this modern infrastructure more than accommodated the needs of New Brunswickers, it was ideal for telecommunication firms which required a communications network that could accommodate vast amounts of data reliably. These features, unique in the country, were exploited by McKenna who saw a natural fit between the communications potential of the province and the changing demands of international businesses. Not only could New Brunswick be sold as a province with state-of-the-art telecommunications but its bilingual workforce, reasonable levels of taxation, educational attainment of the labour force and location made the province an appealing place for certain kinds of businesses to re-locate. Large firms which stressed customer service, such as banks who are entering the era of telephone banking, or firms such as UPS or Purolator, whose services were tied to the need for customers to have up-to-the-minute information, were a natural fit in New Brunswick.

What makes New Brunswick's economic development strategy unique is its reliance on high-tech industries. The rest of this chapter will explain and assess the application of this technology on two significant policy areas, the development of the information highway and the call-centre initiative. Others have documented the influence of technology in traditional industries;[20] the information highway and the call-centre initiative are examples of some important new industries. Moreover, an understanding of these two policy areas tells us something about the potential avenues that may be pursued in the future by other Maritime provinces. With a shrinking natural resource base, industries that are labour intensive and use existing infrastructure provide a certain allure. As we shall see, there are both significant benefits as well as drawbacks associated with taking this path.

THE INFORMATION HIGHWAY

McKenna's government was the first in Canada to have a minister responsible for the information highway; and New Brunswick was the first government to put information about government programs on the Internet.[21] The move was, in fact, more than political symbolism. For the first time in Canada, a provincial government committed its resources to developing the economic potential of this new medium of communication. Prior to discussing how the government has used the information highway, it may be useful to explain exactly what this much (over)-used concept means.

The information highway has been described as

a high-speed communications network capable of carrying voice, text, data, graphics and video services into home and office. It is like a worldwide road system, a globe-encompassing grid that can transport information to and from any destination. As it evolves the Information Highway will link together existing networks of cable, telecommunications, wireless, satellite and computing into an interconnected system.[22]

As such, it integrates computing, communications, consumer electronics, entertainment, and publishing into a one-source provider. Its users will be able to access voice, pictures, and sound from an all-purpose appliance which will serve as a computer, phone, and television all wrapped in one.

Aside from its effects on our leisure-time activities, it has the potential to radically transform democracy. Some see it as an emancipatory tool — making government and democratic discourse accessible to all citizens. Others, however, see computer mediated communications as the commodification of the public sphere — where the gulf between the information rich and information poor grows wider.[23] There are not only important questions of access, but of how political community is possible in a wired world or the effect of this new medium on governments' ability to regulate. These kinds of issues, around which there is a growing literature, are worthy of study but are beyond the scope of this chapter.

Suffice it to say here, however, that the information highway represents a new convergence of telecommunications and capitalism.[24] According to the assistant deputy minister of the information highway, the impetus to develop this new form of technology was to exploit the existing technological infrastructure for the benefit of New Brunswick industry, to market government as a model user of technology and thereby reduce its costs and deliver programs more efficiently, and to educate New Brunswickers of the potential of the information highway.[25] Any analysis of the information highway cannot ignore the enormous transformative potential of this new medium. Not only does it change the way governments do business with their suppliers and their citizens but it also changes the whole range and quality of services that can be offered by government.

According to the Government of New Brunswick, the purposes of this new form of technology are rather prosaic. The report that forms the basis of the government's efforts is called *Driving the Information Highway*. It cites the advantages as:

- an increasing competitive advantage for New Brunswick enterprises;

- opportunity for specific new industry to develop;

- better, more effective and cost-efficient provision of government services and information; and

- improved quality of life and a changed way for New Brunswickers to live, learn, work, and play.[26]

The driving forces behind the information highway were the provincial phone utility, NBTel, and a new entrepreneurial zeal that seized the government. It is described by the assistant deputy minister of the information highway as "running government as a business." In New Brunswick this means treating customers as taxpayers, decreasing costs of the provision of services, increasing revenue and having a greater "customer focus."[27] In fact, the result of this initiative has seen the quality of life improve in some respects for a large number of New Brunswickers.

McKenna's drive along the information highway began in September 1993 when he appointed a steering committee of deputy ministers to "develop a strategy for government to accelerate evolution of the information highway in New Brunswick."[28] From this committee, a task force was created which outlined the current capabilities of the information highway and made recommendations for its future potential. The report, called *Driving the Information Highway,* makes recommendations on using information technology in key government departments such as health, education and government services. The report established four guiding principles with regard to this new technology. They are: first, provincewide availability and affordability; second, open and shared access; third, respect for privacy and security; and finally, standards-based products and services.[29] The first two are substantive goals, the second two are at worst, political rhetoric and at best vague exhortations for the future of the technology.

The first principle of provincewide availability and affordability means that irrespective of geographic location, all New Brunswickers would have access to the same kinds of services "at the lowest possible price over the long term." In this respect, the province has an impressive record. By the end of 1996, all schools in the province will be linked together through the Internet, every classroom from kindergarten to grade five will have its own electronic address and every student from grade six to grade twelve will have his or her own personal e-mail address. This means much greater access to informational resources — from the province's university libraries to libraries around the country and the world. Through a program called TeleEducation NB, college and university courses are offered in 50 sites across the province. The distance education program is the most ambitious of any provincial government in Canada, with teachers and students communicating through "teleconferencing." The existence of fibre optics and broad-band technology means that sound and picture are able to be transmitted across existing telephone lines — something that can be done in few places around the world. Aside from education, New Brunswickers have access to provision of government services in over 100 kiosks across the province, all of which are located in Irving gas stations. At these kiosks, New Brunswickers can do everything from personal property registration to mortgage searches to access road conditions and obtain fishing licences. These sorts of services appear to meet the goal of provincewide access.

The second principle is to ensure that the information highway is accessible "to everyone with a good idea for a product or service to sell."[30] Moreover, the report said that "anyone who wants to form a business to deliver an information product or service across the information highway will be able to do it by paying a fair and equitable price to the communication service providers." The strong free enterprise approach is in keeping with the McKenna government's philosophy. Believing, as the report says, that "[h]ealthy and fair competition will be important to the exploitation of the information highway in New Brunswick" means that the province must open its doors to foreign corporate presence along the information highway. This comes from a realization that the percentage of the Internet traffic that is Canadian is tiny[31] and that in order to recoup their investment, the government must allow firms access to this new resource. While encouraging competition may be a necessary and perhaps laudable goal, there still remains the potential that foreign presence may provide barriers for entry to smaller Canadian firms.

The third and fourth principles are reasonable claims but are beyond the scope of the provincial government's ability. The third principle that forms the cornerstone of the government's approach to the information highway is "respect for privacy and security."[32] These new technologies provide citizens with a powerful new learning tool. They need not leave their own homes to explore the sources of information or entertainment from around the world. This benefit is tempered by an enormous cost discussed in books by Rheingold and Lyon,[33] among others who see the capacity for electronic surveillance a very real threat posed by the Internet. Notwithstanding the provincial government's claims to the contrary, it is inconceivable that a small bureaucracy can tackle this huge problem, assuming it wanted to. In Canada, there is a minor federal regulatory regime (the Telecommunication Privacy Protection Agency) in place which offers the most cursory of protection along the information highway. The anarchic nature of the technology makes government regulatory regimes virtually obsolete in addressing transborder flows of information and data.

The fourth guiding principle is a mere exhortation for "standards-based products and services."[34] In other words, "services and applications developed for New Brunswick's information highway should adhere to nationally and internationally-recognized standards for telecommunications and computing — where standards are available and widely accepted." This has largely been achieved by establishing electronic links with other telecommunication firms on the Internet and using, by necessity, internationally recognized communication protocols.

What then are we to make of the information highway in New Brunswick? Many of its advantages are hard to dispute. In education, the NetLearn project, where distance learning is facilitated over the Internet is a reality. Mount Allison University offers multimedia computing distance education courses in physics and astronomy. It is also the first university in Canada to totally network campus offices, classrooms and all student residences. At the Université de Moncton computer generated TalkMail distributes student grades over the telephone.[35] Government services are now more accessible to those who use the many government kiosks around the province. Government suppliers submit tenders through an electronic bulletin board and government departments order supplies on-line. Internal budgeting and all inter-and intra-departmental correspondence is conducted electronically, so much so that there are no longer paper memos.

There are also benefits to public administration in the province. For example, one feature common to all governments has taken on a modern twist. Discussion groups of deputy ministers, where administrative and management issues are traditionally discussed in a meeting, are done through the Internet, facilitating immediate feedback and a greater sense of conversational continuity. There is an economy of scale working here. With a core civil service of only 1,400 dramatic changes such as these are easier to facilitate. In the area of health care, New Brunswick is leading the country in terms of using the potential of the information highway. Health*Net is a radical way of linking hospitals and other health-related services. In this system, all of the province's health regions are able to communicate through a teleconference, physicians are able to submit medicare claims by computer and a solitary patient record keeps track of a patient's hospital and physician visits regardless of where the patient goes in the province.

It is clear that the information highway is integrated in many aspects of New Brunswick life — both in the private and public sectors. Without a doubt it has revolutionized the way in which the government conducts its business with suppliers and citizens. What is more difficult to understand is the effect of the information highway on the relationship between government and its citizens. Has high technology helped or hindered democracy? Has it made government more accountable? And most important, what are its effects on job creation? Indeed, these impressive technological achievements are little consolation to the 40,000 unemployed who likely do not benefit from this wired world. But the information highway is not without employment opportunities. The employment side of the equation can be found in the way that the information highway has been deployed in the province, through call-centres. In this respect, as we shall see, the quantity of jobs created may be impressive, but the quality is rather modest.

THE CALL-CENTRE INITIATIVE

As alluded to earlier, New Brunswick is fortunate to have "one of the most sophisticated communications infrastructures in North America"[36] and its phone company, NBTel has been described as one of the best telcos on the continent. It is the only phone company in North America to offer a fully digital telephone network. Controlling 95 percent of the long distance market in the province[37] and buoyed for a long time by a few large use customers such as the Irvings, McCains, and the provincial government, NBTel is perhaps unique in the country. These circumstances have made New Brunswick an ideal place for corporations to establish call-centres.

What exactly are call-centres? On one level they are merely places where banks of telephones are staffed by personnel who are able to answer questions about a firm's products. On another level, they are highly technical sources of data — both able to respond to specific customer concerns and establish a database that correlates geographic location (and therefore, socio-economic status) with product use. For the customers who use them, call-centres are just help lines. For the firms who have them, they are a way to use small area demographics to conduct a highly precise and continuous marketing survey on their products. The high-tech part of call firms are the digital switches and fibre optic transmission needed to handle the volume of incoming phone calls. Other features of call-centre telecommunications architecture include automatic call distribution which relocates calls to an appropriate agent and "Telepathic," an application that, for example, automatically connects francophone callers to a francophone agent who has the customer's account information on a computer screen. In short, call-centres are high-tech phone banks designed to provide service for their customers, while also continuously compiling data for the firms who use them.

It was not just Frank McKenna's sales ability that has attracted call-centres to New Brunswick, though his efforts in this regard have been a very public part of the appeal. The convergence of several factors — the existing telecommunications infrastructure, the strong relationship between the provincial government and the phone company, a new public sector ethos and a bilingual workforce — have combined to make the province an ideal place for firms to locate.

The benefits to NBTel are obvious. It gains new large-scale users of an infrastructure already in place. The province too, stands to gain from this initiative. The appeal of call-centres for New Brunswick are manifold. First, they bring large corporations and hence employment and capital to the province; second, call-centres take advantage of existing infrastructure and it is therefore virtually costless in this respect; third, in the age of free trade, where borders are less important to the flow of capital, New Brunswick is able to exploit its bilingual workforce and low cost of living; and fourth, they provide employment which diversifies the provincial economy and requires the kinds of skills possessed by university graduates. As the government's promotional literature states, "[t]here is a steady and stable supply of highly skilled people, ready for specific training or immediate employment."[38] No doubt, the fact that there is a large available job pool of unemployed workers eager to work has not escaped the attention of corporations thinking of locating in New Brunswick.

In many respects the call-centre initiative has been successful. Since its inception, 3,500 jobs have been created through 23 call-centres. Corporations such as the Royal Bank, Canada Trust, Purolator Courier, Northern Telecom, and Federal Express have located their national or international call-centres in New Brunswick. The average wage is $23,000[39] and employees can expect to work in a bright, modern workplace and a chance to break free of employment in traditional natural resource industries. The province, in return, reduces its share of those on welfare benefits and receives an income boost of $75 million in payroll.

The benefits of call-centres are not without cost. The social and economic costs of call-centres are difficult to quantify but may be significant. The jobs created may use high technology but do not provide many new skills for those who occupy them. In many respects, call-centre employees are telephone operators whose average salary is $10,000 lower than the industry average.[40] By directing its energy to this aspect of the industry the government is relegating itself to creating jobs that are low paying, and provide little transferable skills to other industries. New Brunswick may claim to be the only fully digital jurisdiction in North America, and the "call-centre headquarters of the continent" but economists such as Bill Milne wonder about the ephemeral nature of the jobs once other jurisdictions follow suit.[41] For now the province has a strategic advantage. What will happen when other jurisdictions update their communications infrastructure and are able to offer lower salaries and benefits than New Brunswick? This has been a concern of labour leaders who are fearful that call-centres are quick-fix solution. Former president of the New Brunswick Federation of Labour, John McEwen says about the call-centre jobs, "when they move on — and they will — the basis of your economy is gone. We have to look at our fixed assets — our natural resources."[42] Other criticisms have been voiced by other provinces who claim that McKenna is not creating jobs but rather poaching jobs from them and perhaps violating interprovincial trade agreements. Several premiers were outraged when United Parcel Service (UPS) received $6 million in forgivable loans for moving 900 jobs from Ontario, Manitoba, and British Columbia earlier this year.[43]

McKenna's government has not only given many financial incentives to get these call-centre jobs, it has also given up future tax income potential. There are many examples. In the UPS case above, the province provided $10,000 per job for employee training.[44] In other cases, the province provides forgivable loans to call-centre firms. It is, however, in terms of legislation that the province has been vigorous — and vocal — about coming to the aid of private capital. A document from the provincial government given to corporations seeking to locate in New Brunswick boasts that the province "offers the lowest legislated fringe benefit costs in North America for call-centre operations."[45] The same document touts the fact that there is no corporate capital tax or payroll tax.[46] Reforms to the *Workers Compensation Act* removing stress as a legitimate claim have provided further incentives to businesses. By re-classifying call-centre employees, McKenna has reduced the amount of money paid by firms to Workers' Compensation. In New Brunswick, companies pay only 22 cents for every $100 of payroll. This compares to the $6.34 paid in Ontario.[47] All of these efforts indicate a serious willingness on the part of the province to do everything possible to attract call-centres to the province.

These techniques are, of course, not peculiar to New Brunswick. Most governments offer some kind of incentives to lure industry to their jurisdiction. The problem emerges when provinces or states begin a "bidding war" to offer more generous re-location packages or lower tax rates. The tiny province is not able to compete with other jurisdictions, most of which have greater economic clout than New Brunswick and may end up losing in the long run.

With these incentives, one would expect significant benefits to the province. There is, however, a disjunction between the public relations efforts of the McKenna government towards the new technologies and the dividends they have paid. If you were to merely read the popular press and examine government promotional material you would have a distorted view of the province. For all its high technology, New Brunswick is still basically a province dependent upon its primary resources. The information highway and call-centres are merely first steps towards diversifying the economy. The reality is that much of the economy depends on manufacturing and mining. In terms of employment, the results are clear, as shown in Figure 1.

This figure shows that the largest sector of employment is the service sector which is comprised of retail and wholesale trade; finance, insurance, and real estate; and tourism business and personal services. In 1994, employment in this area was 112,000. Trade and manufacturing were second and third at 57,000 and 34,000 respectively. Employment in communication for 1994 was comparatively paltry at 28,000. It is important to note that this latter number includes transportation and utilities. The actual number employed in call-centres and affiliated with the information highway would have been much smaller. More significantly, the trend over the last four years does not show a significant increase of employment in the communications sector.

Employment is, of course, only one way to measure the contribution of an industry to an economic sector. The data for industry value are marginally better for communications but still show a modest contribution to the overall economy. In 1993, the last year for which data are available, manufacturing

Figure 1: New Brunswick Employment by Industry ('000)

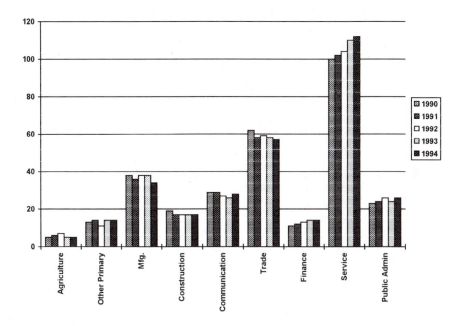

Source: Statistics Canada, cat. 71-529.

and the category of finance, insurance, and real estate each contributed to 13 percent of the provincial gross domestic product (GDP), services were next with 9.8 percent of the GDP, retail trade followed with 7.3 percent while communications as a sector was far behind with 4 percent of the provincial GDP.[48] If employment and economic value were the only ways of assessing the value of the new technologies, it would appear that Premier McKenna is labouring in the wrong area.

CONCLUSION

As stated earlier, it is too early to draw firm conclusions about the role of the information highway in the New Brunswick economy. The province's economic profile is changing. This might be evidence that the province is undergoing a transition or perhaps experiencing a shift from its traditional trajectory. For example, from 1989 to 1993 the economic sector to show the greatest percentage increase was communications, improving 29.5 percent, while the traditional industry of logging and forestry showed a sharp decline of 43 percent. At present, the value of communications is marginal to the province's overall economy. Like Richard Hatfield's attempt to build automobiles, the information highway is a powerful symbol of a province staking its claims in an economic sector that is high in technology and far removed from primary industry. Unlike the ill-fated Bricklin, the information highway is providing some employment. What remains uncertain is the longevity of these new jobs.

New Brunswick under McKenna continues to be a curious blend of the old and new. The kind of economic development that is taking place is new. It remains to be seen whether the application of new technologies will benefit traditional industries such as ship building, aquaculture, pulp and paper or mining. Or perhaps, as has been argued here, the promise of new technology on the new "information industries" may provide an economic solution for traditionally depressed regions such as the Maritimes. This solution is not without cost, what remains to be seen is whether these costs outweigh the potentially significant benefits. In either case, the province is still searching for the elusive magic bullet to take its economy out of the economic doldrums. New Brunswick's history provides examples of a province with a faith in the restorative powers of new technology. In 1947 Hugh Flemming, a Conservative MLA and son of Premier John Flemming, spoke words that are suitable today: "It is obvious that we need something big, something revolutionary, something that will give our people new hope, revive their ambition, and render available worthwhile opportunity."[49] The jury is still out as to whether Premier McKenna is able to deliver.

NOTES

I would like to acknowledge the financial support of Queen's University, Advisory Resarch Council for research support. Thanks go to Doug Brown and two reviewers who provided comments which forced me to re-think some assumptions, though the latter may not think that I have gone far enough. Hugh Mellon was also invaluable in providing critical advice at several stages.

1.   Statistics Canada, *Historical Labour Force Statistics 1994,* cat. 71-201 (Ottawa: Minister of Supply and Services, 1994). During that period, Newfoundland's unemployment rate went from 18 to 20 percent; PEI, 13.1 to 17.1 percent and; Nova Scotia, 12.4 to 13.3 percent. Other data from this paragraph taken from this source.

2. Ibid. From 1987-94 the participation rate went from 58.6 to 59.1 in New Brunswick; stayed constant at 53.6 in Newfoundland; increased from 63 to 65.5 in PEI; and remained essentially constant in Nova Scotia at 60.2 to 60.4.

3. Department of Finance, *The New Brunswick Economy 1995* (Fredericton, NB: New Brunswick Statistics Agency, 1995), Tables 13 and 15.

4. Ibid.

5. See Table 2.5 in Statistics Canada, *Public Sector Employment 1993,* cat. 72-209 (Ottawa: Minister of Supply and Services, 1993).

6. Donald Savoie and Maurice Beaudin, "Public Sector Adjustments and the Maritime Provinces," in George J. De Benedetti and Rodolphe H. Lamarche (eds.), *Shock Waves: The Maritime Urban System in the New Economy* (Moncton: Canadian Institute for Research on Regional Development, 1994), p. 123.

7. See Statistics Canada, *Historical Labour Force Statistics 1994.*

8. See the cover headline of *Maclean's,* "Fast Frank: How New Brunswick's Premier Turned his Province into Canada's Social Laboratory," 11 April 1994. See also "The Energizer Premier," in the *Report on Business Magazine,* March 1993; "McKenna for PM," in the *Financial Post 87:31,* 31 July 1993, p. S3; "The Face of Liberalism in the 90s: Like Bill Clinton, McKenna Has Been Putting Pragmatism over Ideology," in the *Toronto Star,* 26 February 1993, p. A3. More critically, see "Hyping Mr. McKenna," in *This Magazine,* August 1993, pp. 22-25.

9. Dorothy Downing, "High-Tech in Small Towns" in De Benedetti and Lamarche, *Shock Waves,* pp. 141-58.

10. George De Benedetti and Eugen Weiss, "Fredericton: Building on an Intellectual Base," in *Shock Waves,* pp. 249-65.

11. See "NB Pilot Takes Kiosks to New Heights," *Technology in Government* 2, 1 (January 1995): 12-15.

12. Jesse Tatum, "Science, Technology and Government: Re-examining the Relationship," *Technology and Society* 17, 1 (1995): 85-102.

13. "Getting Down to Business in New Brunswick: An Interview with Premier Frank McKenna," *Canadian Business Review,* Winter 1994, p. 7.

14. This point is made by Hugh Mellon, "New Brunswick: The Politics of Reform," in Michael Howlett and Keith Brownsey (eds.), *The Provincial State: Politics in Canada's Provinces and Territories* (Toronto: Copp Clark, 1992), p.100.

15. R.A. Young, "Planning for Power: The New Brunswick Electric Power Commission in the 1950s," *Acadiensis* 12, 1 (Autumn 1982): 99.

16. "Getting Down to Business in New Brunswick," p. 11. Taken from answers to several questions about the information highway.

17. Department of Economic Development and Tourism, *Toward Self Sufficiency: Strategy for Economic Development* (Government of New Brunswick, 1993), p. 6.

18. Ibid., p. 8.

19. Ibid.

20. See De Benedetti and Weiss, "Fredericton Building on an Intellectual Base."

21. The internet news group is nbgov.info.highway. The address is: http://degaulle.hil.unb.ca/NB/info_highway/highway.html

22. Harley Mallory Strategic Communications, *Business Person's Guide to the Info-Highway* (Fredericton: Information Highway Secretariat, 1994), p. 1.

23. This is discussed in Howard Rheingold, *The Virtual Community: Homesteading on the Electronic Frontier* (New York: Harper Perennial, 1993). See ch. 10 "Disinformocracy."

24. For a fascinating account of this, see "So Much for a Cashless Society," *Economist*, 26 November 1994, p. 21.

25. Interview with Jerry Fowler, ADM, Department of Economic Development and Tourism, Information Highway Secretariat, Fredericton, 5 July 1995

26. Department of Economic Development, *Driving the Information Highway: The Report of the New Brunswick Task Force on the Electronic Information Highway,* (Fredericton: Information Highway Secretariat, 1994), p. 4.

27. Interview with Jerry Fowler.

28. *Driving the Information Highway,* executive summary (n.p.).

29. Ibid., p. 10. Other quotes from this paragraph are taken from pp. 10-12 of this report.

30. Ibid., p. 11. Other quotes from this paragraph are taken from p. 10-11 of this report.

31. See the *Economist,* "A Survey of the Internet," 1 July 1995.

32. *Driving the Information Highway,* p. 11.

33. See Rheingold, *The Virtual Community;* David Lyon, *The Electronic Eye: The Rise of Surveillance Society* (Minneapolis: University of Minnesota Press, 1994).

34. *Driving the Information Highway,* p. 12. Other quotes from this paragraph from this source and location.

35. These examples come from *Business Person's Guide to the Info-Highway,* p. 4.

36. Paul DeLottinville, *Shifting to the New Economy: Call-centres and Beyond* (Toronto: Copp Clark Longman, 1994), p. 1.

37. Bruncor *Annual Report,* 1994 , p. 9.

38. Department of Economic Development, *New Brunswick: More than a Location... A Solution* (Fredericton: Government of New Brunswick, 1995), p. 1.

39. Interview with Brian Freeman, Call-centre Coordinator, Fredericton, 5 July 1995.

40. Statistics Canada, cat. 72-002, Table 5, "Employment, Earnings and Hours," September 1994. The average wage for those in the Communications sector is $33, 176 for September 1994.

41. "New Brunswick Hustle" on CBC *Prime Time News,* Transcript, p. 13.

42. Sharon Fraser, "Hyping Mr. McKenna," *This Magazine,* 27 (August 1993): 3.

43. Judy Monchuk, "McKenna Under Attack for Poaching UPS Jobs," *Halifax Chronicle Herald,* 12 January 1995, p. C3. See also "UPS Agreement with N.B. called Theft of Jobs," *The Globe and Mail,* 12 January 1995, p. A4.

44. "The Marketing of New Brunswick" *The Globe and Mail,* 12 January 1995, p. A1.

45. *New Brunswick: More than a Location... A Solution,* p. 2.

46. Ibid., p. 7.

47. "New Brunswick Hustle," p.14

48. Adapted from "Gross Domestic Product by Industry," *The New Brunswick Economy 1995* (Fredericton: New Brunswick Statistics Agency, 1995), p. 55, Table 10.

49. Quoted in "Planning for Power: The New Brunswick Electric Power Commission in the 1950s," p. 76.

9

Assessing the Agreement on Internal Trade: The Case for a "More Perfect Union"

Bryan Schwartz

Issue d'un long processus et prêtant souvent à controverse, les critiques les plus durs de l'Entente sur le commerce intérieur (ECI) la considèrent faible au point où elle pourrait même avoir des effets contraires, alors que même ses partisans la qualifient de première étape modeste. Cet article situe le développement de l'ECI dans son contexte constitutionnel et offre ensuite un exposé, chapitre par chapitre, du contenu de l'entente finale.

L'auteur fournit le contexte juridique et historique qui sous-tend l'ECI; ce faisant il met en lumière la fragilité potentielle de cet accord qui est d'abord et avant tout politique. L'auteur soutient qu'un rôle fédéral plus important est crucial pour s'assurer que les provinces respectent l'entente. L'analyse des pouvoirs fédéraux en matière de commerce suggère que les tribunaux ont une base constitutionnelle suffisante pour permettre d'élargir l'interprétation juridique afin de donner une plus grande marge de manoeuvre à une action fédérale unilatérale qui viserait à parfaire l'union économique canadienne. En l'absence d'une telle action, la tâche reviendrait alors à l'ECI. Cependant, l'entente contient plusieurs exceptions et restrictions alors que bien peu de décisions établissant des précédents ont été prises jusqu'à maintenant. La capacité qu'aura l'ECI de soutenir efficacement l'union économique canadienne reste encore à déterminée.

INTRODUCTION

The Agreement on Internal Trade (AIT), which came into effect on 1 July 1995, is a political accord among Canadian governments to enhance free trade within Canada's own borders. The harshest critics of the accord characterize it as so weak as to be counterproductive; its proponents go no further than to call it a modest first step. The first part of this chapter will attempt to explain why governments have chosen a political accord as opposed to legally binding alternatives to achieving internal free trade. The second part will attempt to explain and assess the actual contents of the agreement.

PROHIBITIONS ON PROTECTIONISM THAT ARE
ENFORCED BY THE COURTS

A national constitution might usefully include a variety of prohibitions against restrictions on free trade, which could be enforced directly by the courts.

The constitution of the European Community[1] is a model that Canadians should emulate. It plainly prohibits states from discriminating against the people, goods, services and investment of another state, and the norm is directly enforceable in the national courts of each state. Disputes over the interpretation of the norm can be referred to the binding authority of the European Court of Justice.

While the American constitution is not as explicitly committed to internal free trade as is the European Union's, the American courts have struck down a variety of protectionist measures by American states on the basis that they intrude on Congress' sole jurisdiction over "interstate" commerce.[2]

Canada's *Constitution Act, 1867* contains only one free trade clause, section 121. It commands that *goods* of each province must be admitted free into another. The courts have not yet used the section to strike down a piece of federal or provincial legislation.

Over 40 years ago, Supreme Court of Canada Justice Ivan Rand in *Murphy v. Canadian Pacific Railway,* offered the individual opinion that:

> I take s. 121, apart from custom duties, to be aimed against trade regulation which is designed to place fetters upon or raise impediments to or otherwise restrict the free flow of commerce across the Dominion as if provincial boundaries did not exist. That it does not create a level of trade activity divested of all regulation I have no doubt; what is preserved is a free flow of trade regulated in subsidiary features which are or have come to be looked upon as incidents of trade. What is forbidden is a trade regulation that in its essence and purpose is related to a provincial boundary.[3]

In another case from that era,[4] Rand held that the structure of the Canadian constitution, with its creation of Canadian citizenship, implied that no province could prevent a resident from another province from immigrating and finding work. Some recent cases[5] in the Supreme Court of Canada have recognized the general concept of the "economic union," and when section 121 is revisited by the Courts, they may be prepared to give it some real teeth. Even if they do, however, the section will still be limited to internal trade issues involving goods (rather than services, capital or human resources) and will be limited to border-related impediments to movement, rather than a variety of other trade barriers.

When it reported in 1985, the MacDonald Royal Commission on the Economy proposed a legally binding free trade agreement with the United States.[6] While calling for this leap of faith in Canada's foreign relations, the commission recommended a more cautious approach to implementing internal free trade. The commission was pessimistic about entrenching free trade norms in the constitution; such a constitutional declaration would end up so riddled with exceptions that it would only legitimize what it was designed to prevent.

Instead the commission proposed cautious incrementalism. First there would be a federal-provincial agreement on an "Economic Code of Conduct" for internal trade. It would be enforceable only through political pressure. Eventually, as confidence in the system developed, a dispute-settling mechanism would be established with the authority to make legally binding orders. Finally, federal and provincial governments would achieve the level of comfort that would permit them to agree to a formal constitutional amendment.

At first glance, the commission's approach seems perverse; could Canadians and the governments be more willing to leap into a legally binding embrace with the United States than to bind themselves to an internal trade agreement? Actual history has shown that the commission's recommendations were not inconsistent with Canadian realities. Canada has indeed entered into two major legally-binding international trade agreements with the United States, first the US-Canada Free Trade Agreement, then NAFTA.

When Prime Minister Trudeau had proposed a constitutionally entrenching "economic union" principle in 1980 as part of his patriation package, provincial opposition forced him to back down almost entirely. Only one small aspect of his package survived in the final version; the *Charter of Rights and Freedoms* now contains individual "mobility rights" — the right to move to cross provincial boundaries to take up residence or work — and these rights are stated in a narrow form and are subject to a variety of qualifications.[7]

In 1991, when the government of Prime Minister Mulroney initiated the discussions that led to the Charlottetown Accord, it again proposed an economic union principle, plus a power of the federal government to further manage the economic union with the consent of the "Council of Federation" (the provincial governments of at least seven provinces and of at least half of the Canadian population) and subject to "opting out" by at least three provinces. Even this attempt to add marginally to Parliament's authority was immediately rejected by politicians from Quebec and elsewhere, and the Mulroney government backed down without a fight.

Now the federal and provincial governments are engaged in stage one of the MacDonald Commission's scenario for internal trade: the Agreement on Internal Trade is the equivalent of the Code of Economic Conduct, and it is not enforceable in the Courts. What theory can explain the paradoxical practice: in the race for free trade, Canada is an enthusiast at the international level, and a stumblebum at home?

Part of the explanation is psychological. In our personal lives, we often tolerate from strangers what we would never accept from friends or family. We are too emotionally engaged, too sensitive to whether we feel affection or respect, to gauge a transaction on purely rational terms. A shared past can build bonds of loyalty, but it can also lead to an accumulation of resentments. Close proximity enhances our fear of being dominated and engulfed. The same emotions tend to apply to international political relations. It may be easier to accept a reciprocal limitation of political sovereignty when the transaction is with an outsider.

Sometimes, closely-related political communities can only get along in the context of a larger organization, composed mostly of outsiders. Their presence renders the aura of objectivity to the decision making of the organization; many "outsiders" are involved in wielding power, and the significance of a closely-related country is diluted, or at least cast in a soft new light. For example, in 1867 the two linguistic communities in the province of Canada attempted to escape from political deadlock by joining with other British colonies in a larger new federation. In Europe, since the Second World War, the German and French political communities have been attempting, with a large measure of success, to dilute their bilateral tensions by joining together in a larger European community.

So it is that the leaders of some of the most "decentralist" provinces, including Alberta and Quebec, have been readily willing to see Canadian sovereignty limited by free trade agreements with the United States and Mexico. Now that the ethos of free trade has been entrenched in that larger context, Canadian political leaders appear ready, at least, to make some modest progress towards promoting it at home.

Part of the explanation for the Canadian paradox (international free trade, internal protectionism) involves legal procedure. The federal government may be able to proceed with an international agreement with a much lower level of provincial consent than is necessary to make progress on internal trade. Like the federal trade and commerce power, the federal power to implement treaties has a curious past and an unclear future. Under the Canadian constitution, the federal executive can enter into any treaty it wishes.[8] In the eyes of international law, the treaty will bind Canada, regardless of any federal-provincial complications. But international treaties do not, by themselves, change Canada's internal law. As far as Canadian constitutional law is concerned, to alter the rights of Canadian citizens within our own borders, there must be an enactment of a duly authorized legislature. Can Parliament implement a treaty in an area that is ordinarily within provincial jurisdiction?

In the Labour Conventions case,[9] the Privy Council said no; the authority to implement treaties strictly follows the ordinary division of powers under the Canadian constitution. In doing so, the court reversed an early Privy Council decision in the Radio Reference,[10] which found that Parliament could implement treaties entered into by the federal government, even in areas of provincial jurisdiction. Each position has its problems. The Labour Conventions rule leaves the federal government unable to consistently ensure that its international commitments are honoured domestically. To the extent that a treaty addresses a matter within provincial authority, a single recalcitrant province can, apparently, violate the treaty and render Canada's federal government liable in international law for the consequences. The rule in the Radio case, on the other hand, might have enabled the federal government to use international treaties for extensive intrusions in provincial matters.

Canadian courts ought to be seeking a new rule in the middle ground. Such a rule would hold that Parliament can implement certain treaties, even in areas of provincial jurisdiction, depending on a number of factors. Among them would be:

- did the federal government enter into the treaty merely as an excuse for interfering with provincial jurisdiction?

- is the implementing legislation actually required by the treaty or could Parliament have implemented the treaty in a manner less injurious to provincial jurisdiction?

- how much interference with provincial autonomy does the implementing legislation actually inflict?

- is the treaty primarily directed towards matters, such as international trade and commerce, that are squarely within federal jurisdiction? If so, the federal order should be permitted some latitude in dealing with the minority of matters that would ordinarily be within provincial jurisdiction.

In any event, let it be supposed that Parliament does not have any authority to implement free trade agreements in matters involving provincial jurisdiction. The fact would remain that most of the issues in a modern free trade agreement, such as tariffs and customs administration, are within the exclusive authority of the federal government. Even when provincial cooperation is required, few Canadian provinces are eager to take responsibility for violating Canada's duties under international law.

By contrast, obtaining agreement on free trade is a tortuous matter, both legally and politically. A constitutional amendment to entrench free trade norms would require the consent of at least seven provinces with half the population, and up to three provinces could "opt out" and thereby virtually negate the practical and symbolic effect of the agreement. A voluntary political accord on free trade cannot pretend to be effective and unifying if any of the largest four provinces were to reject it.

EXERCISING THE FEDERAL POWER OVER TRADE AND COMMERCE

Even if the Canadian constitution were amended to include some "thou shalt nots" on internal trade, enforceable by the courts, the system would remain inadequate. The construction of any economic union requires positive and creative action as well. A fully-integrated economic union must have a central bank and monetary system, and common or harmonized rules on the laws that affect trade and commerce.

In forming a "more perfect [economic] union," a question of fundamental importance is this: to what extent is it legally possible for the federal order of government to proceed unilaterally? The credible threat of unilateral action on the economic union might be a useful tool in persuading provinces to honour the Agreement on Internal Trade (discussed in the next part of this chapter) and to broaden its scope and toughen its enforcement mechanisms. If the threat fails, Parliament may want to impose progress from above. Could it do so?

In the United States, the American Congress has sweeping authority to promote internal economic integration under the Interstate Commerce clause.[11] The constitution of the European Union, the Treaty of Rome,[12] specifically authorizes the central legislative authorities to enact binding, unionwide norms that would establish common or harmonized standards in areas of law such as business, labour, mutual recognition of educational and occupational credentials, transportation, the environment, and taxation.

The story of federal authority over the economic union in Canada is surprising and disappointing. Since the intent of the framers has been largely frustrated by judicial interpretation. This story deserves a brief detour, for, as discussed below, I will suggest that the time has come for Canadian courts to expand their definition of the federal "trade and commerce"[13] power so as to indeed permit more scope for unilateral federal action to perfect the Canadian economic union.

To begin at the beginning: the *Constitution Act, 1867,* appears to have been designed to create an economic union in which leadership would be exercised by the federal order of government. Various provisions limit the ability of provinces to interfere with interprovincial trade and commerce. The constitution guaranteed free movement of goods across provincial boundaries (s. 121). In every case where that authority is assigned to a province, it is limited to matters within the province. Provinces are barred from legislating with respect to indirect taxes (such as customs and excise taxes) whose effects would be passed on in an identifiable form to parties outside the province.[14] Any transportation or communication operation that crosses a provincial boundary is placed under federal jurisdiction.[15] Parliament is authorized to declare even a local operation to be "for the general advantage of Canada" and assume legislative authority over it.[16] The federal executive is also given the authority to veto, in its discretion, any new piece of legislation that emerges from a provincial legislature.[17]

The federal order of government is given the affirmative authority to regulate any matter that is not within the list of exclusive provincial powers. A list of federal powers is included, but it is supposed to be "for greater certainty," but not in any way to impair the overall scope of federal authority.[18] The items on the list are predominantly economic in nature. Parliament has broad authority over taxation, money, banking, and "the regulation of trade and commerce." As the American Constitution had used the more modest mandate of "interstate commerce" to the federal level, it is a reasonable inference that the drafters of the Canadian constitution had in mind a very broad mandate for the federal level. Parliament was specifically authorized to exercise authority over areas of private law where national uniformity was considered important, including bankruptcy and intellectual property.

It is no doubt true that the framers of the constitution imagined some limits on federal authority in the interests of preserving provincial authority, and, in particular, ensuring Quebec could retain its civil law system. Parliament was authorized to render the private laws of the common law provinces uniform — with the consent of those provinces — but it did not occur to the framers that Quebec would ever wish to see its own system entirely supplanted. Nonetheless, a novice reader of the Canadian constitution would likely conclude that the federal government was to have broad authority to promote the Canadian economic union.

The Canadian constitution does not expressly establish the principle that the division of powers would be interpreted and ultimately settled by court decisions. It is possible that the framers thought that the system would be primarily, or perhaps exclusively, policed by the system of disallowance;[19] the British executive could veto overreaching federal laws, the federal executive could veto overreaching provincial laws. In any event, the courts took it for granted that they would have their say on the meaning of the *Constitution Act, 1867,* and the Judicial Committee of the Privy Council — which once served as the supreme court for all the colonies and dominions — exercised its role with an effect that was devastating for federal jurisdiction.

There are a variety of possible explanations for the Privy Council's anti-centralist approach, and no certainty as to which ones were actually at play. As a key member of the court, Viscount Haldane played a major anti-centralist role. Perhaps he was convinced of the provincialist cause as a result of having earlier argued some cases for the provinces as a lawyer. Haldane was much attracted by the philosophy of Hegel,[20] and perhaps Haldane liked the idea of bolstering the provincial side of the power balance in Canada, thereby keeping the federal-provincial dialectic in robust operation. Haldane had also been Secretary of War for Britain, and perhaps he was anxious to keep the dominions within the orbit of the imperial centre; doing so would have been facilitated by keeping the central governments relatively weak.

Some decentralist scholars of the Canadian constitution might suggest that no extra-legal explanation is needed for Haldane and the Privy Council; the original constitution of Canada, they would say, was intended to maintain a reasonably equal balance between federal and provincial authority, and Haldane and his colleagues were legally correct.

In any event, the first major blow to the federal trade and commerce power took place in *Citizen's Insurance v. Parsons*.[21] The case was actually about a very modest point: could Ontario pass a consumer protection law that applied to fire insurance contracts in Ontario? The insurance companies had argued that such legislation "amounted to regulation of trade and commerce" and so was within the exclusive authority of Parliament.

Sir Montague Smith wrote the judgement for the court in the Parsons case. Taking his cue from the terms of the *Constitution Act, 1867,* which repeatedly referred to areas of "exclusive" authority, Smith figured that every piece of legislation must either be within the potential authority of Parliament or of the provinces. In modern times, Canadian courts have tended to find that a great many areas can be regulated by *both* the federal and provincial orders of government, e.g., drunk driving can be regulated by Parliament as a criminal law matter and by the provinces as a highway safety matter. But Smith felt he had to establish conclusively that Parliament did not have the authority to pass the sort of statute that Ontario had passed.

Even at that point, Montague Smith had an easy out; he could simply have said that Parliament could not use its trade and commerce authority to deal with a single industry in a single province. In fact, Smith characterized his own conclusion in these modest terms, and his other comments about the trade and commerce power are tentative and speculative. Nonetheless, they have been taken as the canonical statement of the scope of the federal trade and commerce power. For a century, the Canadian case law has tended to start with Montague Smith's definition of the power, rather than the actual text and structure of the constitution.

Montague Smith arrived at his definition through a series of steps which at first seem to follow a rigorous, quasi-mathematical logic, but which on closer examination prove little or nothing. Smith's conclusions were that the trade and commerce power actually consists of only three branches of authority:

1. "political arrangements with respect to trade requiring the sanction of Parliament."

2. regulation of trade in matters of interprovincial concern;

3. general regulation of trade affecting the whole dominion.

The meaning of the first branch is not clear. When he first introduced the concept, Montague Smith referred to "trade with foreign governments," so evidently he had in mind that Parliament might have to implement international trade treaties.[22] Perhaps Montague Smith did not use the word "treaties" because he was not sure whether Canada had fully acquired the status of an independent state under international law. Some have argued, perhaps too optimistically, that a modern court would interpret the first branch as a full mandate for Parliament to implement treaties such as NAFTA, even in areas of provincial jurisdiction. If they are right, we would reach a doctrine for which there is very little textual support in the constitution — i.e., that Parliament can freely implement trade treaties in areas of provincial jurisdiction, but has no similar authority with respect to any other kind of treaty. It would make more sense for the courts to arrive at a doctrine that would apply to all areas. It would permit Parliament to implement treaties in areas of provincial jurisdiction, but only on certain conditions. An outline of such a doctrine has been suggested earlier in this chapter.

Under the second branch, the courts have not allowed Parliament to regulate interprovincial transactions merely because they are part of an industry that is interprovincial or international in character. Parliament has been allowed to regulate cross-border transactions, but that authority would exist quite apart from the trade and commerce power. Provinces can only legislate matters that are "within the province," and federal authority automatically applies whenever a province is barred from acting. To give some real life to the second branch, the courts could hold that the power authorizes Parliament to insist on compliance with norms that are similar to those included in domestic and international trade agreements, e.g., mutual recognition of occupational credentials, non-discrimination in government procurement, or non-discriminatory treatment of out-of-province emanations once they have entered the local stream of commerce. The fact that a norm is typically included in domestic and international trade agreements suggests that it is indeed a trade and commerce matter, that it concerns a matter where the conduct of one party is of substantial interest to another, and that the norm does not amount to an unreasonable limitation on the sovereign authority of any party.

The meaning of the third branch is still being worked out by the courts. Montague Smith seems to have formulated it on this basis: in the list of federal powers, trade and commerce was placed right near the beginning, with a group of other matters of national and general concern. The framers therefore had in mind "regulations regulating general trade and commerce" as opposed to "minute rules for regulating particular trades."[23] Montague Smith's reasoning in this regard is specious. Trade and commerce is placed with other important subject matters, such as taxation. No one has ever suggested that Parliament's power over taxation does not include the ability to make very specific rules for specific industries. In principle, the fact that the subject is of national and general importance hardly means that it should be addressed, or even can be effectively dealt with, by means of general norms. If you are given authority to manage a forest, you may not be able to adopt and implement a norm that applies equally to all trees, let alone all vegetation.

Finally, in his interpretation of Montague Smith's third branch of the trade and commerce power, Viscount Haldane was prepared to allow very little scope to the central order. Unless there was a need for trade and commerce legislation that amounted to a national emergency, legislation would not be characterized as satisfying the test.

More recently the Supreme Court of Canada has cautiously revived the third branch.[24] The court has said that five tests must be considered in deciding whether Parliament can act under its general trade and commerce power:

- the enactment amounts to a national regulatory scheme;
- the enactment establishes a national regulatory agency;
- the enactment is concerned with trade in general rather than an aspect of a particular business;
- the provinces do not have constitutional authority to pass the enactment;
- if one or more provinces proceed with the enactment, the failure of other provinces to follow suit would render their effort futile.

The presence or absence of any single factor is not decisive, according to the Supreme Court of Canada, in arriving at the overall determination of whether an enactment is a legitimate use of the federal power over "general trade and commerce affecting the whole dominion."

The first two tests are sensible. The constitution speaks of the *"Regulation of Trade and Commerce."* If an enactment establishes norms that apply between private parties, and are enforced by private lawsuits, it would seem to interfere with provincial authority over Property and Civil Rights.

The third test should be given far less importance. As already explained, to deal with the forest effectively, you sometimes have to address individual species of tree. The requirement that a federal norm apply to all industries, rather than specific ones, has led to absurd results. The Supreme Court of Canada has said that Parliament cannot define and enforce a national product standard with respect to an item that never crosses a provincial boundary.[25] It makes no difference, apparently, that the item is also traded interprovincially, and that it is costly and confusing for producers and consumers to have to contend with differing provincial standards. Obviously, product standards vary from product to product.

The fourth and fifth tests, according to the judge who formulated them (former Chief Justice Dickson) are the most important ones. They seem to draw on a subsidiarity rationale: that is, the idea that local commerce should presumptively be dealt with by provincial governments, unless there is some special call for national regulation. That idea is not unreasonable; in the Maastricht Treaty, the parties to the European Union agreed that matters should generally be left to national governments, unless the "scale or scope of the effects"[26] requires a Union-level response.

Tests four and five, however, suggest a version of the subsidiarity principle that is unduly biased against the central government. The operative question seems to be: if most of the provinces wanted to deal with this problem, would they be able to do so? Or would their efforts fail, due to constitutional limitations on provinces or the undermining effect of hold-out provinces? It may be that provinces could deal with a problem, but they choose not to — at great cost to the public interest. It may be that some provinces can proceed by themselves — but the overall national interest is undermined by the passivity of others. A more balanced formulation of subsidiarity would be this: Does the nature of the commerce issue involved here create a strong need for a coherent, nationwide, policy?

Suppose now that there are frequent violations of the Agreement on Internal Trade, and that scheduled talks to expand and toughen the agreement produce few results. Parliament then enacts its own legislation to promote the internal union. It applies to both provinces and to industries that ordinarily operate within provincial jurisdiction. The federal legislation includes a number of general norms, which apply to goods, services, labour, and investment. The norms apply to the federal and provincial governments and agencies, and to private enterprises and their self-regulating bodies. Included among the norms are these:

- no one can engage in commercial discrimination on the basis of province of origin;
- laws or industrial practices should not obstruct internal trade more than is necessary to achieve their legitimate objectives;
- government and industry must give due recognition to the educational and occupational credentials acquired in other provinces;
- government and industry must give products and people from Canada treatment that is at least as favourable as that which is promised to outsiders under various international trade agreements or which is extended to foreigners in practice.

While these norms presumptively apply to all industries, the hypothetical federal enactment does include a variety of special provisions for particular industries. These special provisions may provide for more detail on how the norms apply, or allow for various exemptions and qualifications with respect to the application of the general norms.

The hypothetical enactment, as described above, creates a national regulatory body, the Internal Trade Commission, with the authority to hear complaints and order remedies pursuant to the legislation. Ought the courts to uphold such a provision? My answer would be that the courts should find such an enactment to be a valid exercise of federal authority. Their primary justification ought to be the federal Trade and Commerce power.

In interpreting and applying that power, the courts ought not to consider
Montague Smith's "three branches" one at a time. Instead, they should consider the combined effect of the three aspects of federal authority as outlined
by Montague Smith.

Under Smith's first branch, Parliament has primary authority over international trade policy and agreements. It should have the accompanying authority
to cope with the most urgent consequences of those agreements on the Canadian economy and polity, and, specifically, the vital need to ensure that
Canadians can trade with each other at least as freely as with outsiders. Under
the second branch, i.e., trade in matters of interprovincial concern, the courts
should allow Parliament to insist on norms such as non-discrimination against
residents of other provinces and due recognition of occupational credentials
acquired in another province.

As argued earlier, under the third branch, i.e., general trade and commerce,
the courts should recognize that internal trade barriers are a matter in which
there is a special justification for intervention by the central authority. Local
authorities are too likely to yield to local pressures for protectionism. The
central authority is most likely to have the broad national perspective needed
to push for internal free trade. The federal government also has a bigger revenue base, more levers of legal authority and a more diverse electorate from
which to draw support than any single province. As a result, the federal government is more likely to be able to resist protectionist pressures from any
particular special interest group.

In considering the third branch, the courts should not condemn the federal
enactment merely because it contains specific provisions for various industries, as well as broad national norms. As already discussed, a purist insistence
that problems be dealt with by applying general norms can render the federal
government incapable of enacting legislation that is intelligent and effective.

THE CONTENTS OF THE AGREEMENT ON INTERNAL TRADE

From the broad discussion of the legal parameters for the application of existing — and potential — constitutional principles to the subject of internal trade,
we now turn to examine the specifics of the agreement which took effect on
1 July 1995.

The Agreement on International Trade is closely modelled, in both form
and substance, on international trade agreements, including the GATT[27] and
NAFTA.[28] The first three chapters set out operating principles, definitions and
constitutional powers and responsibilities. For our purposes here, these can
be skipped.

Chapter 4: General Rules sets out the basic principles of the agreement. These
principles or General Rules, are phrased so as to be applicable to the four

areas that are commonly identified as being the pillars of an ideal free trade agreement: free movement of goods, services, people, and investment.[29] They include: "reciprocal non-discrimination," "free entry," "no obstacles," "reconciliation" and "transparency." These terms are discussed below.

Reciprocal non-discrimination combines two of the founding principles of the GATT system: most-favoured nations and national treatment. Under the most-favoured nations principle,[30] each party to the GATT must give every GATT partner the best treatment it extends to the goods of any other party. This most-favoured nations idea is a *force multiplier* for freer trade because the trade liberality among the whole gamut of GATT partners must always be ratcheted up to a new peak established with respect to the gains achieved by any individual GATT partner. Under the national treatment principle[31] of the original GATT, once goods are admitted into a state, they must be treated as favourably as the state's own products.

Under the reciprocal non-discrimination principle[32] of the AIT, each party can demand that its own emanations (goods, services, people or investments) be given the best treatment that another AIT partner affords to a local equivalent or an equivalent from another province. For example, if Quebec allows locally produced wines to be sold in grocery stores, it would have to permit the same of Ontario or British Columbia wines. Manitoba may not produce any wines, but if it allows Quebec wines to be sold at the annual folk festival, it would have to do the same for British Columbia or Ontario wines.

Free entry means that the emanations of a province must be admitted into another. In other words, it is made clear that the reciprocal non-discrimination principle cannot be evaded by barring goods from initial entry into a party's local market. Depending on how they are interpreted, the norms of non-discrimination and free entry would still not necessarily be sufficient to prescribe a functioning regime of internal free trade. A party might maintain legal measures that extend the same treatment to all, but whose practical effect is to stifle imports.

For example, suppose that Alberta adopted a law that prohibited the sale of bottled water that falls short of a certain standard of purity. Further suppose that the laws are easily met by Alberta products, which come from glaciers, but not by products from many other provinces, which come from springs. The scientific evidence is that the purity law does not have any significant effect on protecting public health. A regime of free trade might reasonably require Alberta to modify its laws so as to facilitate the entry of out-of-province competitors.

Perhaps to address the sort of concern just identified, among others, the AIT expressly states the principle of *no obstacles*: a party must ensure that any measure it adopts does not operate to create an obstacle to internal trade.[33] It is not clear whether the principle of no obstacles would apply to a measure that equally stifles local and imported trade. An affirmative answer makes more sense to me, but others might insist that a local measure is immune from challenge under the AIT regime if it does as much harm to local trade as it does to imports.

The *General Rule of Reconciliation* means that parties are committed to reducing trade friction caused by varying standards. The parties undertake to reduce these measures through means such as harmonization (making standards identical or similar) and mutual recognition (parties accept each other's standards for their own internal purposes). The General Rule of transparency means that parties undertake to make their rules and operating procedures public and readily accessible to other parties and individuals.

Of the five General Rules stated above (reciprocal non-discrimination, free entry, no obstacles, reconciliation and transparency) the first three may be avoided as exceptions provided that they meet the criterion set out for legitimacy. The AIT enumerates these exceptions. A free-trade norm can be infringed if:

- the objective behind the measure is legitimate. The AIT clearly states that except where expressly provided to the contrary, the protection of a party's production is not a legitimate objective. The objectives that are legitimate are stipulated: public order and safety, protection of the health and safety of humans, plants and animals, consumer protection, protection of the health, safety and well-being of workers, and affirmative action programs for disadvantaged groups;

- the measure does not unduly impair free trade in emanations of a party that meet the objective;

- the measure does not limit free trade more than is necessary to achieve its objective;

- the measure is not a disguised restriction on trade.

It must be emphasized that the basic rules of the AIT do not seem to call for a simple balancing of the social benefits of regulations versus the costs flowing from the obstruction of internal trade. There is no clear and specific signal to that effect in the AIT itself. On the contrary, the overall tenor of the AIT is cautious and tentative; it does not characterize itself as legally binding, it is limited in scope and replete with exceptions and qualification.

The basic norms of the AIT seem to be more subtle: given a particular objective by a party, which can generally be as demanding as a party wishes, the party must choose the means of achieving that objective that does not discriminate against outsiders or unnecessarily limit the flow of trade. A party's discretion to define its objectives might not be absolute. One can imagine a party defining its objectives in such a detailed and exacting fashion that it could sustain any measure it chose. The overall spirit and coherence of the AIT would be better served by holding that a party might have to accept at least a very minor modification of its objectives if doing so would produce very substantial gains to free trade.

In interpreting whether the means to an objective unnecessarily limits free trade, dispute-settling panels will have to make some subtle judgement calls.[34] It will frequently be possible to point to an alternative that would be somewhat less obstructive of free trade, but which would be somewhat more costly in terms of regulatory complexity or enforcement.

Under the *Charter of Rights of Freedoms*, a legislative measure can infringe certain fundamental values.[35] (such as free expression) if the social benefits of the measure outweigh the damage it inflicts on basic rights, and if the measure passes the minimal impairment test, that is, there is no alternative measure that would achieve the same objectives but at a lower cost to basic rights. In interpreting the minimal impairment test, Canadian courts have decided that a measure cannot be condemned merely because a judge can imagine an alternative which the judge considers slightly less damaging to basic rights.[36] Each alternative has its own advantages and disadvantages, and a legislature must be allowed a certain margin of appreciation in determining which balance is the most suitable.[37]

None of the AIT's general principles apply directly to any actual trade dispute. Only when a specific chapter of the AIT addresses an issue do the principles come into play. Even then, the application of the principles may in large part be blunted by specific exceptions. There are large inconsistencies in how different chapters treat such issues as whether the AIT applies to municipalities and non-governmental agencies, and how much leeway is allowed for governments to depart from free-trade principles in order to pursue certain policy objectives.

From the discussion of general principles, then, we now turn to an examination of the specific chapters of the AIT.

An annex to chapter four deals with *standards and related measures*. The AIT requires parties to reconcile their standards with respect to goods and services. The definition of "low calorie" peanut butter, for example, may vary from province to province, depending on voluntary industry standards or government regulations.

The AIT says that governments should:

- avoid adopting standards that are more trade restrictive than necessary in terms of their legitimate objectives;

- where appropriate and possible, adopt standards that are based on national or international standards;

- provide expeditious and non-discriminatory avenues for demonstrating that an imported good or service conforms to a party's own standards;

- recognize the standards of other parties, or provide written reasons for refusing to do so;

- work with other parties to harmonize standards (make them identical, or at least minimize the differences).

Annex 405.2 of the AIT requires parties to:

- avoid adopting or maintaining regulatory regimes that damage free trade more than is necessary to achieve a legitimate objective;

- encourage non-governmental regulatory bodies to do the same;

- consult with any other party that believes that a difference in regulatory regimes is creating a substantial obstacle to free trade, and attempt to achieve a mutually satisfactory resolution.

The dispute resolution procedure in the AIT does not apply to conflicts over the interpretation of the commitments in this annex.

Chapter 5: Procurement. The buying of goods and services by government provides enormous opportunities to distribute wealth and opportunity. There is a long Canadian tradition of patronage (rewarding the individual corporate friends of government) and porkbarrelling (attempting to purchase electoral support by funnelling money into selected areas in which voters reside). In addition, governments may attempt in good faith to stimulate the local economy by buying locally.

Whether the intentions of governments are good or bad, the overall effect of "buy local" policies on the Canadian economy is very likely to be negative. Providers of goods and services in one part of the country may benefit from local favouritism, but suffer from the local preferences carried out by other jurisdictions.[38] The elimination of competition from out-of-province tenderers raises the price that governments pay, which may result in higher taxes or poorer services for other sectors of the economy.

As procurement constitutes some of the most powerful levers of government policy and politicking, it is not surprising that it has proven difficult for governments to surrender their freedom of action. The AIT follows the same cautious path that is contained in the U.S.-Canada Free Trade Agreement and the new General Agreement on Trade in Services.[39] Each of them provides a code of non-discriminatory conduct with respect to government purchases. When the code applies to a purchasing entity, that entity must establish an open tendering process. The entities of other parties have the right to participate in the competition on equal terms. All of the agreements provide that a monetary threshold must be met before the code kicks in. In the case of the AIT, the procurement code does not operate on government purchases of goods that are worth less than $25,000, or services and construction worth less than $100,000.

Each agreement provides an appeal process for dissatisfied tenderers. In the AIT system, the dissatisfied party can appeal to an impartial dispute-settling panel or reviewing authority, which can assess whether the AIT has been breached, and can recommend an accommodation. "Recommend" in this circumstance means that the decision of the appeal body is not legally binding, a fact that may deter dissatisfied parties with meritorious complaints. After an enterprise has spent its money and hopes on preparing a tender, and then been spurned by a government that has acted unfairly, should it risk more resources in the hopes that the same government will accept a non-binding opinion by an impartial body?

The AIT does authorize a government party to take countermeasures against another party (government) that has shown a disregard for the government procurement regime. But an individual party cannot count on its own government to have the will or the economic power to effectively retaliate in such a manner.

In none of the agreements is the ban on discriminatory treatment all-encompassing. Instead, each party to the various agreements provides a list of government departments or government-controlled entities which must engage in non-discriminatory purchasing. The list of government-controlled entities to which the agreement applies varies drastically from province to province. Quebec, for example, has included a long list of government departments and agencies, but has excluded from the application of the procurement code two enormous entities: the Caisse de Dépôt and Hydro-Québec.[40] Over time it is hoped that parties will unilaterally add to their lists, or negotiate reciprocal additions with their trade agreement partners.

Chapter 6: Investment. This chapter specifically applies the general norms of the AIT, such as reciprocal non-discrimination, to the area of investment. Parties are given until the end of 1995 to compile a list of their programs that they can exempt unilaterally from the application of these norms.

Chapter 6 also lists some particular rules concerning investment. Parties are prohibited from requiring that an investor be a resident of a province in order to do business there. The parties must further undertake to try to reconcile their laws with respect to the local registration of companies who are incorporated elsewhere.

Chapter 6 also addresses the issue of beggar-thy-neighbour incentives to investment. Some heated controversies have erupted in Canada of late over efforts by various provinces to lure investment by offering incentives. The consequence may be the loss of existing or potential investment in other provinces. Private sector concerns are able to play off provinces against each other and may enjoy the spectacle of bidding wars between provinces over how generous the welcoming package will be.

The "Code of Conduct on Incentives"[41] provides that parties may generally continue to use incentives as part of their economic development programs. In doing so they must take into account the interests of other provinces. Parties promise to "endeavour to refrain" from certain kinds of incentives, including those that would promote enterprises that are not economically viable or add more productive capacity than is warranted by market conditions. They must also try to steer clear of "engaging in bidding wars to attract prospective investors seeking the most beneficial incentive package."[42]

The code provides that the "endeavour to refrain" commitments cannot be referred to dispute-settling panels. The investment code is, in principle, one of the most innovative, needed, and laudable aspects of the new AIT. It is unfortunate that the parties have reduced most of the norms in the code to the level of hortatory rhetoric. The code does, however, contain two outright prohibitions. First, a party cannot use incentives to lure an enterprise from one province to another; second, if another province is tendering a contract, a party cannot help a favoured enterprise outbid its competitors. These prohibitions actually are subject to the formal process of dispute resolution.

As with so many AIT matters, the parties promise to carry out further work. They will cooperate in compiling an annual report on the major incentive programs offered by each party.

Chapter 7: Labour Mobility. Chapters of the AIT often start off by enunciating powerful and inspiring norms, and then tail off with a spate of qualifications and exceptions. Chapter 7, by contrast, begins with the exceptions. It says that most of the general norms of the AIT, including reciprocal non-discrimination and no obstacles, do not apply. Furthermore, the chapter does not even address "difference in social policy measures, including labour standards and codes, minimum wages, unemployment insurance qualification periods and social assistance benefits."[43]

Chapter 7 does, however, offer several specific commitments. The parties do promise not to make local residence a condition of obtaining employment opportunities, and not to discriminate against out-of-province employees. The prohibition on local favouritism is subject to laws that have legitimate objectives and do not impair labour mobility more than is necessary to achieve those purposes.

It is not clear whether, in general, promotion of local employment can be one of the "legitimate" objectives that justifies discrimination against non-resident workers. The definition of "legitimate objectives" in chapter 4 includes "worker well-being" but excludes "protection of local production." Does protection of local jobs count as the former or the latter? Chapter 7 does make it clear that in case of a "severe economic dislocation" a party can excuse a party from honouring one or more of its chapter 7 obligations.[44]

The most important commitment in chapter 7 is that parties undertake mutual recognition of each other's occupational qualifications.[45] The regulation of professions and trades in Canada is almost entirely within provincial jurisdiction. A person can qualify for an occupation in one province, and then find it impossible to work in another province without going through a prohibitively long and expensive process of re-qualification. The damage to an individual's ability to make the most of his talents can be grievous, and Canadian society may sustain a wholly unwarranted loss of economic productivity.

Under the AIT, each party undertakes to examine its occupational qualifications, and determine whether they have a high degree of commonality with those of other parties. If so, a party must recognize those qualifications. If there is a moderate or low level of commonality, parties should strive to revise their standards so as to make them mutually acceptable. In the interim, each party will continue to apply its own occupational qualifications to workers who have arrived from another province, but in doing so will try to make accommodations that give appropriate recognition to the skills and experience the worker has acquired elsewhere.

Most professions and occupations are self-regulated primarily by administrative agencies operated by persons in the sector, rather than by government itself. In the AIT, the parties promise, through appropriate measures to seek compliance with its provisions by municipal governments and non-governmental organizations. Self-regulating bodies in the various provinces can be highly protectionist, and it will likely be necessary for provincial governments to take strong measures to ensure compliance. Each province might wish to consider setting up a specialized administrative tribunal which would monitor compliance with the mobility provisions of the AIT and which would have the authority to order them, where necessary, to enhance their recognition of out-of-province credentials and experience. Better still, the federal and provincial governments could establish a single national administrative tribunal with the authority to oversee and order progress on the part of various self-regulating bodies.

Chapter 7 of the AIT concludes with a commitment that the Forum of Labour Market Ministers will meet annually to review the operation of the chapter, including the extent of cooperation with its objectives by non-governmental organizations.[46]

Chapter 8: Consumer-related Measures and Standards. This chapter applies the basic AIT norms (reciprocal non-discrimination, free entry, no obstacles) to consumer-related standards. It purports to modify, however, the definition of the permissible exceptions to those norms. Ordinarily, the minimal impairment test requires that a measure which has a legitimate objective be no more trade restrictive than necessary to achieve that legitimate objective. In chapter 8, "legitimate objective" is replaced with "the level of consumer protection that it considers appropriate."

As far as I can determine the implication is this: when it comes to consumer protection laws, no other party will be able to undermine a consumer protection regulation merely by claiming that its underlying objective could be achieved in a less trade restrictive way. For example, suppose that British Columbia wished to require that soft drinks and fruit juice must contain less than x percent lead. The practical effect of the measure is to discourage imports from several other provinces, where bottlers use local water that has higher-than-x lead content. These provinces would not be able to mount a challenge on the "minimum impairment" principle.

In the hypothetical situation just cited, objecting provinces would still have the right to rely on the principle that a measure cannot be a disguised barrier to trade. The word "disguised" might be interpreted as suggesting bad faith. If it could somehow be shown that British Columbia had introduced its highly purist anti-lead laws for the purpose of favouring local bottlers, the objecting provinces might be able to prevail. However, finding evidence of a government's motives is difficult, and a dispute settlement panel may, out of sense of diplomacy, be reluctant to making a finding of bad faith even when the evidence is strong. Still, one could imagine circumstances in which the evidence would be almost overwhelming, for example, if it were shown that British Columbia's government had been lobbied extensively by local bottlers, and that the emerging regulations were concerned only with the one contaminant, lead, in which British Columbia waters happen to be unusually pure, while at the same time ignoring other contaminants for which British Columbia waters happen to be on the higher side of normal.

A set of annexes to chapter 8 contain specific commitments by parties to harmonizing consumer standards in three areas: direct selling, upholstered and stuffed articles, and cost-of-credit disclosure.

Chapter 9: Agriculture and Food Products. The regulation of agriculture is almost always a particularly difficult issue in trade negotiations. Farming is always a risky activity since uncontrollable forces of nature, both at home and in competing countries, can drastically vary the economic returns in a given year for the farmer and prices for consumers. There is, accordingly, an unusually strong case for at least some forms of governmental intervention to help stabilize prices. It is not so easy, even in principle, to rule out various forms of subsidies and quotas. Furthermore, farmers can be an exceptionally forceful lobby group for protectionist measures. Most political systems include voting on the basis of geographical constituencies, and farmers usually dominate a large number of such ridings. Finally, it can be difficult to make progress on agriculture at the level of internal or regional trade negotiations when the participants must cope with protectionist measures from competitors in other countries.

Agriculture was the most bitterly contested issue in the Uruguay Round of GATT negotiations. The United States pushed hard for a drastic reduction of protectionism, the European Community (under pressure from France, and in particular, French farmers) resisted. The turbulent state of the world negotiations while the AIT was being negotiated may account in large part for the tentative nature of its provisions.

Chapter 9 of the AIT says that the General Rules do not immediately apply to most agricultural trade. Only with respect to technical barriers to trade (e.g., product standards) do General Rules have immediate effect. With respect to other matters, chapter 9 consists primarily of a work plan:

- parties will not alter their existing laws "so as to restrict internal trade in an agricultural or food good";
- parties will attempt, within five years of the AIT's coming into force, to adopt common national standards on technical issues related to agriculture;
- parties, through their ministers of agriculture, will participate in a review of internal trade barriers to trade in agriculture; and attempt, by 1 September 1997, to adopt a set of measures to reduce internal trade barriers.[47]

As an aside, the world trade negotiations did result in an agreement at the end of 1993, and the results were dramatic. States will have to replace import quotas on agricultural products with tariff barriers. Under NAFTA, it may be illegal for Canada to maintain even tariff barriers with respect to American and Mexican imports. In light of the international trend towards liberalization, Canadian governments should be moving quickly to fill in the "agriculture" chapter of the AIT with some robust commitments to barrier-free internal trade.

Chapter 10: Alcoholic Beverages. Alcoholic beverages have been the subject of exceptionally intensive government regulation and control in Canada. Governments have been anxious about the impact of alcohol on public health and safety and, at the same time, eager to reap the rewards that come from owning a monopoly over a lucrative product.

Chapter 10 of the AIT provides that the General Rules apply to alcoholic beverages — except for right of entry and exit. Perhaps the parties wanted to make it clear that federal laws can continue to require that the trade in wholesale quantities of alcohol be conducted only by provincial monopolies or authorized dealers. The application of the General Rules is made subject to the province-by-province list of exceptions, the collective effect of which does not appear to seriously undermine the liberalizing impact of chapter 10 as a whole.

The results of GATT decisions and of the NAFTA have been to extensively limit the ability of provincial monopolies to engage in protectionist practices at the expense of external competitors. Article 1004(2) of the AIT states that a province must extend the favourable treatment required by international trade agreements to imports from other provinces. This concept (i.e., that the level of internal free trade in Canada must at least match the standard set by international agreements) ought to be a cornerstone of all future developments of the internal market in Canada. If necessary, the federal government ought to unilaterally enact and enforce this principle under the mandate of its "trade and commerce" power.

Chapter 11: Natural Resources Processing. Chapter 12: Energy. Chapter 11 begins by extending the general rules of the AIT to the processing of forestry, fish, and mineral production. It then provides a very broad list of exceptions. The AIT does not apply to measures to lease harvesting rights to private operators, or to conservation measures, or to water in general. In chapter 12, the subject of energy is put off entirely to future negotiations.

As the general rules of the AIT include the right to make exceptions in the pursuit of legitimate objectives, such as conservation, there does not seem to be any objective justification for the debilitating list of exceptions to chapter 11.

No doubt some governments were loathe to accept any constraints in the area of natural resources and energy. These areas are the foundation of a number of provincial economies. Provincial governments own the crown land within their boundaries, which are often vast. There can be a strong government interest as proprietor, in addition to that of regulator and tax harvester.

Precisely because of the high stakes and heavy government entanglement in the resource and energy area, there is a strong temptation for government policy to be influenced by local partisan politics and pressure from powerful private interests. The application of the AIT would have subjected government decision making to more scrutiny and market-oriented discipline, and would have subjected locally powerful special interests to more competition.

Chapter 13: Communications. This area is primarily regulated by the federal government, with the assistance of regulatory agencies such as the Canadian Radio-television and Telecommunications Commission and the Canadian Transport Commission. Federal policy of late has tended to favour opening up markets to competition. In the AIT, the parties agree that the General Rules apply to communications, and that provincial monopolies in the area will not use their positions to engage in anti-competitive practices.

Chapter 14: Transportation. With respect to railway and air transport, the predominant authority of the federal government has enabled some uniformity of safety and business regulations. With respect to highway transport, however, the mixture of federal and provincial authority has produced a complex and costly mix of regulations. An interprovincial trucking business may be regulated by the federal government with respect to its business and labour relations, but may have to cope with a tangle of provincial laws that are intended to ensure that drivers are qualified and that vehicles are operated in a manner that is safe and does not inflict excessive damage to the roads and surrounding environment.

Chapter 14 is one of the more inspiring chapters for the AIT. It enhances the principles of the General Rules by stating clearly that the parties aim to produce a "seamless, integrated, Canadian transportation system" that is safe, responsive to the needs of shippers and travellers and that will promote "a competitive, productive and sustainable economy throughout Canada." The parties promise not only to honour chapter 14 themselves, but to ensure compliance by crown corporations and municipalities.

In several transport sectors, including air and rail, Parliament has predominant authority, and the federal level of government has been able to reduce complexity and costs by enacting uniform national legislation and moving towards free and open market policies. The AIT may have a greater beneficial impact with respect to highway transport, where the federal-provincial division of responsibility has resulted in a tangled web of varying regulations. Parliament does have extensive authority to regulate the business of interprovincial transport, but the provinces have primary authority over matters such as highway safety.

Chapter 15: Environmental Protection. This chapter extends the General Rules of the AIT to environmental protection. While affirming the usual norm that parties can set their own particular standards, as long as they avoid unnecessary restrictions on trade, the AIT calls for all parties to maintain high standards and to improve them over time.

Chapter 16: Institutional Provisions. Chapter 17: Dispute Settlement Procedures. These chapters establish the institutional framework for implementing and developing the AIT. A Committee on Internal Trade, a federal-provincial committee at the ministerial level, has the general supervisory mandate and must meet at least once a year. The chair of the committee is rotated among the parties.[48] The dispute-resolution provisions of the AIT, which are established in chapter 17, raise the issue of whether the whole deal is not a "toothless tiger."

Actually, given its limited scope of application and many exceptions, the AIT is a smallish and rather mild-mannered tiger. When it becomes clear that the terms of the agreement are offended, the guilty party is expected, as a matter of honour, to mend its ways. If it does not do so, the agreement may be cited to bring public attention to the offender's shameful conduct. If the offender is still unrepentant, the agreement can provide no further relief except that the victimized party is authorized to retaliate.

In other words, the AIT generally works like this: if one party believes that another has breached the agreement, the party can request the alleged offender to engage in consultations with a view to reaching an amicable settlement. If that process fails, the complaining party can refer the matter to a dispute resolution panel. This impartial body is supposed to determine whether the AIT has been breached. The offending party is supposed to comply with its recommendations. If the party fails to comply, the panel report will be made public, thereby subjecting the offender to public embarrassment. The issue will also be placed on the agenda of the trade committee's annual meetings, where it will remain until the problem is resolved. The complaining party also has the option of retaliating against the wrongdoer by denying it a trade benefit of equivalent value.

The retaliatory remedy is unlikely to be used often or effectively. A party that restricts trade with another is likely to injure its own economic interests. Third parties can also move in and scoop up the benefits of the bilateral trade war. If two provinces deny each other access to government contracts, bidders from other provinces may take advantage of the reduced competition and charge higher prices.

It could be possible to structure a retaliatory system that would be less burdensome to the innocent party and more chastening to the offender, e.g., require all the parties to collectively retaliate against a wrongdoer. The problem would remain, however, that retaliation is a economically and emotionally destructive means of obtaining compliance.

An alternative approach would be to make some, or all, of the norms of the AIT legally binding. Complaints of breach could be brought directly to the courts, or alternatively, ad hoc panels could be authorized to register their decisions as court orders. A wrongdoing party would be presented with a court declaration that its conduct has been in breach of its legal obligations, with a legally binding order to pay appropriate compensation for the consequences of its wrong. The AIT norms instead amount to a political agreement, and as such governments will feel themselves justified in violating it more than if it were in some degree legally binding.

Chapter 18: Other Provisions. True to the hesitant spirit of the AIT as a whole, its final chapter stipulates further exceptions to the General Rule. Regional economic developments, at both the federal and provincial levels, are exempted from the application of the AIT. The exemption applies as long as two conditions are met: the measure does not "impair unduly" the market access of another party, and the measure is not more trade restrictive than necessary to achieve its objectives.[49]

As regional development can be the excuse for porkbarelling programs that result in massive economic waste, it is disappointing that the AIT does not impose better defined constraints on such programs, and put more of a burden on governments to explain and justify them on a case-by-case basis.

Chapter 18 also contains a wholesale exemption for any measure that applies to culture or cultural industries. Even the North American Free Trade Agreement does not allow for such a sweeping exemption. Does it make any sense for provinces to be more protected from the cultural influences of other Canadians than from foreigners?

Measures with respect to Aboriginal Peoples are also entirely exempted from the application of the AIT.[50] Granted that the issue of aboriginal self-government is currently under discussion, it may have been premature to address aboriginal issues in the AIT, and representatives of aboriginal governments should be at the table when the matter is finally addressed in a Canadian free trade agreement. On the other hand, the issue cannot be avoided indefinitely. Free trade between aboriginal communities and the rest of Canada may be essential for improving prosperity in many of those communities, and for checking the tendency of the local government to completely dominate both political and economic life. Furthermore, Canadian policymakers must eventually address the extent to which aboriginal communities will operate as tax or regulatory havens.

CONCLUSION

The AIT contains some welcome features, such as the commitment to expedite the mutual recognition of occupational credentials, and the reduction of favouritism in government procurement. The agreement is disappointing, however, in many respects.

The form of the agreement will make it unnecessarily difficulty to understand and use. It is lengthy, sometimes legalistic, and riddled with lists of exceptions and qualifications. Various chapters define the meaning or application of the most basic norms in subtly, even obscurely, different ways. The scope of its application is too limited; an AIT should generally apply to all levels of government, including municipal governments, and to the private sector as well. Too many sectors (culture, agriculture, energy) and governmental activities (taxation, regional economic development) are immune, or almost entirely immune, from its applications. There are too many detailed exceptions in the areas to which the AIT does have some effect. The enforceability of the provisions of the AIT are also weak; no party can obtain a legally binding declaration that another party is in breach.

The AIT is deficient compared to international trade agreements, such as NAFTA, to which Canada is a party. Canada's economic union should be consistently more integrated than regional and international arrangements. It is sad to report that the AIT in some respects maintains the bizarre and divisive status quo, in which Canadians may find it easier, legally as well as practically, to transact business with foreigners than with residents of other provinces.

Despite the weakness of the AIT, there appear to be strong prudential reasons in favour of the decision by the parties, including the federal government, to proceed with it. At the time of signing, the government of Quebec was heading into an election campaign against an outright separatist opposition party. A concrete demonstration of the creative potential of cooperative federalism was needed. Premier Daniel Johnson characterized the AIT as "a perfect illustration of how federalism should work."[51] It was not an appropriate time for the federal government to threaten unilateral action, and some provincial governments were still smarting from the threats of unilateral action by the Mulroney government during the negotiation of the Charlottetown Accord.[52] The actual enactment of unilateral federal legislation would have soured the atmosphere for further federal-provincial negotiations and provided ammunition for Quebec separatists.[53]

Defenders of the AIT are optimistic about the longer process in which it is only the first step. John Manley, the federal minister of industry, defended the deal in these terms:

> I am convinced that, once this agreement is in place on 1 July of next year, there will be no turning back. But unlike the General Agreement on Tariffs and Trade (GATT), which took 47 years to achieve its current state of imperfection, we shall be able to move ahead surely and quickly.[54]

Such predictions may be the triumph of hope over experience. If the parties do not in fact make rapid progress towards implementing the AIT in its current form, and towards expanding its scope and enforceability in future negotiations, the time for cooperative federalism will be over. The federal government will be obliged to threaten unilateral action, and, if necessary, to carry out that threat. "To deny the legitimacy of federal authority in this respect is nothing less than to deny the existence of the Canadian nation."[55]

NOTES

The author wishes to thank the Legal Research Institute of the University of Manitoba for its support, and to students who have assisted me on my various trade law projects over the past few years, including Denis Guenette, Brian Jones, Allen Kirk and Philip S. Brooks.

1   *Treaty of Rome*, 25 March 1957, art. 3, as amended by the *Single European Act* (SEA), February 1986.

2.   *United States Constitution*, art. 1, s.8(3), (known as the Interstate Commerce clause).

3.   *Murphy v. C.P.R.* [1958] S.C.R. 626, 15 D.L.R. (2d) 145.

4.   Winner v. S.M.T. (Eastern) [1951] S.C.R. 889, at 920.

5.   *Black v. Law Society of Alta.*, [1989]1 S.C.R. 591. and *Hunt v. T&N plc*, [1993]4 S.C.R. 289.

6.   Royal Commission on the Economic Union and Development Prospects for Canada, *Report* (Ottawa: Minister of Supply and Services, 1985), vol.III, ch. 22.

7.   B. Schwartz, *Opting In*, (Hull: Voyageur Publishing, 1992), (see ch. II review of recent constitutional history).

8.   *Letters Patent constituting the office of the Governor General of Canada* , R.S.C. 1985, Appendix II, No.31.

9.   *A.-G. Can. v. A.-G. Ont.* (Labour Conventions) [1937] A.C.326.

10. *Radio Reference* [1932] A.C. 304.

11. Note 2, above.

12. Note 1, above.

13. *Constitution Act, 1867,* s.91(2).

14. Ibid., s.92(2).

15. Ibid. s.92(10)(a).

16. Ibid. s.92(10)(c).

17. Ibid. s.90, (this power has not been exercised since 1943 and recent Supreme Court dicta in *The Queen v. Beauregard* [1986]2 S.C.R. 56, 72 suggests that in terms of political reality the federal power to veto or disallow provincial legislation is now virtually obsolete).

18. Ibid., in the preamble to s.91.

19. Ibid. s.55, s.56, s.57 and s.90.

20. Mark MacGuigan, "The Privy Council and the Supreme Court: A Jurisprudential Analysis," 1966, 4 *Alberta Law Review*, p.419.

21. *Citizen's Insurance Co. v. Parsons* (1881)7 App Cas. 96.

22. Ibid.

23. Ibid.

24. *General Motors v. City National Leasing* [1989]1 S.C.R. 641.

25. *Labatt Breweries v. A.-G. Can.* [1980]1 S.C.R. 914.

26. *General Motors v. City National Leasing.*

27. General Agreement on Tariffs and Trade (hereafter GATT), Uruguay Round, 15 April 1994, art. I, (this eighth and most recent GATT was signed by 124 "contracting nations" and non-contracting participants).

28. North America Free-Trade Agreement (hereafter NAFTA), 1 January 1994, (Canada, United States, Mexico).

29. Canadian Agreement on Internal Trade (hereafter CAIT), 1 September 1994, art. 101(3).

30. GATT, art. I.

31. Ibid., art. III.

32. CAIT, art. 401.

33. Ibid., art. 403.

34. Ibid., art. 1600(b).

35. *R. v. Oakes*, [1986]1 S.C.R. 103.

36. *Black v. Law Society of Alta.*, [1989]1 S.C.R. 591. and *Hunt v. T&N plc*, [1993]4 S.C.R. 289.

37. *R. v. Edward's Books & Art*, [1986]2 S.C.R. 713, (Dickson,C.J. at p.781-82).

38. Also potentially significant is CAIT, art. 401(3) which would make the federal government more accountable in procurement practices such as the controversial early 1980s CF-18 maintenance contract which was awarded to a Quebec aerospace firm over a superior Manitoba bid. Also CAIT Annex 502.1A.

39. GATT, Annex 1B

40. CAIT, Annex 502.2A.

41. Ibid., Annex 607.3.

42. Ibid., art. 607.3.4

43. Ibid., art. 702(2).

44. Ibid., art. 710(1).

45. Ibid., Annex 708.

46. Ibid., art. 712(1c)(5).

47. Ibid., art. 902(3).

48. Ibid., art., 1601

49. Ibid., art., 1801(2).

50. Ibid., art., 1802.

51. *The Globe and Mail*, 19 July 1994, p.A4.

52. *The Globe and Mail*, 18 July 1994, p.B1, quoting a provincial negotiator.

53. While I have argued for the constitutionality and, in some circumstances, appropriateness of unilateral federal action to strengthen the Canadian economic union, I have some reservations about Bill C-88. It would authorize the federal executive to retaliate against violations of the AIT by selectively suspending the operation of federal laws. The statute does not contain adequate safeguards. There should be a requirement for the executive to give notice before a specific retaliatory measure is taken, and to allow input from potentially affected parties. There should also be guaranteed access to the courts to overturn retaliatory measures that are disproportionate or based on extraneous considerations. (If the federal executive takes undue retaliatory actions for violations of NAFTA or the GATT agreements, an aggrieved state can seek a remedy before an internal dispute-settling panel, and the remedy will be binding under international law. The AIT, by contrast, does not provide for legally-binding remedies for excessive retaliation.) The prospect of having Canadian governments engaging in mutually destructive bouts of violation and retaliation is not an attractive one. It would be far better to rely on the rule of law, and establish legally binding norms and remedies.

54. *The Globe and Mail*, 5 July 1994, p. A17.

55. Andrew Coyne, *The Globe and Mail*, 5 July 1994, p.A17.

V

Chronology

10

Chronology of Events July 1994 – June 1995

Andrew C. Tzembelicos

An index of these events begins on page 251

3-6 July 1994
Agriculture

After a three-day meeting in Winnipeg, Canada's agriculture ministers near the realization of a national farm income protection policy which will provide a "whole farm safety net" to cover all or most farm commodities. The proposed safety net is created to shield farmers from the traditional vagaries associated with farming such as crop failures and market downturns.

5 July 1994
Justice

The federal government announces the creation of a national crime prevention council to help combat the social causes of crime. The creation of the council fulfils a Liberal election promise but is viewed with scepticism given its operating budget of only $4 million over a five-year period.

6 July 1994
Environment

Federal Environment Minister Sheila Copps and her Ontario counterpart Bud Wildman sign an agreement committing both parties to the cleanup of some 40 environmental "hotspots" in the province by the year 2000, with joint government spending at $1.6 billion over the six-year period.

7 July 1994
Aboriginal Peoples

Ovide Mercredi, national chief of the Assembly of First Nations, begins his second term in the position. To recapture his title Mercredi receives 273 votes on the third ballot compared to Wally McKay, chief of Sachigo Lake in north-western Ontario at 175. Mercredi is supported by 61 percent of the 449 chiefs — a mere one percent more than the 60 percent required to head the group, which represents 533,000 status Indians.

13 July 1994
Aboriginal Peoples

A report prepared by the Royal Commission on Aboriginal Peoples concludes that Ottawa "coerced" Inuit families into moving to the High Arctic in the 1950s, misleading them about the reasons why. Although the commissioners resist assigning blame to the government, the report suggests that in addition to offering an apology to the Inuit the federal government should also provide a compensation package.

13 July 1994
Transportation

In a sweeping reform of air policy, Transport Minister Doug Young announces that the federal government plans to save $100 million per year by leasing all of Canada's major airports to local authorities in addition to eliminating subsidies for more than 100 smaller regional airports. The new policy requires all large airports to become self-sufficient not only in paying for any new facilities, but also in day-to-day operation.

18 July 1994
Trade –
Interprovincial

After seven years of negotiation, the first ministers sign the Agreement on Internal Trade, a national trade agreement which is also expected to provide support for the federalist forces in Quebec. The accord, to take effect 1 July 1995, will serve to:

- facilitate the sale of goods and services between provinces;
- open government buying practices;
- place limitations on the use of incentives such as tax breaks, to lure businesses from other provinces;
- attempt to standardize consumer protection regulations that would allow the freer movement of goods across Canada;
- standardize trucking industry regulations, thereby allowing the industry to become more competitive; and
- offer clear administrative provisions for effective dispute resolution based on negotiation.

18 July 1994 *Reduction of* *Government* *Duplication*	Minister of Intergovernmental Affairs Marcel Massé, announces that the federal government has signed agreements with eight of the provinces in order to reduce duplication and overlap within government. The agreements are signed by Prime Minister Jean Chrétien and the first ministers from: Ontario, Nova Scotia, New Brunswick, Manitoba, British Columbia, Prince Edward Island, Saskatchewan, Newfoundland, and the Yukon.
19 July 1994 *Federal-Provincial* *Relations – Quebec*	An agreement between the federal and Quebec governments gives the Collège militaire royal de St-Jean, Quebec, a new lease on life. The terms of the agreement stipulate that Ottawa will provide Quebec with $5 million annually for five years to run a modified program at the former military college, which had previously been scheduled to close.
21 July 1994 *Aboriginal Peoples –* *Quebec*	The Inuit of Quebec take a significant step towards self-government with the conclusion of an agreement with the Government of Quebec which offers the Inuit the opportunity to create their own elected assembly with wide-ranging powers. The deal also allows the Inuit to assume greater control over key areas such as policing, wildlife management, and education.
22 July 1995 *Sovereignty –* *Quebec*	A poll commissioned by *The Globe and Mail* and *Le Devoir* says that 51 percent of decided voters will vote for the PQ in the upcoming election, compared to 44 percent for the Liberals. The poll also indicates the primary objective of a majority of voters for good government (at 56 percent, compared to 36 percent for whom the goal was to move to sovereignty).
24 July 1994 *Elections – Quebec*	Quebec Premier Daniel Johnson dissolves the Quebec legislature, calling for an election on 12 September — an election which some analysts claim will provide Quebecers with a choice between federalism and independence.
25 July 1994 *Economy – Quebec;* *Sovereignty –* *Quebec*	A study conducted for the Caisse de dépôt et placement du Québec in Montreal concludes that Quebec has profited more from the Canada-U.S. Free Trade Agreement than Canada as a whole. The report shows that between 1988 and 1992 Quebec's exports to the United States grew

43 percent compared to a national figure of 33 percent, allegedly substantiating the argument made by sovereignists for an independent and economically viable Quebec.

3-6 August 1994 *Trade – Canada-U.S.;* *Disputes*	A six-year dispute between Canada and the United States over softwood lumber under the Free Trade Agreement ends in Canada's favour. A three-member panel consisting of two Canadian jurists and one American concludes that Canadian softwood lumber is not subsidized and therefore the United States must cease the imposition of a 6.51 percent tariff on Canadian imports.
8 August 1994 *Elections – Quebec*	After entering the Quebec election fray, Bloc Québécois Leader Lucien Bouchard alters the course of the Parti Québécois campaign by emphasizing good government first and sovereignty afterwards. Bouchard's strategy surprises many, since it not only attacks the past record of the provincial government but it also targets the Chrétien government, claiming that a vote for the Quebec Liberals is a vote for massive federal invasion into Quebec.
8 August 1994 *Infrastructure* *Program*	As part of a $6 billion national infrastructure program, federal Treasury Board President Art Eggleton announces that the federal and Ontario governments will team up to fund a new $173 million trade centre designed to attract large trade and consumer shows to Toronto in addition to creating employment. The trade centre is the second largest project to be approved under the infrastructure program.
10 August 1994 *Fiscal Policy –* *Provinces*	A report by the Toronto Dominion Bank suggests that for the first time this decade, every province in Canada was able to cut its deficit in the past year — reducing the total of the annual provincial deficits from $25 billion to $19.5 billion.
16 August 1994 *National Unity*	At the first Acadian World Congress in Moncton, Prime Minister Jean Chrétien promotes a united Canada as the best means of preserving French culture in North America, citing the Acadians as an example. The same day, Heritage Minister Michel Dupuy announces a new federal policy promoting both French and English minority language groups across Canada.

25 August 1994 *Justice*	Justice Minister Allan Rock tells the annual convention of the Canadian Association of Chiefs of Police in Montreal that there is much work to be done to make the streets of Canada safe. In a closed session, the chiefs approve resolutions supporting broader gun controls, more severe treatment of immigrants who commit crimes, and the prohibition of "serial killer" trading cards.
29 August 1994 *Elections – Quebec*	Quebec Premier Daniel Johnson is aggressive in a televised leaders' debate, defending himself against attacks by Parti Québécois Leader Jacques Parizeau, although analysts agree that Johnson's performance is unlikely to stem the sovereignist tide in the 12 September election. Johnson emphasizes to Quebecers that their choice is between a free-market, federalist Liberal party and an interventionist, sovereignist PQ.
31 August 1994 *Senate – Appointments*	Prime Minister Jean Chrétien makes his first Senate appointment selecting Jean-Louis Roux, a renowned Quebec actor, writer, and director. Roux's appointment brings standings in the Upper House to 56 Conservatives, 41 Liberals, and three independents, with four vacancies.
1 September 1994 *Premiers – Annual Conference*	Canada's premiers conclude their two-day annual conference in Toronto. The main achievements of the meeting include an agreement to establish a task force on aboriginal self-government and treaty rights; a commitment to greater information sharing to reduce welfare fraud; and an affirmation of support for a proposal by Quebec Premier Daniel Johnson to create a new mechanism for provincial cooperation on issues of national importance.
9 September 1994 *Social Assistance – Manitoba*	In a joint effort, Human Resources Minister Lloyd Axworthy announces that the federal and Manitoba governments are committing $2.6 million to a new five-year program designed to help 4,000 single parents on welfare find employment.
12 September 1994 *Elections – Quebec*	After a seven-week election campaign, Quebecers hand the Parti Québécois a majority government with 77 seats to 47 for the Liberals, one for the Parti Action Démocratique, and a complete shut-out for the Equality Party. Despite capturing a majority of the 125 seats in the

legislature, the PQ surprises political observers in that it receives 44.7 percent of the popular vote, only 0.4 percent more than the Liberals. The media interpret the election results as an indication that Quebecers are not ready to separate from Canada, and are likely to vote against sovereignty in the upcoming referendum.

13 September 1994
Elections – Quebec

Prime Minister Jean Chrétien reacts to news of the Parti Québécois victory by saying that the election results are the best he could have hoped for without achieving a Liberal victory. Chrétien expresses confidence in the strong Liberal showing and suggests that Quebecers will choose to remain a part of Canada at referendum time. In a conference call nine provincial premiers agree that the election results do not give the PQ a mandate to break up the country, nor do they entitle Quebec to "special deals" to remain a part of Canada. The premiers urge the PQ to hold the referendum as soon as possible. However, they are adamant that there will not be another round of constitutional negotiations.

14 September 1994
*Sovereignty –
Quebec; Federal-
Provincial Relations
– Quebec*

In his first news conference as Quebec premier-designate, Jacques Parizeau announces that the Parti Québécois will maintain its referendum timetable, holding its critical vote on independence sometime in the coming year. Parizeau also states that he and his ministers will attend only those federal-provincial conferences that are in Quebec's interests, and will refuse to participate in any major reforms that encroach on areas of provincial jurisdiction, such as initiatives to revamp Canada's social programs.

14-15 September 1994
Health Policy

Federal and provincial health ministers end a two-day conference in Halifax. Issues discussed at the meeting include: regulation of the development of private clinics in Canada; a review of proposed federal legislation regarding the use of generic drugs; and issues concerning Canada's blood system.

15 September 1994
*Senate –
Appointments*

Prime Minister Jean Chrétien appoints three prominent Liberal women to the Senate: Sharon Carstairs, former Manitoba Liberal leader; Lise Bacon, a former deputy premier of Quebec; and Landon Pearson, a daughter-in-law of former Prime Minister Lester Pearson.

18 September 1994 *Sovereignty –* *Quebec*	At the annual meeting of the Canadian Chamber of Commerce in Quebec City, Prime Minister Jean Chrétien says that he will promote Canadian federalism through economic incentives such as deficit reduction and job creation; he also suggests that part of the government's strategy is to provide Quebecers with better government in Ottawa. Chrétien also says that he intends to be a vocal critic of the referendum since it is important to all Canadians, not just Quebecers.
26 September 1994 *Aboriginal Peoples*	Health Minister Diane Marleau announces that the federal government plans to give native communities $243 million over the next five years to confront problems of alcoholism, solvent abuse, suicide, and family violence. This is in addition to the annual $500 million contribution which Ottawa spends on non-insured health service for Aboriginal Peoples.
27 September 1994 *Education*	The Council of Ministers of Education meets in Charlottetown to discuss a national education agenda. The ministers agree to publish a report card on Canadian schools in order to make provincial school systems more accountable for their performance.
28 September 1994 *Federal-Provincial* *Relations – Quebec*	In a news conference Quebec Premier Jacques Parizeau says that Quebec will decide to participate in federal-provincial and interprovincial conferences on a case-by-case basis, depending on whether or not its interests are at stake.
28 September 1994 *Sovereignty –* *Quebec*	Quebec Premier Jacques Parizeau declares that the referendum on sovereignty will be held by 31 December 1995, thus rejecting a proposal made by Bloc Québécois Leader Lucien Bouchard to postpone the referendum until the PQ is certain of victory.
29 September 1994 *Federal-Provincial* *Relations – Quebec*	Intergovernmental Affairs Minister Marcel Massé announces that the federal government has agreed to comply with the demands of the Parti Québécois and the Bloc Québécois and will fulfil a promise made by the former Conservative government to compensate Quebec for that province's 1992 referendum on the Charlottetown Accord. While the PQ government demands $47.2 million in

remuneration, the federal government agrees to a sum of $34 million.

5 October 1994
Social Programs –
Reform

Human Resources Minister Lloyd Axworthy unveils the federal government's plans for a major overhaul of Canada's social programs. In order to reduce the deficit and potentially cut $3 billion in federal spending per year, the government proposes radical reforms of federal spending on welfare, unemployment insurance, and postsecondary education — with a specific emphasis on improving job training and making programs more efficient. Among the proposals in the Axworthy plan:

- a two-tiered unemployment insurance system for occasional and chronic claimants and a restriction on admissibility criteria;
- a reduction in federal support for postsecondary education; but a proposal for increased student loans through an income-contingent program;
- revision and reduction of Canada Assistance Plan payments to the provinces, with provincial governments assuming greater control over welfare and social services;
- increased child tax benefits to the most needy.

6 October 1994
Environment

Federal Environment Minister Sheila Copps announces the proclamation of the *Canadian Environmental Assessment Act*, which requires environmental assessment of major projects in every region of the country and also replaces the Federal Environmental Assessment Review Office with the Canadian Environmental Assessment Agency. The Act is denounced by Quebec Minister of the Environment Jacques Brassard as an intrusion into provincial jurisdiction.

12 October 1994
Sovereignty –
Quebec

Pierre Fortin, an economics professor at the University of Montreal, releases a study which suggests that separation from Canada could cost Quebecers an extra $3.4 billion annually. According to Fortin, who supports neither the Parti Québécois nor the Quebec Liberals, the additional costs would be attributed to a variety of factors including: the costs associated with starting up a new country; a substantial slowdown in the Quebec economy; and the burdens incurred in funding all social security programs in the province.

12 October 1994
Sovereignty –
Quebec

Prime Minister Jean Chrétien announces that the federal government does not have a backup plan in the event that Quebecers opt to separate from Canada in the upcoming referendum, instead expressing confidence that such a scenario is unlikely.

13-14 October
Fiscal Policy

Canada's finance ministers, including Jean Campeau of Quebec's Parti Québécois government, meet in Toronto to discuss public finances. The ministers discuss proposals to eliminate the goods and services tax, an election promise made by the federal government, although Finance Minister Paul Martin announces that the Chrétien government has abandoned a deadline of 1 January 1996 to replace the tax.

18 October 1994
Fiscal Policy

Finance Minister Paul Martin announces that the federal government requires an additional \$9.4 billion in spending cuts or additional tax revenues over the next two years to meet his target of slashing the federal deficit to \$32.7 billion in 1995-96, and \$25 billion in 1996-97, 3 percent of Canada's gross national product (GNP).

20 October 1994
Health Policy –
Reforms

Prime Minister Jean Chrétien opens a \$12 million National Health Care Forum in Ottawa without provincial representation. The purpose of the forum, consisting of 22 health-care experts and spanning a period of five years, is to search for more efficient means of providing health care. The lack of provincial representation is attributed to the federal government's decision not to appoint any provincial representatives to the panel or to the position of vice-chair and the provinces' rejection of the federal government's intervention in an area that is traditionally under provincial jurisdiction.

20 October 1994
Aboriginal Peoples

In a demonstration on Parliament Hill, aboriginal groups protest new guidelines established by Revenue Canada which will force thousands of native persons to pay income tax. The guidelines were conceived after a Supreme Court ruling which decided that the tax status of Aboriginal Peoples should be based on three factors: location of residence, location of work, and location of employer. Originally proposed by the Conservative government in 1992, the guidelines were then denounced by Prime Minister Jean Chrétien who served as opposition leader at the time.

In an unrelated development, the federal government announces that it will relinquish control of manpower training to the Mohawks of the Kahnawake in order to create more effective employment programs. The government commits $3.8 million in funds to the Kahnawake through 1997 in order to help reduce unemployment.

24 October 1994
Trade – Quebec

The Quebec government signs a trade agreement with the Chinese province of Hubei, designed to promote exchange in the areas of business, science, technology, and education. In keeping with earlier statements the Quebec government will not participate in an upcoming trade visit to China by Prime Minister Jean Chrétien and Canada's nine other premiers.

25 October 1994
Tourism

Prime Minister Jean Chrétien announces the creation of a national tourism commission with an initial annual budget of $50 million, to promote Canada as a tourist destination, noting that Canada has a balance of payments deficit in tourism of nearly $8 billion.

27 October 1994
Taxation – Ontario

An agreement between the federal and Ontario governments commits both parties to the goal of reducing tax evasion, smuggling, and the black market, which traditionally result in a loss of $2 billion in federal taxes. The governments agree to share information to identify cases of tax evasion, and to cooperate on audits and collection activity.

29 October 1994
Sovereignty –
Quebec

Prime Minister Jean Chrétien says that he will not interfere with Quebec Liberal Leader Daniel Johnson's efforts to maintain a united Canada. Chrétien also reiterates that no new constitutional offers will be made to the province before the referendum.

4 November 1994
Aboriginal Peoples –
Nova Scotia, Self-
Government

Federal Indian Affairs Minister Ron Irwin signs an historic accord giving complete control of education to Nova Scotia's Micmacs. The agreement in principle, which is the first to relinquish control over education on reserves to natives in the province, will mean that the Micmacs negotiate directly with school boards on issues such as subject matter and tuition, and are given the freedom to emphasize their language and culture within the school curricula.

7 November 1994
Environment

The Government of Quebec refuses to participate in a meeting of the Canadian Council of Ministers of the Environment in Bathurst, New Brunswick to discuss the harmonization of environmental policies. It feels that harmonization offers the federal government a greater opportunity to encroach upon areas of provincial jurisdiction.

10 November 1994
Trade – International

Prime Minister Jean Chrétien, and Canada's premiers, with the exception of Quebec Premier Jacques Parizeau, return from a six-day trade mission to China known as "Team Canada." The group is successful in negotiating potentially $9 billion in commercial agreements, and considers adopting a similar strategy in the future to tap markets in India or South America.

10 November 1994
Federal-Provincial
Relations – Quebec

Richard Le Hir, PQ minister responsible for restructuring, releases 42 studies prepared by the former Liberal government suggesting that spending by the federal government is $3 billion a year less than it should be considering Quebec's share of Canada's population. Liberal critic Jean-Marc Fournier suggests that the figures do not include equalization payments or large areas of federal spending such as postsecondary education.

15 November 1994
Sovereignty –
Quebec

In an address to the Montreal Chamber of Commerce Quebec Premier Jacques Parizeau denounces the federal system, alleging that it: restricts the province's ability to grow by blocking its initiatives in areas such as labour training and communications; and penalizes its success, through reductions in equalization payments.

15 November 1994 *Fisheries – Reforms*	Fisheries Minister Brian Tobin releases a discussion paper committing the federal government to establishing a clear set of rules governing natural resources of the seas within Canadian territory. Under a new oceans act the management strategy would seek to:

- conserve and protect the ocean environment;
- assert Canada's sovereignty and environmental control within the 200-mile nautical limit;
- create a federal agency responsible for oceans management; and
- establish a series of economic and environmental guidelines for ocean management.

18 November 1994 *Energy – Hydro-Quebec*	The Quebec government decides to terminate the $13 billion, "Great Whale" hydroelectric project undertaken by Hydro-Québec, the second phase of the James Bay development project. The decision to scrap the project is interpreted by the media as partly to meet the objections of Quebec's native population, which has been vocal in its opposition to the notion of an independent Quebec.
22 November 1994 *Sovereignty – Quebec*	In Toronto, Quebec Premier Jacques Parizeau promises that the constitution of a sovereign Quebec will give anglophones in the province veto power over any reduction of their rights.
24 November 1994 *Fisheries – East Coast; Disputes*	Fisheries Minister Brian Tobin announces that the U.S. government has formally recognized Canadian jurisdiction over Icelandic scallops in international waters off the East Coast, thereby ending a four-month dispute between the two countries.
27 November 1994 *Sovereignty – Quebec*	Concluding a weekend policy meeting of the Bloc Québécois in Mont-Ste-Anne, Quebec, Bloc Leader Lucien Bouchard officially declares the referendum season open, committing his party to an agenda of attacks on the federal system. Bouchard says that the initiatives by the Chrétien government to produce social reform, develop a national sales tax, and tackle Canada's debt will ultimately serve to weaken Quebec's ability to act within its jurisdiction.

30 November 1994
Sovereignty –
Quebec

In his inaugural address to the National Assembly, Quebec Premier Jacques Parizeau reaffirms that the referendum will be held in 1995. Parizeau adds that he is in favour of maintaining an economic association with Canada in addition to using Canadian currency; he also suggests that Quebecers will be consulted on the sovereignty issue in the months ahead.

30 November 1994
Justice – Reforms

Justice Minister Allan Rock tables a sweeping package of controversial reforms aimed at improving gun control in Canada. The justice minister argues that a registration system for firearms is required since many crimes are committed in Canada each year using weapons stolen from legitimate owners, and a registration system could help to facilitate the apprehension of criminals. Among the stipulations: compulsory registration of all firearms in Canada within a specified time frame, a widespread ban on civilian ownership of handguns, new mandatory sentencing for serious offences committed with weapons and possession of smuggled firearms, and the imposition of age restrictions on the sale of ammunition.

1 December 1994
Party Leadership –
Bloc Québécois;
Sovereignty –
Quebec

The effectiveness of the Bloc Québécois in Parliament and in the upcoming referendum campaign is questioned after leader Lucien Bouchard loses his left leg and nearly his life to a viral disease. He is absent from the House of Commons until 22 February 1995.

6 December 1994
Sovereignty –
Quebec

Quebec Premier Jacques Parizeau tables a draft bill in the National Assembly stating that Quebec is a sovereign country, proposing a referendum to seek public approval of the bill, and demarcating the Parti Québécois strategy for the referendum campaign. The legislation also accomplishes several other goals:

- it establishes a $2-million system of regional forums and public hearings to encourage the participation of Quebecers in drafting a declaration of sovereignty to be included in the bill's preamble;
- it authorizes the government to negotiate an economic association with the rest of Canada and it stipulates that Quebec will continue to use the Canadian dollar as its legal currency;

- it indicates that Quebec citizens will be able to retain their Canadian citizenship;
- it reaffirms Quebec's intentions to apply, as a sovereign state, to international organizations such as the United Nations; and
- the bill also calls for a new Quebec constitution including a Charter of Rights, and protection of the rights of Aboriginal Peoples and the English-speaking community.

7 December 1994
Fiscal Policy –
Stabilization
Payments

Finance Minister Paul Martin announces that the federal government will pay $782.4 million in stabilization claims to eight provinces as compensation for losses in revenue incurred as a result of the recent recession. More than half of the total, or $484.4 million, goes to Ontario while Quebec, which receives $125 million, counters that it has been shortchanged and opts to take the matter to arbitration. Other provinces that receive payments are Newfoundland, $31.1 million; Prince Edward Island, $ 9 million; Nova Scotia, $55 million; New Brunswick, $25 million; Manitoba, $42.9 million; and Saskatchewan, $10 million.

7 December 1994
Aboriginal Peoples –
Self-Government

The federal government signs an unprecedented agreement with Manitoba native leaders which outlines the process for dismantling the Indian Affairs Department in that province. The agreement is claimed to mark a significant step in the goal of aboriginal self-government.

13 December 1994
Aboriginal Peoples –
Quebec

At a meeting of the Assembly of First Nations, Chief Ovide Mercredi asks Prime Minister Jean Chrétien to protect the rights of Aboriginals in Quebec in the event that Quebec separates from Canada, which Mercredi suggests the federal government can circumvent by opening constitutional discussions with Quebec.

14 December 1994
Sovereignty –
Quebec

Quebec Liberal Party Leader Daniel Johnson declares that he will not ask the federal government to open constitutional negotiations on renewed federalism until after the referendum has taken place.

15 December 1994
Aboriginal Peoples –
Quebec, Self-
Government

The Parti Québécois offer two of the province's aboriginal groups, the Atikamekw and the Montagnais, a self-government deal that would give the groups exclusive jurisdiction over 4,000 square kilometres of land, the revenues from natural resources, and $342 million in financial compensation. The offer is viewed with scepticism by some other aboriginal communities, which see it as a means of dividing Quebec natives on the subject of sovereignty for the province.

15 December 1994
Federal-Provincial
Relations – Quebec

The Quebec government demands $79 million in compensation from the federal government to cover the costs associated with the provision of provincial police services during the Oka crisis of 1990. Intergovernmental Affairs Minister Marcel Massé says that the federal auditor-general will decide whether or not Quebec receives the payment.

19 December 1994
Sovereignty –
Quebec

The Quebec government tables enabling legislation to ensure the application of provisions that fall within its constitutional bounds under international trade agreements such as the North American Free Trade Agreement (NAFTA) and the General Agreement on Tariffs and Trade (GATT). The legislation is designed to provide Quebecers with greater participation in liberalized trade and trade bodies; it also claims that a sovereign Quebec should not be denied entry to international agreements. Quebec is the first province to introduce enabling legislation.

19 December 1994
Agriculture –
Federal-Provincial
Relations

Canada's agriculture ministers conclude a framework for a new farm safety net designed to facilitate planning by farmers in the long term. The optional program replaces a number of existing programs, allowing farmers to deposit money into an account during prosperous times and to make withdrawals when income drops below an established level during harder times. The new plan places more responsibility on producers, and attempts to make them less dependent on government bailouts in times of difficulty.

20 December 1994 *Sovereignty –* *Quebec; National* *Unity*	In an interview with CTV, Prime Minister Jean Chrétien says that it is illegal and "non-constitutional" for Quebec to separate from Canada, whether the sovereignists achieve a majority vote on the upcoming referendum or not. Chrétien also dismisses claims made by the PQ that Quebec will automatically become part of international trade agreements negotiated by Canada such as the North American Free Trade Agreement. Chrétien reiterates that he expects the federalist forces to win the referendum.
21 December 1994 *Sovereignty –* *Quebec*	Federal Finance Minister Paul Martin admits that Ottawa cannot stop an independent Quebec from using the Canadian dollar, however, Martin believes that Quebec would consequently lose its economic sovereignty since it would have no control over the Canadian dollar.
4 January 1995 *Sovereignty –* *Quebec*	Moody's Investor Service, a leading American debt-rating agency, cautions the Quebec government against pursuing its separatist agenda at the expense of a credible deficit-reduction program if the province wishes to maintain its A1 rating.
6 January 1995 *Health Policy –* *Funding*	Health Minister Diane Marleau declares that any province that allows private clinics to charge facility fees will be denied transfer payments of equal value beginning 15 October. According to Marleau, facility fees engender a two-tiered system of health care which threatens Canada's publicly funded system.
10 January 1995 *Sovereignty –* *Quebec*	Mario Dumont, leader of the Parti Action Démocratique, announces that his party is drafting its own referendum question based on the vision of a European-style association between a sovereign Quebec and Canada. In other developments regarding sovereignty, a study released by the C.D. Howe Institute suggests that Quebec independence will produce a constitutional, political, and economic crisis that will lead to hardship for all Canadians, rivalling the Great Depression in scope.
10 January 1995 *Social Programs –* *Reform; Maritime/* *Atlantic Provinces –* *Cooperation*	In light of the federal government's proposals of October to reform Canada's social policy, governments in Atlantic Canada join together in order to protect their mutual interests. Of particular concern are plans to restrict unemployment insurance, proposals to change educational

funding, and initiatives designed to encourage welfare recipients to work.

11 January 1995
Trade –
Interprovincial;
Disputes

Dissension among the provinces occurs when it is announced that courier giant United Parcel Service Canada Ltd. is to receive $6 million from the government of New Brunswick in worker training incentives, for moving almost 900 jobs to that province from across Canada. The other provincial governments, most notably those of British Columbia and Ontario, argue that this "job poaching" violates the spirit of an interprovincial trade agreement signed six months earlier by the first ministers, to take effect on 1 July.

12 January 1995
Sovereignty –
Quebec

Quebec Liberal Party Leader Daniel Johnson says that he will embark on a cross-Canada tour in the months before the referendum meeting with all of Canada's premiers, in order to show Quebecers that dialogue between Quebec and the rest of Canada is possible, and that other provinces also support Johnson's bid for a modified federalism.

13 January 1995
Sovereignty –
Quebec

At a news conference in Montreal, Quebec Liberal Leader Daniel Johnson says that a vote against independence in the coming referendum will be a vote for a better Canadian union in the future. At the conference Johnson tries to appeal to undecided voters by suggesting that changes to Confederation are required and are expected in the future. He also announces the creation of a Liberal party committee to assemble arguments against separation and provide a perspective on what a vote against sovereignty will offer Quebecers.

16 January 1995
Sovereignty –
Quebec

Prime Minister Jean Chrétien suggests that he is willing to consider constitutional change as an option in the future, saying that it can be accomplished through the constitutional amending formula. He also indicates that the federal government might limit its involvement in areas such as higher education and social welfare, but that its role in health care is non-negotiable.

24-25 January 1995
Justice

Canada's justice ministers end a two-day conference in Victoria and agree to adopt several recommendations of a task force on dangerous offenders, including reclassifying repeat violent offenders as long-term offenders who would remain in prison longer, a revision of sentencing provisions for dangerous offenders, and use of a police information databank to track individuals considered to be dangerous.

27 January 1995 *Sovereignty –* *Quebec*	Quebec Premier Jacques Parizeau ends a four-day visit to Paris and is confident that France will recognize a sovereign Quebec if the referendum results favour independence.
1 February 1995 *Social Programs –* *Reform*	Human Resources Minister Lloyd Axworthy announces that proposals introduced in October to reform the federal government's social programs will be postponed until there is "clear fiscal stability" in Canada, implying that the reforms will occur only after the government's deficit-reduction plans are in place.
6 February 1995 *Sovereignty –* *Quebec*	The Quebec government opens a series of hearings by 16 regional and two special-interest commissions intended to boost support for independence before the referendum. Some commission hearings are criticized for not providing federalists with an equal opportunity to participate.
8 February 1995 *Governor-General*	Romeo Leblanc is installed as Canada's new governor-general. At the investiture Leblanc, the first Acadian to assume the position, promotes national unity by discussing Acadian history and how his people overcame French-English differences and learned to coexist peacefully.
9 February 1995 *Aboriginal Peoples –* *Quebec, Self-* *Government*	Native leaders from the Atikamekw community reject an offer made by the Quebec government which would realize major land claims and self-government. The leaders charge that the offer was extended in order to gain aboriginal support for the referendum on Quebec sovereignty; they also say that the offer does not respect fundamental native rights. The Montagnais, another native community, reject the same offer a month earlier.
10 February 1995 *Sovereignty –* *Quebec*	Prime Minister Jean Chrétien addresses the Canadian Chamber of Commerce in Montreal and warns that Quebec's international trade will suffer extensively if the

province separates from Canada. Chrétien also says that not only will a sovereign Quebec have to negotiate its entrance into trade pacts of which Canada is already a member, such as the North American Free Trade Agreement (NAFTA), but Quebec also risks losing special protection for cultural industries, dairy products, and provincial crown corporations.

13 February 1995
Elections – Federal Byelections

The federal Liberals win three byelections, the biggest accomplishment being that of Denis Paradis over Bloc Québécois candidate Jean-François Bertrand in the Quebec riding of Brome-Missisquoi, a seat previously held by the Bloc. The party also gains seats in the traditional Liberal strongholds of St-Henri-Westmount and Ottawa-Vanier. Prime Minister Chrétien touts the victories as an indication that the federalist forces will stem the separatist tide in the upcoming referendum on Quebec sovereignty.

14 February 1995
Electoral Reforms

Members of the House of Commons agree in principle, by a vote of 176 to 54, to the addition of six MPs to the House in time for the next federal election; this brings the number of MPs to 301, from the present 295. Members also agree that riding boundaries will be redrawn, before the next federal election, to reflect the latest changes in census data.

15 February 1995
National Unity

The federal government spends $1.1 million on ceremonies commemorating the 30th anniversary of the Canadian maple leaf flag. Chrétien uses the celebration to further the cause of Canadian unity.

16 February 1995
Language Policy

A study released by the Office of the Commissioner of Official Languages concludes that francophones continue to have difficulties in obtaining service in French from federal government offices.

20 February 1995
Sovereignty – Quebec

Bloc Québécois Leader Lucien Bouchard makes several statements questioning the referendum strategy of its provincial counterpart, the Parti Québécois, indicating that Quebec Premier Jacques Parizeau should only call the referendum when support for sovereignty is strong.

22 February 1995
Federal Cabinet –
National Unity

At the House of Commons, Lucienne Robillard, a victor in the recent byelections, is installed in Prime Minister Jean Chrétien's Cabinet as labour minister and the minister responsible for the Quebec referendum.

22 February 1995
Pension Reform –
Members of
Parliament

Treasury Board President Art Eggleton announces the federal government's plans to reform the pension plan of members of Parliament, which will save taxpayers $3.3 million per year. The reforms include an end to double dipping, a practice that allows former MPs to collect pensions while working in another government job; the establishment of age eligibility criteria in order to receive a government pension; and the provision of greater benefits to those MPs who work longer.

24 February 1995
Canada Pension
Plan

A report from the Office of the Superintendent of Financial Institutions says that the Canada Pension Plan will run out of money by the year 2015 unless premiums rise faster than projected or benefits are reduced.

27 February 1995
Budgets – Federal

Federal Finance Minister Paul Martin introduces a budget designed to reduce the federal deficit to $24.3 billion in two years. The budget meets the federal government's medium-range deficit-reduction plans, and is critically acclaimed by the financial community. Martin proposes to accomplish the goal of deficit reduction largely through $10.4 billion in cuts to government spending and through modest tax increases, although the budget does not call for any personal income tax increases. The budget announces that the Established Programs Financing (EPF) and the Canada Assistance Plan (CAP) will be combined in fiscal year 1995-96, and the total entitlement reduced from $32.7 billion in 1995-96 to $24.3 billion in 1996-97. The new program, to be called the Canada Social Transfer (later re-named the Canada Social and Health Transfer), will be the subject of negotiations with the provinces regarding potential conditions as well as the formula for determining interprovincial shares. Among other budget highlights:

- a $975 right-of-landing fee for adult immigrants in addition to increases in citizenship fees;
- a $1 billion corporate tax increase over two years;

- privatization of CN and the sale of remaining shares of Petro-Canada;
- substantial cuts in business, dairy, and transportation subsidies;
- a 21-percent cut in foreign aid spending over three years;
- more cuts and closures of military facilities;
- a rollback of RRSP contribution limits;
- promises of further reform of the unemployment insurance system; and
- promises of a restructuring of the Canada Pension Plan.

28 February 1995
Justice – Reforms

The House of Commons passes amendments to the *Young Offenders Act* which double maximum sentences for teenagers convicted of first-degree murder to ten years, while raising sentences for second-degree murder from five years to seven. The amendments also create provisions to try older teenagers charged with serious violent offences in adult court, serving a new minimum of at least ten years before parole eligibility.

2 March 1995
Budgets – Federal;
Fiscal Policy

The Canadian Bond Rating Service (CBRS) gives its first encouraging report of federal finances in five years as a result of the budget brought down by Federal Finance Minister Paul Martin.

3 March 1995
Budgets – Federal

In a visit to New York City, Finance Minister Paul Martin's attempts to sell his budget are met with enthusiasm by Wall Street, although the financial community expresses concern regarding investment prospects in Canada in view of Quebec's separatist aspirations.

8 March 1995
Fisheries – East
Coast

Canada's first Round Table on the Future of the Atlantic Fishery meets in Montreal, where fishermen, processors, natives, and government officials meet to decide the best means of preserving Atlantic fish stocks. Among the conclusions were: an essential decrease in capacity by all fleets and in all regions and provinces, stricter management of quotas, and distribution of unemployment insurance primarily to full-time fishermen. The group also agrees that it is largely Ottawa's responsibility to manage and conserve the resource.

9-10 March 1995
Sovereignty –
Quebec

After a two-day caucus meeting in Drummondville aimed at boosting the morale of Parti Québécois MNAs disheartened by sagging support for sovereignty, Premier Jacques Parizeau says that the referendum will be held within the year as originally planned. Parizeau quells speculation, including that of Bloc Québécois Leader Lucien Bouchard, that the referendum will be delayed or that the nature of Quebec sovereignty will be diluted to appease soft nationalists. Parizeau admits that the regional commissions created to promote Quebec independence failed to produce the surge in support that was hoped for.

13 March 1995
Sovereignty –
Quebec

The Quebec government releases a study by a New York law firm which says that economic self-interest would likely ensure that a separatist Quebec would remain in any trade or defence-related agreements negotiated by Canada, and that the United States would likely extend coverage of existing treaties and agreements to a sovereign Quebec.

14 March 1995
Sovereignty –
Quebec

Furthering the sovereignist cause, Premier Jacques Parizeau tells the opening of the spring session of the Quebec legislature that it is not independence that will inevitably cause Quebec's economic downfall but the burden of the massive Canadian debt.

21 March 1995
Senate –
Appointments

Prime Minister Jean Chrétien makes two more appointments to the Senate: Celine Hervieux-Payette, a former federal Cabinet minister; and Rose-Marie Losier-Cool, a former teachers' union leader and women's advocate. The new standings in the Upper House, after several appointments, are: Conservatives, 52; Liberals, 47; Independents, three; and two vacancies.

22 March 1995
Fiscal Policy –
Federal-Provincial

Dominion Bond Rating Service announces that Canada's four richest provinces will shoulder a disproportionate share of the federal government's cutbacks of $5.3 billion in transfer payments over the succeeding three years.

23 March 1995
Aboriginal Peoples

A report of the Royal Commission on Aboriginal Peoples on treaty-making as an alternative to the extinguishment of aboriginal title, says that Ottawa must stop trying to buy out Aboriginal Peoples with land and cash and start negotiating with them as partners. The report also recommends joint land management by Aboriginal Peoples and other governments, with self-government as a part of the treaties.

27 March 1995
Sovereignty –
Quebec

In a statement, Quebec's Deputy Premier Bernard Landry suggests that the referendum on independence will most probably be delayed until sometime after June due to a lack of support for the separatist cause. Landry's statements along with remarks made by Premier Jacques Parizeau, suggest that a fall referendum is likely. In order to boost support for the sovereignist movement, which is estimated to be well below the 50 percent level, the Parti Québécois plans a massive information campaign for households in order to allay the fears and concerns of Quebecers.

4 April 1995
Defence

The Public Works Department announces that it will pay Unisys GSC Canada Inc. of Montreal $68 million in return for cancelling a $5.8 billion deal made by the former Conservative government for the purchase of new shipborne and search and rescue helicopters.

5 April 1995
Sovereignty –
Quebec

During a speech to the "South Shore" Chamber of Commerce in Quebec, Premier Jacques Parizeau announces that the referendum on independence for the province will be held in the fall. Parizeau justifies the delay by saying that Quebecers need more information about separation. The announcement is said to surprise the federal government, although it continues to ready its arguments for the spring.

6 April 1995
Justice – Reforms

A package of controversial gun-control reforms passes second reading in the House of Commons by a vote of 175 to 53, with the Bloc Québécois supporting the bill and all but one Reform MP voting against it.

7 April 1995
Sovereignty –
Quebec

Bloc Québécois Leader Lucien Bouchard incites dissension within the separatist movement when he challenges Parti Québécois Premier Jacques Parizeau to take a "virage" (change in direction) proposing a closer political economic and political union between a sovereign Quebec and Canada.

10 April 1995
Health Policy

Canada's health ministers sign an agreement with the Canadian Red Cross Society and the Canadian Blood Agency that will improve the safety of Canada's blood supply by clearly defining the roles of the two organizations.

11 April 1995
Aboriginal Peoples –
Newfoundland

After a 16-month absence the RCMP returns to the Labrador community of Davis Inlet a month after signing a joint policing agreement with the Innu which gives the Aboriginal People a greater role in policing. The RCMP were originally ordered to leave the community because of Innu demands for a native justice system.

11 April 1995
Agriculture

Agriculture Minister Ralph Goodale announces that the federal government will pay a total sum of $1.6 billion to Prairie farmers who rent their land as compensation for the elimination of grain transportation subsidies.

13 April 1995
Budgets – Federal

Sceptical of the federal government's commitment to deficit-reduction and the likely success of Finance Minister Paul Martin's plan as announced in the recent budget, Moody's Investors Service downgrades the federal government's Canadian-dollar bonds from triple-A to double-A1. It also cuts the ratings on bonds issued in foreign currencies from double-A1 to double-A2.

13 April 1995
Health Policy

In Edmonton, Prime Minister Jean Chrétien denounces proposals suggested by Alberta Premier Ralph Klein that would allow for the privatization of some health-care services, saying that the *Canada Health Act* does not allow for private clinics or the unilateral de-insuring of medical services. The Alberta proposals attempt to make health-care services more efficient through such means as offering certain medical services on a "user-pay" basis and selling surplus hospitals to private groups.

15 April 1995
Fisheries – East
Coast

Federal Fisheries Minister Brian Tobin announces that a tentative agreement has been reached between Canada and the European Union after a month-long dispute over turbot fisheries in the area just outside Canada's 200 mile limit. In the agreement Canada realizes key demands for tougher enforcement and conservation measures and new limits on minimum fish size. In return, Canada agrees to give the EU 6,000 tonnes of its turbot quota for the year, putting Canada and the Union on a par with 10,000 tonnes each.

19 April 1995
Sovereignty –
Quebec

The provincial commission on the future of Quebec releases a report drawing conclusions from the 18 commissions that solicited the opinions of Quebecers during the winter. The report is significant in that it proposes a political union with Canada after sovereignty. Other key conclusions are that the Quebec government should negotiate its fair share of the national debt and an independent Quebec should guarantee the historical rights and identity of both its anglophone minority and its Aboriginal Peoples.

23 April 1995
Sovereignty –
Quebec

A Quebec public affairs program, L'Évènement, makes public a document suggesting that the Quebec Liberal Party believes Quebec should adhere to the 1982 constitution with three conditions: that Quebec regains its constitutional veto, that the trend to decentralization leads to concrete measures to divide powers among the levels of government, and that there be a renewed emphasis on making each level of government accountable to its citizens.

25 April 1995
Elections – Manitoba

The Conservative government of Manitoba, led by Premier Gary Filmon, returns to power for a third consecutive term. The Conservatives get a majority government capturing 31 of the legislature's 57 seats; the New Democrats solidify their position as official Opposition, with 23 seats; the Liberals win only three seats. Seats at dissolution were: Conservatives, 29; NDP, 20; and Liberals six, with two vacancies.

26 April 1995
Justice – Reforms

Alberta Justice Minister Brian Evans declares that the Alberta government supports a proposal put forth by the Government of Saskatchewan to opt out of federal gun-control legislation.

28 April 1995
Pension Reform –
Members of
Parliament

Legislation aimed at reforming the pension plan for members of Parliament is introduced in the House.

28 April 1995
Sovereignty –
Quebec

With support for sovereignty declining, Premier Jacques Parizeau decides to employ suggestions by Bloc Québécois Leader Lucien Bouchard and other Quebec sovereignists proposing a closer political union with Canada in order to gain the confidence of Quebecers. Prime Minister Jean Chrétien dismisses Parizeau's about face as an attempt to dupe the people of Quebec, saying "Why leave just to come back?" Chrétien is also adamant that the federal government will not negotiate any special agreements with Quebec.

3 May 1995
Sovereignty –
Quebec

At a Liberal fund-raising dinner in Montreal, Prime Minister Jean Chrétien accuses Premier Jacques Parizeau of attempting to "trick" Quebecers into voting for sovereignty in the upcoming referendum, by offering economic and political association with the rest of Canada. Chrétien insists that it is a decision for the rest of Canada to make, not Quebecers.

5 May 1995
Maritime/Atlantic
Provinces –
Conference of
Atlantic Premiers

The 13th session of the Conference of Atlantic Premiers is held in Halifax in conjunction with the 93rd session of the Council of Maritime Premiers. The premiers agree to cooperate in several areas, including distance education, regional development, the creation of an Atlantic investment fund, and the establishment of a computer service to market and sell government information.

9 May 1995
Budgets – Quebec

Finance Minister Jean Campeau delivers the Parti Québécois' first budget, promising much financial hardship for Quebecers in the event that the vote to separate from Canada fails in the referendum. Campeau says that sovereignty will protect Quebecers from the federal government's tax increases and deep spending cuts, claiming that Quebec will have to compensate for Ottawa's cuts in equalization payments. The budget forecasts a deficit of $3.98 billion for 1995-96, down from $5.7 billion for the previous year, but fails to cut government spending . The PQ is careful to avoid any major tax increases for potential referendum voters; however, it targets big business with an increase in capital taxes and other measures designed to net $677 million.

10 May 1995	The governments of Manitoba and the Yukon join their
Justice – Reforms	counterparts in Alberta and Saskatchewan in opposing the

10 May 1995
Justice – Reforms

The governments of Manitoba and the Yukon join their counterparts in Alberta and Saskatchewan in opposing the federal government's reforms to gun-control legislation. Yukon Justice Minister Douglas Phillips, like Alberta and Saskatchewan, also asks for exclusion from the legislation, arguing that it will infringe on the treaty rights of natives to hunt.

10 May 1995
Federal-Provincial
Relations – Quebec;
Disputes

Quebec Intergovernmental Affairs Minister Louise Beaudoin claims that the federal government owes the province $333 million for expenses on the education of aboriginal children, stabilization payments falling under a federal revenue-sharing program, and costs associated with the Oka Crisis.

11 May 1995
Fiscal Policy

In an address to the Quebec association of economists, Premier Jacques Parizeau proposes that the federal government leave all income tax collection to Quebec in a scheme similar to the single sales tax system.

15 May 1995
Social Programs –
Reform

Human Resources Minister Lloyd Axworthy announces to the House of Commons that he has abandoned one of the key tenets of his social program reforms announced in October, the idea of establishing a two-tiered system of unemployment insurance that would differentiate between repeat users and occasional users.

23 May 1995
Aboriginal Peoples –
Quebec

The Quebec government and the Cree announce that, after a six-year dispute, the parties have signed an accord committing both sides to participation in formal talks regarding future development in northern Quebec. Among the topics to be discussed are the issues of native self-government; improved housing and infrastructure and joint partnership in natural resources development. The agreement benefits the government in that it serves to postpone a legal challenge by the Cree regarding Hydro-Québec's Great Whale hydroelectric project; it also demonstrates good faith on the part of the government, which is looking to gain support for its soubereignist movement — although the issue of Quebec independence does not make the agenda.

24 May 1995
Justice – Reform

Prime Minister Jean Chrétien declares that the federal government will cover the costs associated with the creation of a national gun registry, one of the key proposals in Justice Minister Allan Rock's controversial package of gun control reforms. Although the bill has passed second reading and is being examined by a Commons committee, Rock offers several amendments easing the conditions of the legislation in order to alleviate the concerns of backbench Liberals, police, and the legal community. Among the changes are limitations on the power of police to inspect the homes of gun owners and reduction in the penalty for first-time gun registry violations.

28 May 1995
Sovereignty –
Quebec

At a meeting of the Parti Québécois' national council in Quebec City, Premier Jacques Parizeau works through proposals aimed at creating an association between Canada and an independent Quebec. Parizeau says that he is prepared to reconcile and work with the federal government for up to one year after a positive vote in the critical referendum declaring Quebec to be a sovereign nation.

29 May 1995
Aboriginal Peoples

Health Minister Diane Marleau announces the creation of the Aboriginal Head Start program, a four-year, $84 million initiative established to finance local projects to motivate young Aboriginals and to promote health and education.

30 May 1995
Sovereignty –
Quebec

Intergovernmental Affairs Minister Marcel Massé confirms that the federal government will make no new constitutional offers to Quebec before the referendum on independence.

2 June 1995
Transportation –
Reforms

Transportation Minister Doug Young announces that the federal government will no longer finance small ports across Canada. Under the initative the ports are to be divided into three classes. While key ports are to remain under federal jurisdiction, management of others is relinquished to provincial and municipal governments as well as private individuals.

6 June 1995
Fisheries –
West Coast

More than 300 fishermen in British Columbia file a class-action suit in B.C. Supreme Court against federal Fisheries Minister Brian Tobin and his department for the alleged mismanagement of the B.C. salmon fishery. The fishermen are challenging a 1992, five-year initiative of the former Conservative govenment which afforded special fishing rights to native fishermen, claiming that the initative has cost them money and that native fishermen have been taking advantage of the agreement by fishing illegally.

8 June 1995
Elections – Ontario

In an overwhelming sweep Mike Harris leads the Conservatives to a majority government, defeating the NDP government led by Premier Bob Rae and capturing 82 of the province's 130 seats. It is the first time that the Conservatives have been in power in Ontario for ten years. The Liberals retain their position as the Official Opposition with 30 seats, while the New Democrats kept only 17. Standings at dissolution of the legislature were: NDP, 69; Liberals, 34; Conservatives, 21; and Independents, two, with four vacancies.

8 June 1995
Premiers'
Conferences

Quebec Premier Jacques Parizeau irritates his Canadian colleagues at the 21st conference of eastern premiers and New England governors in Portsmouth, New Hampshire by bringing up the issue of Quebec independence among other issues discussed including energy, the environment, and economic development. The conference also produces resolutions on overfishing off the Grand Banks of Newfoundland, and a United Nations treaty on high-seas fishing.

8 June 1995
Sovereignty –
Quebec

Ghislain Dufour, president of Quebec's largest employers' group, the Conseil du patronat, says that a number of companies are postponing major investments in the province until after the referendum on independence.

12 June 1995
Sovereignty –
Quebec

The leaders of the Bloc Québécois, Parti Québécois, and Parti Action Démocratique ratify an agreement in Quebec City after announcing that their parties are to be united in the common goal of achieving sovereignty for Quebec. In addition to affirming the common front of the three parties, the text of the tripartite agreement proposes several measures designed to develop a partnership with the Canadian federation in the event of separation. Among the measures proposed in the event that Quebecers vote for sovereignty:

- negotiation of a political and economic partnership treaty with the rest of Canada within one year of the referendum;
- maintenance of the Canadian dollar as the official currency of a sovereign Quebec;
- the creation of a Partnership Council with decision-making powers over the implementation of the partnership treaty;
- establishment of a Parliamentary Assembly to examine draft decisions of the Partnership Council and to make recommendations;
- creation of a tribunal to resolve disputes relating to the treaty; and the
- organization of an orientation and supervisory committee to oversee the negotiations.

13 June 1995
Justice – Reforms

Bill C-68, the federal government's package of legislation designed to reform gun control is passed by a majority of MPs in the House of Commons with a vote of 192 to 63.

14 June 1995
Social Program – Reforms

The National Council of Welfare, an independent agency appointed by the federal government, denounces federal plans to consolidate transfer payments for health, postsecondary education, and social assistance into one package. The Council claims that under the initiatives of the new federal budget, the provinces will be provided with greater opportunites to limit spending on welfare.

15 June 1995
Budgets – Quebec

Moody's Investors Service downgrades the rating on long-term bonds in that province from A1 to A2, given the minimal progress made in the area of deficit-reduction within the last three years and the service's concerns over the government's preoccupation with its separatist agenda.

Chronology: Index

Maritime/Atlantic Provinces 10 January 1995, 5 May 1995

National Unity 16 August 1994, 20 December 1994, 15 February 1995

Party Leadership 1 December 1994

Pension Reform 22 February 1995, 28 April 1995

Premiers' Conferences 1 September 1994, 8 June 1995

Senate 31 August 1994, 15 September 1994, 21 March 1995

Social Assistance 9 September 1994

Social Programs 5 October 1994, 10 January 1995, 1 February 1995, 15 May 1995, 14 June 1995

Sovereignty – Quebec 22 July 1994, 25 July 1994, 14 September 1994, 18 September 1994, 28 September 1994, 12 October 1994, 29 October 1994, 15 November 1994, 22 November 1994, 27 November 1994, 30 November 1994, 1 December 1994, 6 December 1994, 14 December 1994, 19 December 1994, 20 December 1994, 21 December 1994, 4 January 1995, 10 January 1995, 12 January 1995, 13 January 1995, 16 January 1995, 27 January 1995, 6 February 1995, 10 February 1995, 20 February 1995, 9-10 March 1995, 13 March 1995, 14 March 1995, 27 March 1995, 5 April 1995, 7 April 1995, 19 April 1995, 23 April 1995, 28 April 1995, 3 May 1995, 28 May 1995, 30 May 1995, 8 June 1995, 12 June 1995

Taxation 27 October 1994

Tourism 25 October 1994

Trade 18 July 1994, 3-6 August 1994, 24 October 1994, 10 November 1994, 11 January 1995

Transportation 13 July 1994, 2 June 1995

List of Titles in Print

The Following Publications are Available From:
Renouf Publishing Co. Ltd.
1294 Algoma Rd.
Ottawa, Ontario K1B 3W8
Tel.: (613) 741-4333 / Fax: (613) 741-5439

Canada: The State of the Federation

Douglas M. Brown and Janet Hiebert, eds., *Canada: The State of the Federation, 1994.* ($20)

Ronald L. Watts and Douglas M. Brown, eds., *Canada: The State of the Federation, 1993.* ($20)

Douglas Brown and Robert Young, eds., *Canada: The State of the Federation, 1992.* ($20)

Douglas M. Brown, ed., *Canada: The State of the Federation, 1991.* ($18)

Ronald L. Watts and Douglas M. Brown, eds., *Canada: The State of the Federation, 1990.* ($17)

Ronald L. Watts and Douglas M. Brown, eds., *Canada: The State of the Federation, 1989.* ($16)

Peter M. Leslie and Ronald L. Watts, eds., *Canada: The State of the Federation, 1987-88.* ($15)

Peter M. Leslie, ed., *Canada: The State of the Federation 1986.* ($15)

Peter M. Leslie, ed., *Canada: The State of the Federation 1985.* ($14)

Canada: L'état de la fédération 1985. ($14)

Conference Proceedings

2. Douglas Brown, Pierre Cazalis and Gilles Jasmin, eds., *Higher Education in Federal Systems*, 1992. ($20). French version: *L'enseignement supérieur dans les systèmes fédératifs* ($30)

1. Out of Print.

Research Papers/Notes de Recherche (Formerly Discussion Papers)

32. Robert Young, *The Breakup of Czechoslovakia*, 1994. ($12)

31. Steven A. Kennett, *The Design of Federalism and Water Resource Management in Canada*, 1992. ($8)

30. Patrick Fafard and Darrel R. Reid, *Constituent Assemblies: A Comparative Survey*, 1991. ($7)

29. Thomas O. Hueglin, *A Political Economy of Federalism: In Search of a New Comparative Perspective With Critical Intent Throughout*, 1990. ($10)

28. Ronald L. Watts, Darrel R. Reid and Dwight Herperger, *Parallel Accords: The American Precedent*, 1990. ($6)

27. Michael B. Stein, *Canadian Constitutional Renewal, 1968-1981: A Case Study in Integrative Bargaining*, 1989. ($12)

26. Ronald L. Watts, *Executive Federalism: A Comparative Analysis,* 1989. ($6)

25. Denis Robert, *L'ajustement structurel et le fédéralisme canadien: le cas de l'industrie du textile et du vêtement*, 1989. ($7.50)
24. Peter M. Leslie, *Ethnonationalism in a Federal State: The Case of Canada*, 1988. ($4)
23. Peter M. Leslie, *National Citizenship and Provincial Communities: A Review of Canadian Fiscal Federalism*, 1988. ($4)

Reflections/Réflexions

14. Roger Gibbins, *The New Face of Canadian Nationalism*, 1995. ($15)
13. Daniel J. Elazar, *Federalism and the Way to Peace*, 1994. ($20)
12. Guy Laforest and Douglas Brown, eds., *Integration and Fragmentation: The Paradox of the Late Twentieth Century*, 1994. ($15)
11. C.E.S. Franks, *The Myths and Symbols of the Constitutional Debate in Canada*, 1993. ($9)
10. Out of print.
9. Donald J. Savoie, *The Politics of Language*, 1991. ($4)
8. Thomas J. Courchene, *The Community of the Canadas*, 1991. ($5)
7. Gordon Robertson, *Does Canada Matter?* 1991. ($3)
6. Thomas J. Courchene, *Forever Amber: The Legacy of the 1980s for the Ongoing Constitutional Impasse*, 1990. ($5)
5. Patrick J. Monahan, *After Meech: An Insider's View*, 1990. ($6)
4. Albert Breton, *Centralization, Decentralization and Intergovernmental Competition*, 1990. ($3)
3. Peter M. Leslie, *Federal Leadership in Economic and Social Policy*, 1988. ($3)
2. Clive Thomson, ed., *Navigating Meech Lake: The 1987 Constitutional Accord*, 1988. ($4)
1. Allan E. Blakeney, *Canada: Its Framework, Its Foibles, Its Future*, 1988. ($3)

Bibliographies

Aboriginal Self-Government in Canada: A Bibliography 1987-90. ($10)
Aboriginal Self-Government in Canada: A Bibliography 1986. ($12)
Bibliography of Canadian and Comparative Federalism, 1986. ($20)
Bibliography of Canadian and Comparative Federalism, 1980-1985. ($39)

Aboriginal Peoples and Constitutional Reform

Evelyn J. Peters, ed., *Aboriginal Self-Government in Urban Areas*, 1995. ($20.00)

Douglas Brown, ed., *Aboriginal Governments and Power Sharing in Canada*, 1992. ($7)

Thomas J. Courchene and Lisa M. Powell, *A First Nations Province*, 1992. ($7)

Background Papers

16. Bradford W. Morse, *Providing Land and Resources for Aboriginal Peoples*, 1987. ($10)
15. Evelyn J. Peters, *Aboriginal Self-Government Arrangements in Canada*, 1987. ($7)
14. Delia Opekokew, *The Political and Legal Inequities Among Aboriginal Peoples in Canada*, 1987. ($7)

The Following Publications are Available From:
The Institute of Intergovernmental Relations
Queen's University
Kingston, Ontario K7L 3N6
Tel.: (613) 545-2080 / Fax: (613) 545-6868

Institute of Intergovernmental Relations, *Annual Report to the Advisory Council*, for the following years: *1991-92, 1992-93*, and *1993-94* / Institut des relations intergouvernementales, *Rapport annuel au Conseil consultatif*, pour les années suivantes: *1991-1992, 1993-1994*, et *1993-1994*. (Charge for postage only)

William M. Chandler and Christian W. Zöllner, eds., *Challenges to Federalism: Policy-Making in Canada and the Federal Republic of Germany*, 1989. ($25)

Peter M. Leslie, *Rebuilding the Relationship: Quebec and its Confederation Partners/ Une collaboration renouvelée: le Québec et ses partenaires dans la confédération*, 1987. ($8)

A. Paul Pross and Susan McCorquodale, *Economic Resurgence and the Constitutional Agenda: The Case of the East Coast Fisheries*, 1987. ($10)

Bruce G. Pollard, *Managing the Interface: Intergovernmental Affairs Agencies in Canada*, 1986. ($12)

Catherine A. Murray, *Managing Diversity: Federal-Provincial Collaboration and the Committee on Extension of Services to Northern and Remote Communities*, 1984. ($15)

Peter Russell et al., *The Court and the Constitution: Comments on the Supreme Court Reference on Constitutional Amendment*, 1982. (Paper $5, Cloth $10)

Allan Tupper, *Public Money in the Private Sector: Industrial Assistance Policy and Canadian Federalism*, 1982. ($12)

William P. Irvine, *Does Canada Need a New Electoral System?* 1979. ($8)

The Year in Review

Bruce G. Pollard, *The Year in Review 1983: Intergovernmental Relations in Canada*. ($16)
Revue de l'année 1983: les relations intergouvernementales au Canada. ($16)

S.M. Dunn, *The Year in Review 1982: Intergovernmental Relations in Canada*. ($12)
Revue de l'année 1982: les relations intergouvernementales au Canada. ($12)

S.M. Dunn, *The Year in Review 1981: Intergovernmental Relations in Canada*. ($10)

R.J. Zukowsky, *Intergovernmental Relations in Canada: The Year in Review 1980, Volume I: Policy and Politics*. ($8) (*Volume II not available*)

Discussion Papers

22. Robert L. Stanfield, *National Political Parties and Regional Diversity*, 1985. (Charge for postage only)

21. Donald Smiley, *An Elected Senate for Canada? Clues from the Australian Experience*, 1985. ($8)

19. Thomas O. Hueglin, *Federalism and Fragmentation: A Comparative View of Political Accommodation in Canada*, 1984. ($8)

18. Allan Tupper, *Bill S-31 and the Federalism of State Capitalism*, 1983. ($7)

17. Reginald Whitaker, *Federalism and Democratic Theory*, 1983. ($7)

16. Roger Gibbins, *Senate Reform: Moving Towards the Slippery Slope*, 1983. ($7)

14. John Whyte, *The Constitution and Natural Resource Revenues*, 1982. ($7)

13. Ian B. Cowie, *Future Issues of Jurisdiction and Coordination Between Aboriginal and Non-Aboriginal Governments*, 1987. ($7)
12. C.E.S. Franks, *Public Administration Questions Relating to Aboriginal Self-Government*, 1987. ($10)
11. Richard H. Bartlett, *Subjugation, Self-Management and Self-Government of Aboriginal Lands and Resources in Canada*, 1986. ($10)
10. Jerry Paquette, *Aboriginal Self-Government and Education in Canada*, 1986. ($10)
9. Out of print.
8. John Weinstein, *Aboriginal Self-Determination Off a Land Base*, 1986. ($7)
7. David C. Hawkes, *Negotiating Aboriginal Self-Government: Developments Surrounding the 1985 First Ministers' Conference*, 1985. ($5)
6. Bryan P. Schwartz, *First Principles: Constitutional Reform with Respect to the Aboriginal Peoples of Canada 1982-1984*, 1985. ($20)
5. Douglas E. Sanders, *Aboriginal Self-Government in the United States*, 1985. ($12)
4. Bradford Morse, *Aboriginal Self-Government in Australia and Canada*, 1985. ($12)
2. David A. Boisvert, *Forms of Aboriginal Self-Government*, 1985. ($12)
1. Noel Lyon, *Aboriginal Self-Government: Rights of Citizenship and Access to Governmental Services*, 1984. ($12)

Discussion Paper

David C. Hawkes, *The Search for Accommodation*, 1987. ($7)

Position Papers

Inuit Committee on National Issues, *Completing Canada: Inuit Approaches to Self-Government*, 1987. ($7)
Martin Dunn, *Access to Survival, A Perspective on Aboriginal Self-Government for the Constituency of the Native Council of Canada*, 1986. ($7)

Workshop Report

David C. Hawkes and Evelyn J. Peters, *Implementing Aboriginal Self-Government: Problems and Prospects*, 1986. ($7)

Bibliographies

Evelyn J. Peters, *Aboriginal Self-Government in Canada: A Bibliography 1987-90*. ($10)
Evelyn J. Peters, *Aboriginal Self-Government in Canada: A Bibliography 1986*. ($12)

Final Report

David C. Hawkes, *Aboriginal Peoples and Constitutional Reform: What Have We Learned?* 1989. ($7)